AUG 1 8 2017

# MUSTANG
## CHRONICLE

BY JERRY HEASLEY
AND THE AUTO EDITORS OF CONSUMER GUIDE®

PUBLICATIONS INTERNATIONAL, LTD.

Contributing author: Jerry Heasley

Copyright © 1998 Publications International, Ltd. All rights reserved. This book may not be reproduced or quoted in whole or in part by any means whatsoever without written permission from:

Louis Weber, C.E.O.
Publications International, Ltd.
7373 N. Cicero Avenue
Lincolnwood, Illinois 60646

Permission is never granted for commercial purposes.

Manufactured in U.S.A.

8  7  6  5  4  3  2  1

ISBN: 0-7853-3262-6

The editors gratefully acknowledge the cooperation of the following people who supplied photography to help make this book possible. They are listed below, along with the page number(s) of their photos.

Special thanks to Dan R. Erickson, Ford Photographic Services.

Front cover: Ford Public Relations
Back cover: Jerry Heasley; Ford Public Relations

**Alex Gabbard:** 38, 65 **Sam Griffith:** 88, 207, 213, 214 **Thomas Glatch:** 89, 117, 234 **David Gooley:** 12, 17 **Jerry Heasley:** 32, 33, 34, 35, 36, 37, 38, 39, 40, 41, 42, 46, 47, 58, 59, 66, 67, 68, 72, 73, 78, 79, 81, 82, 85, 86, 87, 92, 93, 94, 95, 97, 109, 110, 113, 114, 120, 121, 122, 123, 137, 144, 145, 187, 189, 206, 208 **Roland Flessner:** 236 **Mitch Frumkin:** 230, 238 **Bud Juneau:** 11, 13, 62, 85, 93, 97 **Milton Gene Keift:** 17 **Dan Lyons:** 11, 64, 94, 95, 233 **Vince Manocchi:** 11, 12, 13, 14, 16, 44, 123 **Ron McQueeney:** 229 **Doug Mitchel:** 12, 19, 33, 64, 97 **Mike Mueller:** 7, 56, 60, 61, 69, 70, 71, 83, 99, 177 **Brenda Priddy:** 231 **Chris Poole:** 228 **Rick Popely:** 231 **Phil Toy:** 94 **Joseph H. Wherry:** 14 **Nicky Wright:** 32, 33, 34, 35, 45, 47, 54, 55, 60, 62, 63, 65, 68, 69, 70, 86, 91, 93, 95, 96, 98, 105, 106, 107, 108, 110, 113, 115, 116, 118, 119, 120, 144, 145, 184, 232, 233, 235

OWNERS
Special thanks to the owners of the cars featured in this book for their enthusiastic cooperation.

CHAPTER 1: Unique Motor Car; Dennis Murphy; Dr. Ernie Hendry; William E. True; M. Randall Mytar; Joe Gonzalis; Everett Faulkner; Robert & Diana Adams; Darl & Mary McAllister; Richard Carpenter; Jose & Leann Compean; Jim Davidson; Larry & Sandra Van Horn; Les Huckins; Les Rave; Deer Park Car Museum, Escondido, CA; Bob Heffman; Ray Somers; Bob Patrick

CHAPTER 2: Ed Coughlin; Richard A. Emry; Alice Greunke; Gerald King; George Lyons; Ronald E. Miller; Rick Mitchell; Alan Nelson; Jay F. Painter; Vince & Helen Springer; Wendy Talarico

CHAPTER 3: Michele King; Ron Wold; Ed & Debbie Werder; Ken Baker; David L. Robb; Charles & Marie Cobb; Jerry Gibino; Louise Gibino; Michael Baker; Chris Plylar; Edward J. Wey; Gary Emerson; Joe Antrican; Winfred & Betty Keep; Kurt A. Havely; Sam Pampanella; Gerald King; Duane Mann; Joe Infinger; Thomas S. Rapala; Dennis Begley

CHAPTER 4: Brian & Elvira Torres; Tom Hasse; Bruce Weiss; Nelson Cardadeiro; Chris Duwalt; Steve Doley; Leroy Lasiter; Dixon Polderman; Mark Johnstad; Greg & Rhonda Haynes; Robert Augustine; Lewis H. Hunter; Thomas & Carol Podemski; Walter P. Wise; Bill Collins; Jeff Knoll; Steve Ames

CHAPTER 5: Doug & Teresa Hvidston; Don Bergman; Don & Karen Kerridge; Thomas & Carol Podemski; Thomas S. Rapala; Gary Pattee; Ron Edgerly; Dan Dixon; Frank Trummer; Ronald E. Miller; Gary M. Gunushian; Ray P. Fisher; Jeff Fowler; Sandra Nadolski

CHAPTER 6: D.L. Bohart; Thomas & Carol Podemski

CHAPTER 8: Doug & Teresa Hvidston; Mitch Lindahl

CHAPTER 9: Tony Kanzia; Dave Schmerler, Schmerler Ford, Elk Grove Village, IL

CHAPTER 11: Frank Trummer; Thomas & Carol Podemski

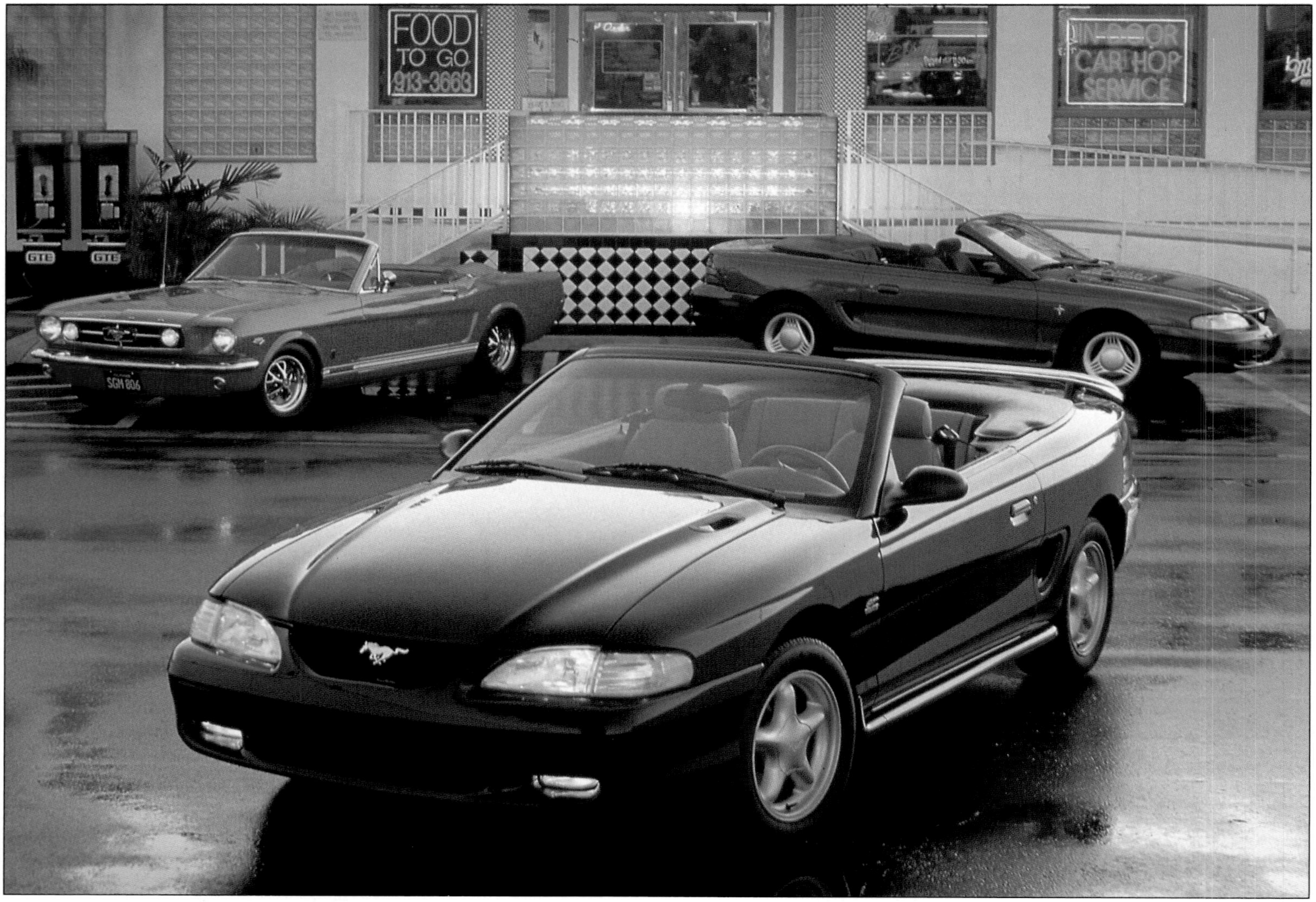

The present-generation Mustang *(center and right)* isn't just a thoughtful update of the fabulous 1964½ original *(left)*, but also proof that the thirtysomething ponycar is in the prime of its life.

# CONTENTS

THE FIRST MUSTANG, WHICH WAS formally introduced to the public in April 1964, was many things: the catalyst of a great marketing strategy; a great sales success; a great personal triumph for Lee Iacocca and Henry Ford II; a great vindication of the gut instincts of the car's designers and engineers; and a source of great excitement within and without the auto industry. That first Mustang, however, was not a great car. Mustang's true greatness came later.

Buyers of early Mustangs seemed not to mind (or, more likely, were not aware) that the car's rakish long hood/short deck body disguised mundane Falcon mechanicals and a set of undeniable compromises. But the thing that people were buying, and what Ford promoted with energy and immense cleverness, was the promise of speed, freedom, and youthful good times.

A vital component of this image was the Mustang name. As the project developed in 1962-63, "Mustang" was favored by Iacocca, and his point of view was echoed by the research of Ford ad man John Conley, who offered a whole slate of "horsey" names. "Mustang" stuck, conjuring visions not only of the wide-open American west, but—for countless citizens then old enough to remember—a remembrance of America's P-51 Mustang fighter plane, which was largely responsible for cementing Allied air superiority over Europe during the latter years of World War II. Frisky and aggressive; beautiful and potentially intimidating—the Mustang name said it all.

Of course, a clever name cannot guarantee the success of any automobile.

### FOREWORD
# Journey to Greatness

Mustang succeeded because its inspired moniker was wedded to striking looks and to handling and performance that were never less than competent, and that, thanks to a mile-long options list, could be made downright impressive.

Buyers could personalize their cars and "build" just the Mustang they wanted. Everything from interior appointments to engines could be ordered in packages or à la carte. Easygoing drivers chose from a selection of tame but pleasant V-6s while more adventurous buyers demanded available V-8s often installed in Carroll Shelby's legendary Shelby Cobras. Rated horsepower on Mustang V-8s ranged from 164 to a thumping 390. As muscle-car fever gripped young America in the Sixties, Mustang was right in the thick of things.

Mustang's success prompted other automakers to offer competing "ponycars" that ranged from frisky to brutish. Many of these pony-come-latelys—AMC's Javelin and AMX, GM's Camaro and Firebird, Chrysler Corporation's Barracuda and Challenger—found followings of their own, yet somehow lacked the special allure of Mustang. At this writing, only Camaro and Firebird remain to challenge Mustang's sales tallies—and to challenge them rather weakly, at that.

From the start, Mustang was as much an *image* as an automobile, and although that image waxed and waned over the decades, it retains a remarkable potency. Indeed, the passing years have only burnished Mustang's reputation—this despite some unfortunate lapses in the car's integrity that occurred along the way: the oversized, steroid 'Stangs of the early Seventies (a particularly regrettable example of the "mess with success" syndrome that periodically afflicts Ford); the flashy but embarrassingly weak-sister Mustang IIs of 1974-78 (mandated in large part, of course, by increasingly stringent federal guidelines and by gasoline shortages); and the unfortunate lack of a convertible body style from 1974 through 1982.

Today's Mustang is less a hot rod than a nimble, brisk *boulevardier* that strikes a satisfying balance between comfort and performance. Mustang continues to offer a power-to-price ratio that's difficult to ignore and even harder to resist. And in a positive signal sent to the car's many fans, buyers can choose a more powerful Mustang with "New-Edge" styling for 1999.

Because of the enormous popularity of sport-utility vehicles, some observers have predicted the end of the small coupe. Are they correct? Will Mustang go away? Not likely. Mustang is very much a FoMoCo "franchise" product, a priceless imagemaker. And given the considerable expense of the aforementioned facelift, Ford seems to have made a commitment to the car's continued existence.

A tip for the smart wagerer: Mustang will drive smartly into the new millennium.

Mustang made its debut on April 17, 1964, at the New York World's Fair. Two models were offered initially, a convertible (*above, foreground*) and a two-door hardtop. More than 30 years later, America's premier ponycar still sizzles in a variety of guises, including a swoopy ragtop (*above, background*).

## CHAPTER 1

# Gearing Up for Mustang

The 1948 Ford Sportsman combined the paneled look of a station wagon with the open-air luxury of a convertible. Ads called it "Something really new!"

ALTHOUGH THE MUSTANG IS commonly viewed as a creation of the Swingin' Sixties, this revolutionary, hugely successful car actually traces its origins to 1946, when America—and the American auto industry—strode victorious from World War II, full of energy, enthusiasm, and a level of optimism unprecedented in the nation's history. People wanted consumer goods—cars in particular.

Once the huge, pent-up demand of consumers for new cars began to be satisfied, though, the seller's market waned and buyers started hungering for new engineering and new styling. Ford and Mercury introduced zesty wood-bodied Sportsman convertibles in 1946, but it wasn't until 1949 that Ford and the other members of the Big Three, Chrysler and General Motors, offered entirely new models. Ford's offerings helped save the company, while GM had success with its pillarless "hardtop convertibles," a sporting body style Ford attempted to imitate with limited editions for 1950: the Ford Custom Crestliner, Mercury Monterey, and the Lincoln Lido and Capri. Ford responded more directly to GM's initiative in 1951, when it brought out the hardtop Victoria.

Aside from Nash's Suburban, the independents offered no noteworthy limited editions before 1949, when newcomer Kaiser-Frazer, which began production in 1946 at Willow Run, Michigan, weighed in with the Kaiser Virginian. It was followed in 1951 by the DeLuxe-derived Dragon, "Mark II" Dragon, Jade Dragon, and "Hardtop" Dragon. Although essen-

tially trim packages—and slow sellers at that—these cars were early examples of "personal" automobiles, and thus legitimate antecedents of the Mustang.

Stylish examples from other automakers included Packard's Caribbean, Cadillac's Eldorado, Buick's Skylark, Oldsmobile's Fiesta, and Chevrolet's Corvette, all of which bowed for the 1953 season.

Besides big convertibles and hardtops, sports cars were also enjoying a burst of popularity in the U.S., thanks largely to the enthusiasm of GIs who brought them home from England. Notable players included the Triumph TR2, Austin-Healey 100, Alfa Romeo Giulietta, and Mercedes-Benz 190SL. Although sports

cars accounted for only .027 percent of the U.S. market in 1953, there was a growing fascination with "foreign" features like bucket seats, floor-mounted gearshifts, and lithe two-seat bodies on chassis that offered exceptional handling.

Sports cars soon appeared from two independents: the Anglo-American Nash-Healey of 1951 and the fiberglass-bodied, sliding-door Kaiser-Darrin of 1954. An even more colorful attempt was the very low-volume Hudson Italia of 1954-55, a four-seat grand touring coupe with jazzy, rectilinear American styling executed by Italy's Carrozzeria Touring on the compact Hudson Jet chassis. We should also not forget 1953's new low-slung Starlight coupe and Starliner hardtop from the Raymond Loewy studios at Studebaker, which looked very European even if they weren't pure sports cars. But the independents were simply too strapped for money to compete with European sports cars head-on. They had to be more concerned with the higher-volume family models on which their profits and survival depended.

Chevrolet's Corvette, on the other hand, sprang from America's best-selling single make and the world's most successful car company, GM. Nevertheless, it was something of a hurry-up job, introduced as a Motorama showpiece in early '53 and rushed into limited production six months later. Power was provided by a low-suds six-cylinder engine mated to an uninspired two-speed automatic transmission, while unorthodox fiberglass body construction contrasted sharply with old-fashioned side curtains and a fairly rudimentary top.

Jaguar was just one British make that benefited from postwar American interest in sports cars. This is a '52 XK-120 roadster.

With all this, the first Corvette was less a sports car than a rather unsporting tourer, and initial sales were slow. By early 1954, GM was ready to drop the Corvette, but two-seat activity at Ford and lobbying by GM Design director Harley Earl and Chevy chief engineer Ed Cole won the car a reprieve—and further development. Corvette thus got its first V-8, the classic 265-cid Chevy small-block, for 1955, followed by smooth new styling for '56 and optional fuel injection for 1957. The result was a true sports car that endures to this day.

At Ford Motor Company's Dearborn headquarters, where GM's every move was carefully watched, the Corvette's highly publicized arrival sparked a good deal of debate. Should Ford now field a challenger to the low-volume plastic sports car?

The answer was *yes*, and it appeared at the end of 1954: the Thunderbird, an all-new, steel-bodied two-seater available with a 292-cid Mercury V-8; a six would not even be available. Roll-up windows, plus optional automatic transmission and a bolt-on hardtop, made for a car that was sporty, elegant, and recognizably Ford.

At $2944, the T-Bird was price-competitive with the new V-8 Corvette, and sold 16,155 copies for 1955, to a puny 674 Corvettes. By 1957, more than 21,000 Thunderbirds were sold. Surprisingly, an all-new four-seat replacement was being prepared for 1958, even as the first T-Bird rolled off the line.

Ford Division general manager Robert S. McNamara—a no-nonsense type famous for his obsession with the bottom line—had looked at the Thunderbird and realized he had three options. He could continue with a two-seater as a prestige item, selling it at a loss or perhaps a small profit; he could drop it entirely; or he could remake the T-Bird into something that would sell in greater numbers than the two-seater. Given McNamara's orientation, the choice was obvious, and a four-seat model got the green light for 1958.

McNamara knew what he was doing, and the 1958 Thunderbird was a sweeping sales success. It was offered as a convertible and as a new fixed-roof hardtop with a handsome, wide-quarter roofline destined to be imitated by Ford and others. The "Squarebird" was intended not just to build showroom traffic but to sell in high volume.

**1904**

- Henry Ford's 999 racer sets a world speed record of 91.4 mph

**1932**

- Ford introduces an affordable V-8 that turns the make into a synonym for performance

**1945**

- World War II ends in Europe in May; in the Pacific in August

----

- Henry Ford II, grandson of Henry Ford, is named president of Ford Motor Company

**1953**

- The Korean War ends when an armistice is finally signed on June 26
- Chevrolet's fiberglass-bodied, two-seat Corvette debuts
- Studebaker introduces the stunning Starlight and Starliner coupes, designed by Bob Bourke under the guidance of Raymond Loewy

**1954**

- Red-baiting Wisconsin senator Joe McCarthy is formally censured by his peers
- Kaiser introduces the uniquely styled Kaiser-Darrin

**1955**

- Martin Luther King, Jr., leads a black boycott of the Montgomery, Alabama, bus system

----

- Ford introduces the sporty, two-place Thunderbird

**1958**

- Nikita Khrushchev becomes premier of the Soviet Union

- Thunderbird is redesigned and becomes the four-place "Squarebird"

**1959**

- Cuban president Batista is overthrown by rebels led by Fidel Castro
- Driver Carroll Shelby wins the 24 Hours of Le Mans

**1960**

- John F. Kennedy narrowly defeats Richard Nixon to become President of the United States

----

- The Big Three introduce appealing new compacts: Chevy Corvair (available in sporty Monza trim); Ford Falcon; Mercury Comet; Plymouth Valiant
- Health problems force noted racer Carroll Shelby to retire from competition
- Ford VP Lee Iacocca is named Ford Division general manager

**1961**

- Anti-Castro Cuban exiles mount a disastrous, U.S.-backed invasion of Cuba at the Bay of Pigs

----

- A Ford styling study called Avanti appears; revised versions from 1961-62 are called Avventura and Allegro II

**1962**

- President John F. Kennedy faces down Soviet premier Nikita Khrushchev, who removes Soviet missiles from Cuba
- Marilyn Monroe dies at her home in Brentwood, California
- American Motors rejects the Budd XR-400, a Rambler-based, 2+2

convertible that predicts much of the look and philosophy of the Mustang

----

- More sporty Allegro styling studies—most with long hood/short deck proportions—are unveiled; in all, Ford will create 13 with that name
- At Watkins Glen, Ford unveils the experimental, mid-engine Mustang I, a two-seater with engineering supervised by Herb Misch, styling overseen by Eugene Bordinat
- Ford's Falcon Futura features bucket seats and four-on-the-floor
- On August 16, a styling study by a design group headed by Joe Oros gets the nod from Lee Iacocca and Henry Ford II
- Carroll Shelby drops a Ford 289 into an AC sports car body and creates the first Shelby Cobra

**1963**

- President John F. Kennedy is assassinated in Dallas
- The Buick Riviera mixes luxury and sportiness

----

- A clay mock-up called Torino is completed in May; it carries Mustang-style side scoops and three-piece taillights
- Fall brings a running prototype called Mustang II
- A later production prototype looks very much like the first-generation Mustang, except for a cougar emblem, instead of a mustang, in the center of the grille
- A running fastback prototype called Cougar II is shown late this year and early in 1964

Perhaps the most significant "personal-car" response from GM was Chevy's Corvair, which included the sporty Monza model for debut model-year 1960 and followed up with the Monza Spyder two years later. Monza's success revealed the existence of a brand-new market that was soon joined by a diverse array of sporty cars: the compact Plymouth Valiant V-200 hardtop coupe and Dodge Lancer 770 hardtop coupe, a "non-letter" Chrysler 300 series, the Buick Special Skylark, Pontiac Tempest Le Mans, Oldsmobile F-85 Cutlass, and Studebaker Lark Daytona and Gran Turismo Hawk.

Ford countered Monza with the interesting and worthy Falcon Futura and Futura Sprint, but realized that if it was to effectively compete in this new market, it would need a brand-new product, one designed especially for its market, just as the four-seat Thunderbird had been. Fortunately for Ford, the corporation had risen to robust financial health during the Fifties and continued strong into the early Sixties. Thus Ford decided in 1961 to create its niche-marketed car.

One reason for Ford Division's good fortune in these years was McNamara's successor as general manager. McNamara was an able leader, but he wasn't a lifelong auto enthusiast. His replacement, however, was: a hard-working salesman blessed with both astute business sense and an enthusiast's appreciation of automotive design. That man, as auto enthusiasts know, was Lee Iacocca. In fact, some people "know" this a bit too well, assuming that Iacocca was almost solely responsible for the Mustang.

In truth, Iacocca's contribution to Mustang was as chief mover-and-shaker. It's doubtful that the idea was his alone, but because of his position, Iacocca received media credit as principal architect once the Mustang debuted.

Nevertheless, as a sales-savvy executive who's always been what we now call a

Model-year 1953 brought top-down excitement from General Motors: Cadillac Eldorado (*top*), Oldsmobile 98 Fiesta (*middle*), and Buick Skylark (*above*). Although not true sports cars, these good-looking convertibles nevertheless epitomized the youthful notion of sporty "personal" motoring.

"car guy," Iacocca couldn't help but leave his personal imprint on the original pony-car, though a great many others did, too, as we'll see. Yet because his input and decisions were crucial to the car's development, it's appropriate to look at Iacocca's career in the years leading up to the Mustang's genesis.

Iacocca was car-crazy from an early age. Exceedingly bright, he was in the auto-rental business while an adolescent and breezed through high school, Lehigh University, and Princeton, where he earned a master's in mechanical engineering while on a scholarship. After joining the Ford sales force in a tiny outpost in Pennsylvania, Iacocca devised a novel sales scheme: $56 a month for a '56 Ford. Robert McNamara liked the idea, liked Iacocca, and applied the 56/56 plan to the entire country.

Iacocca was a Ford vice president by age 35, and a year later, in 1960, he replaced McNamara as Ford Division general manager when McNamara turned his attention to politics.

The Mustang reflected Iacocca's hunch that there must be a market looking for a sporty, low-cost compact; that is, a car that would offer flash and performance at a price that would appeal to the masses.

Once installed as general manager, Iacocca started sprucing up the Ford line that McNamara had made profitable but dull. Iacocca arrived too late to do much about the 1961-62 line, but he made changes for mid-year 1962 and again for "1963½." He approved dropping a V-8 into the Falcon, okayed fastback roofs for some big Fords, and plunged the division back into racing in a big way. With the blessing of Henry Ford II, Dearborn re-

The personal-car idea picked up momentum as the Fifties progressed. The fiberglass, I-6 Corvette (*top left*) was introduced in 1953 and failed to impress buyers, auto writers, and even some Chevy dealers. However, it did boost interest in sporty imports such as the '53 Austin-Healey 100M (*above left*). Domestic automakers responded with the '54 Kaiser-Darrin (*top right*), which had unique sliding doors, and the drop-dead gorgeous '56 Continental Mark II (*above*), which blended luxury with performance, thanks to a 368-cid V-8 rated at 285 horsepower.

entered NASCAR competition and was very successful on the big Southern tracks. By 1965, Ford had also won Sebring and Indianapolis and had almost won Le Mans. It was all part of Iacocca's strategy to "think young."

Iacocca first broached the subject of a youth-oriented sporty car at a 1961 meeting of top Ford execs and representatives from the division's ad agency. Ford market research, under the direction of marketing manager Chase Morsey, Jr., was soon underway. At the same time, a team of young engineers and designers got to work under the supervision of Donald N. Frey, who was Iacocca's product planning manager. Although Frey later downplayed the extent of market research, Ford could see that the postwar Baby Boom generation was approaching car-buying age by 1960. Further, the 15-29 age group would swell by about 40 percent between 1960 and 1970, while the number of 30-39-year-olds would actually decrease by nine percent in the same period. Buyers between 18 and 34 were expected to account for more than half the projected increase in new-car sales in 1960-70, and many in that age group—notably those under the age of 25—were eager to drive a car with a stickshift and sporty performance. These potential buyers were educated and more willing than older buyers to purchase cars that were "image extensions."

Most importantly, more families would have more money. The number with incomes above $10,000 was expected to rise by a whopping 156 percent between 1960 and 1975. Thus, more households would be able to afford second and even third or fourth cars. Women and teenagers were the family members who most wanted cars of their own.

So a potential and sizable market definitely existed. The question faced by the planners of the project that had been dubbed T-5 was, what should that car be? An earlier proposal, never seriously considered for production, was the experimental Mustang I, a two-seat, rear-drive sports car with an engine based on the 1927-cc, 60-degree V-4 used in the front-drive Cardinal. The car had begun development in 1959 as a test bed for a subcompact intended to slot below Falcon in the Ford lineup. For the Mustang I, supervising engineer Herb Misch saw that

Traditional sports-car fun was provided by the '57 Triumph TR3 (*top left*). It was nimble but not as quick as the two-seat V-8 '57 Ford Thunderbird (*top right*). The 'Bird was upsized for 1958 and carried on similarly for '59 (*middle right*). Studebaker's Golden Hawk looked good in '57 (*middle left*), and the '59 Corvette (*above*), now with V-8 power, was a force to be reckoned with.

the engine was tuned to produce 90 bhp with a small, single-throat Solex carburetor. A competition version with dual Weber carbs topped 100 bhp.

Under the direction of stylist Eugene Bordinat, Mustang I went from sketch to approved clay model in just 21 days.

Thanks to product planner Roy Lunn (who laid out the basic design), the car met *Federation Internationale de l'Automobile* (FIA) and Sports Car Club of America (SCCA) racing regulations.

The Mustang I made its public debut at the United States Grand Prix at Watkins

Glen, New York, in October 1962, where racer Dan Gurney drove it around the circuit to the cheers of fans. *Car and Driver* later tested the car in 90-bhp form and found it as fast as Ford claimed. Zero to 60 acceleration was about 10 seconds, yet fuel economy was as high as 30 miles per gallon.

Innovative and exciting though it was, the Mustang I was a false start that Ford never intended to produce.

Another early-Sixties two-seat proposal, the Falcon-based XT-Bird, also came to naught. The car was an exercise in production engineering by the Budd Company, a long-time Ford supplier that had built the original 1955-57 Thunderbird bodies. A prototype XT-Bird was duly run up on a Falcon chassis, with much of its underbody structure intact. Styling was updated by shearing off the '57 tailfins and lowering the front fenders. Budd ingeniously managed to retain the original

dashboard and cowl, but in deference to contemporary tastes, the wrapped windshield and its severe dogleg gave way to less-angled A-pillars, and front quarter vents were added. Like the '57, the XT-Bird had a steel body with a soft top that folded down into a well ahead of the decklid. Unlike the original, it had a small rear jump seat that could carry children or be folded down into a luggage platform.

Budd made an aggressive sales pitch, promising that "total tool, jig, and fixture costs . . . would not exceed $1.5 million." In the end, though, the XT-Bird was only wishful thinking. Lack of full four-passenger capacity was its main limitation, though dumpy lines didn't help.

The Fairlane group also passed over two other two-seat designs, an open racer called Median and a sports model called Mina. By 1962, dozens of four-seat packages—paper renderings and quarter- and full-scale clays—had been designed.

After reviewing them all, management asked that one, a four-seater dubbed "median sports car," be worked up into a coupe and convertible, feeling that its styling captured some of the original T-Bird's personal flavor. It was also mocked-up as a two-seater, a 2+2 with jump seats, and a 2+2 with cramped rear bucket seats.

This exercise led to another round of studies under the name Avventura, and a dozen different clay models. One of these became the Allegro X-car, publicly shown in August 1963. Actually, there were 13 Allegros, each differing slightly in dimensions and interior packaging. By labeling Allegro a "styling experimental car," Ford as much as admitted that none would ever be produced.

Indeed, Ford had decided in August 1962 to start over with a new series of clays. Another set of dimensions was laid down, and four styling teams were invited to submit proposals. Specifications now

The Mercedes-Benz 190SL was introduced in 1955 and was the automaker's first high-volume sports car. By 1960 (*above left*), it had become a pleasant tourer. For brute power, buyers could strap on the '59 Chrysler 300-E (*above middle*), which cranked out 380 horses with its 413-cid V-8. The 1961 MGA 1600 (*above right*) ran with a 99-cid inline four and stressed style and handling over acceleration. The '61 Olds Starfire (*right*) was a convertible-only subseries of the Super 88 line. It ran with a 394-cid, 325-horse V-8—Olds's largest eight.

called for a target price of $2500, a 2500-pound curb weight, a 180-inch maximum overall length, four seats, floorshift, and the use of mostly Falcon mechanicals. Styling character would be "sporty, personal and tight." Finally, Ford tossed in a marketing brainstorm: an arm-long option list that would let the buyer tailor the car for economy, luxury, performance, or any combination. If any car was designed to be "personal" in nature, the Mustang was that car.

The studios that went to work represented Ford and Lincoln-Mercury Divisions, Corporate Projects, and Advanced Design. All, of course, were guided by Bordinat, who gave them just two weeks to come up with suitable clays. Seven were ultimately submitted, and on August 16 all were gathered in the Ford Design Center's outdoor viewing area for management perusal. One leaped out from the rest. "It was the only one in the courtyard that seemed to be moving," Iacocca said later. Henry Ford II agreed.

The eye-catching proposal came from the Ford Division studio under Joe Oros (later executive director of Ford and Lincoln-Mercury design), studio manager Gale Halderman, and executive designer L. David Ash. The group had talked about the assignment at length before anyone even put pencil to paper. They talked so much, in fact, that once they started, they needed only three days to draw the shape that so impressed Iacocca.

The proposal looked very much like the eventual production Mustang, but lacked a front bumper and wore Cougar emblems. As development progressed, the name was changed to Torino, then Turino. Finally, and confusingly, it was labeled Mustang II. (Iacocca, Frey, and others wanted the name "Mustang" from the start.) Oros deliberately painted the clay white so it would stand out at the showing and increase his team's chances of winning the intramural competition. That tactic—and the car's styling—succeeded handsomely.

The Mustang was introduced in 1964, but its evolution began three years before. A July 1961 rendering of a two-place sportster (*top left*) carried a "Thunderbolt" moniker—appropriate since the front and rear were reminiscent of that era's Thunderbird. *Top right:* Ford design chief Eugene Bordinat (standing) was a prime mover behind the Mustang I, a 1962 pre-Mustang exercise. Another two-place concept, the Ford Cougar of 1962 (*above left and above*), charted a course Ford chose not to follow.

Like the Budd XT-Bird, the Cougar/Torino/Mustang II was designed around the Falcon floorpan, though the Oros team planned for drivetrains up to and including the 289-cid, 271-bhp V-8, and 4-speed all-synchromesh transmission from Ford's mid-size Fairlane. To provide true four-passenger seating, wheelbase was pegged at 108 inches, only 1.5 inches shorter than the Falcon's. Track was 56 inches front and rear. Overall length was 186.6 inches, a bit more than the specified maximum.

**15**

In 1963, a running prototype based on the Oros design and also called Mustang II was built and displayed around the country. Like Mustang I, it was first shown at Watkins Glen, before the U.S. Grand Prix.

Meanwhile, Oros and company had one more fling with a two-seater, called Cougar II. This running prototype, shown in late 1963 and early '64, was a fastback coupe with exciting lines not unlike those of the 1963 Corvette Sting Ray split-window coupe. And though Ford didn't mention it, the Cougar II was dimensionally quite close to the rip-snorting A.C. Cobra: 90-inch wheelbase, front/rear track of 50.5/52 inches, 66.5-inch width, 48-inch height, 168-inch overall length. Chassis features included the Fairlane 260 V-8, four-speed all-synchromesh gearbox, and all-independent suspension.

The Cougar II was certainly the closest thing to a genuine street sports car yet seen from Dearborn (not counting Carroll Shelby's Ford-powered, British-built Cobra), with the smoothest styling of any prototype developed in these years. But it suffered the same problem that weighed against the Mustang I and XT-Bird: Ford just didn't think a two-seater would sell in sufficient numbers to assure a satisfactory return on tooling costs. Also, the Cougar II didn't fit Iacocca's idea for a low-cost personal four-seater, and its styling was probably too close to the Sting Ray's for the comfort of many in Dearborn.

On September 10, 1962, the original white Cougar clay model that had wowed the company brass a few weeks earlier was "validated" for production. Only now did Ford Engineering get involved.

*Top:* Ford enjoyed sales success with the compact Falcon, which became the underskin basis for the first Mustang. This is a sporty '62 Futura. *Middle:* The Chevy II was Chevy's retort to the Falcon. This top-of-the-line '62 Nova 400 carries the standard 120-bhp inline six. *Left:* Studebaker's '62 Gran Turismo Hawk provided sporty luxury.

This was unusual, because engineers are typically called in at a much earlier stage in a vehicle's development. The need to keep styling options open was probably the reason behind this. Except for routine compromises needed to adapt a styling prototype for mass production (conventional bumpers, round headlights, a less rakish windshield), the Oros design saw few changes. Engineering bent over backward, in fact, to keep the styling intact.

The Mustang was mainly a body engineering job, because its basic chassis, engine, suspension, and driveline were, by design, off-the-shelf Falcon and Fairlane components. At 181.6 inches, its overall length was identical to the 1964 Falcon's. Wheelbase, at 108 inches, remained 1.5 inches shorter. The Mustang could have shared some Falcon sheetmetal, too, but that idea didn't last long.

Though the notchback hardtop would always be the best-selling Mustang body style, Ford was still playing around with two-seaters and other variations of the

new sporty compact. Except for a 2+2 fastback idea, all of these went unrealized.

A rigid frame, improved suspension, and other mechanical concerns were attended to by the engineering team, but the problem of finding a suitable name remained. Although "Mustang" had been seriously considered early on, as shown by the mid-engine two-seater, it didn't take hold for some time. Different departments had applied a variety of working titles to the project which was known for a time as "Special Falcon." Henry Ford II favored "T-Bird II" or "Thunderbird II." Iacocca favored "Mustang."

To get additional ideas, John Conley of Ford's ad agency was dispatched to the Detroit Public Library. Earlier, he'd combed through lists of bird names to come up with Falcon for Ford's 1960 compact. This time, Conley was interested in horses, considering Colt, Bronco, Pinto, and Maverick. All four would eventually appear: Colt by Dodge; Bronco, Pinto, and Maverick by Ford, of course.

*Top row, from left:* Chevy's stylish and sophisticated Corvair Monza for 1963; designer Bill Mitchell's stunning '63 Buick Riviera; the beautiful and ill-fated 1963 Studebaker Avanti. *Above:* The XT-Bird was proposed by the Budd Company as an economical way for Ford to create a sporty car by using Falcon mechanicals and '57 Thunderbird body tooling. The XT's so-so lines (*shaded area*) and limited passenger room made it a no-sale.

Mustang, however, soon became the clear choice. In many ways it was a natural. It conjured up visions of cowboys, prairies, movie adventures, and the romantic West. It was easy to spell and easy to remember. As one Ford ad man said, "It had the excitement of the wide-open spaces, and it was American as all hell." Thus, the wild, free-spirited horse of the Western plains was carved out of mahogany as a template for the soon-to-be-familiar chrome sculpture that graced the first prototype. The Mustang was ready, and a revolution was about to begin.

AUTOMAKERS ARE OLD HANDS at promoting their wares, and are particularly adept at baiting the press. An information leak here, an "unauthorized" photo there—voilá!—instant publicity. Ford utilized these tricks in early Mustang promotion and went one better on the evening of April 16, 1964, with the purchase of commercial time during the 9 P.M. slot on all three television networks; an estimated 29 million viewers were treated to the Mustang's unveiling without ever leaving their living rooms. The next morning, 2600 American newspapers carried announcement ads and articles. As the capper, Ford arranged for Mustang to be officially introduced at the April 17 opening of the New York World's Fair.

The publicity mill continued to grind as some 150 newspaper and magazine journalists were invited to Detroit to drive virtual hand-built Mustangs. The scribes raved about the car, and Mustangs quickly went on display in airport terminals, hotel lobbies, and dealer showrooms across the country. Base price was boldly advertised everywhere. And why not? At just $2368 f.o.b. Detroit for the hardtop, the Mustang was a tremendous bargain.

Long before all this, Ford had projected first-year Mustang sales of 100,000 units. As announcement day approached, Lee Iacocca upped the estimate to 240,000 and switched his division's San Jose, California, plant to Mustang production. Iacocca had been conservative: Only four months were needed to sell 100,000 Mustangs. For the full 1965 model run—April 1964 through August 1965—a total of 680,989 were

## CHAPTER 2
# 1964½-66: Out of the Gate

sold, an all-time industry record for first-year sales. By March 1966, the one-millionth Mustang had rolled off the line.

Most automotive experts greeted the Mustang with qualified enthusiasm, which partly reflected the nature of the car. Underneath that striking new shape was little more than just another Detroit compact—and a humble Falcon at that. But most critics were willing to forgive this, because performance and handling equipment was available to make any Mustang a competent grand tourer.

Standard equipment on the early "1964½" models included the 170-cubic-inch Falcon six, 3-speed manual floorshift transmission, full wheel covers, padded dash, bucket seats, and carpeting. From there, you were on your own. A sampling: Cruise-O-Matic, 4-speed manual, or 3-speed overdrive transmissions (around $180 depending on engine); three V-8s ($106-$328); limited-slip differential ($42); Rally-Pac (tachometer and clock, $69); power brakes ($42); front disc brakes (from late 1965 on, non-assisted, $58); deluxe steering wheel ($32); power steering ($84); air conditioning (except with the "Hi-Performance" V-8); full-length center console ($50); vinyl roof covering for the hardtop ($74); push-button AM radio with antenna ($58); knock-off-style wheel covers ($18 the set); 14-inch wire-wheel covers ($45) and styled steel wheels (with V-8 only, $120); and a profusion of tires (including whitewalls and larger rubber up to 6.95 × 14).

Buyers could also grapple with option *packages*: Visibility Group (mirrors and wipers, $36); Accent Group (pinstriping and rocker panel moldings, $27); special handling package (for V-8s only, $31); Instrument Group (needle gauges for fuel, water, oil pressure, and amperes, plus round speedometer, $109); and a GT Group (disc brakes, driving lights, and special trim, $165). The most expensive single option, air conditioning, listed at a reasonable $283, and many of the more desirable individual items—such as the $107 "Pony" Interior Decor Group with horses embroidered on the seatbacks—were well within the reach of most buyers.

Engine options played a big role in determining a Mustang's personality. During the long 20-month 1965 model run, powerplant offerings were shuffled slightly. The original standard engine, the 101-bhp Falcon six, was dropped after September 1964 (considered the accepted break between "1964½" and the "true" 1965 models). Its replacement was a 200-cid six with 120 bhp. The 200 was an improvement on the 170 because of its higher compression, redesigned valvetrain, and seven (instead of five) main bearings. It also featured an automatic choke, short-stroke cylinder block for longer piston and cylinder wear, hydraulic valve lifters, and an intake manifold integral with the head.

The first-generation Mustang electrified the public and kicked off the "ponycar" craze.
Although it was eventually imitated by Camaro, Barracuda, Javelin, and others, Mustang
remained preeminent and, like this '66 GT convertible, timeless.

The smallest V-8 initially offered was the modern 260-cid "thinwall" unit from the Fairlane, rated at 164 bhp. A bore enlarged from 3.80 to 4.00 inches made it a 289 (on the same 2.87-inch stroke), offering 195 bhp with the two-barrel carburetor or 210 bhp with an optional four-barrel carb (for an additional $158). A "Hi-Performance" (HP) four-barrel version delivered 271 bhp; price was $276 with the GT Group, $328 without. After September 1964, the 260 was discontinued and a 200-bhp, two-barrel 289 became the base V-8 option (at $106). Output of the standard four-barrel unit was then boosted to 225 bhp, while the "Hi-Po" version was unchanged.

The four-barrel engines achieved their extra power by increased carburetor air velocity matched to the engine's performance curve. They also had valve timing different from that of the two-barrel engines, plus a higher compression ratio that demanded premium fuel.

Ordering the High-Performance 289 meant buyers also had to take the extra-cost 4-speed gearbox, which made the latter a "mandatory option"—a contradiction in terms but an arrangement much-beloved by Detroit automakers in the Sixties. The HP was also the only engine offered with optional "short" rear axle ratios (3.89:1 and 4.11:1) favored by drag racers. Standard ratios were 3.20:1 with the six, 2.80:1 with the two-barrel V-8, 3.00:1 with the four-barrel V-8, and 3.50:1 with the HP.

For real performance, of course, buyers could spring for the most "special" of Mustangs: the GT-350 Shelby Cobra. A creation of Carroll Shelby—a lanky Texan who had been a roustabout, chicken farmer, and champion driver—the GT-350 was instigated by Ford, which was looking for a car capable of whipping Corvettes in Sports Car Club of America (SCCA) B-Production competition. Shelby's participation also brought the Cobra name, which

had rocketed to prominence beginning in 1962, when Shelby dropped a Ford 289 into a lightweight AC Ace roadster and called it the AC/Shelby Cobra.

Final specs for the GT-350 were determined by the fall of 1964, and a dozen cars were subsequently built by hand at Shelby's small production facility in Venice, California. In addition, 88 of 100 production Mustangs shipped by Ford to Venice for homologation purposes had been transformed by New Year's Day, 1965. The GT-350 was unveiled at Riverside Raceway on January 27, 1965.

The "full-strength" GT-350R (R for "racing") was conceived as a competition car; the street GT-350 was simply a less extreme, more tractable version of it. A beefed-up suspension that included a steel brace running between the shock towers improved handling and limited body flex. Rolling stock comprised hefty 15 × 6-inch Shelby-made wheels shod with 7.75 × 15 Goodyear Blue Dot performance tires.

Underhood modifications included aluminum high-rise manifolds, wilder camshaft profile, and a larger Holley carb fed by a functional scoop in a hood made of fiberglass instead of steel. These changes, plus a less restrictive exhaust system, boosted the HP 289 to an honest 306 bhp. (The competition version was tweaked to 340-360 gross horsepower.)

All 1965 GT-350s were painted white; no other colors were available. All Ford and Mustang badging and insignia were removed, but the blue rocker-panel stripes prominently displayed the GT-350 name. The back seat was removed, but Shelby offered a bolt-on bench kit for useful "+2" seating.

The street GT-350 went for $4547, about $1500 more than a standard V-8 Mustang. From a standing start, 60 mph came up in an average of 6.5 seconds. Top speed was 130-135 mph, and the car handled like a true race machine. And at $5950, the competition-only R version

was a real bargain capable of going directly from showroom to winner's circle.

Although the Shelby was not an easy car to drive, demand for the street version quickly exceeded the capability of Carroll Shelby's facility, prompting Shelby American, Inc., to move from Venice to two huge hangars at Los Angeles International Airport in the spring of 1965.

Meanwhile, the "regular" Mustang continued to evolve. Front disc brakes built by Kelsey-Hayes were offered beginning late in the '65 model year, and a new model came along, too: a snazzy Mustang coupe with semi-fastback styling that arrived with the rest of the '65 Ford line in autumn 1964. Several names were considered, including GT Limited, Grand Sport, and, ironically, GTO, but the final nameplates read "2+2." That was apt, because rear leg room was scant—even less than in the hardtop or convertible. But there was compensation in an optional fold-down rear seat, with a partition in the trunk bulkhead that dropped forward to create a long load platform that could accommodate skis or fishing rods. Instead of rear-quarter windows, the 2+2 had gill-like C-pillar air vents, part of the flow-through ventilation system.

The first Mustang was undeniably attractive, but the fact remains that it was more an example of brilliant marketing than a piece of revolutionary design and engineering. The body carried too many non-functional "gingerbread" touches, and utilization of interior space, given the 108-inch wheelbase, wasn't exactly a model of practicality.

With standard suspension, Mustang offered a wallowing, sometimes floaty ride that fell short of the car's sporting pretensions. The 210-bhp 4-speed managed the 0-60 sprint in nine seconds, performance that failed to impress *Road & Track*. The magazine's opinion changed radically, though, when a tester laid hands on a 271-bhp Hi-Performance V-8 and took it from rest to 60 mph in 8.3 seconds. *Motor Trend* made the same run in 7.6 seconds.

The HP engine was good, but changes wrought by the optional and inexpensive handling package were even more impressive. Stiff springs and shocks, a large-diameter front anti-sway bar, 5.90 × 15 Firestone Super Sports tires, and a quicker steering ratio (3.5 turns lock-to-lock) brought noticeably improved roadworthiness. The ride was occasionally harsh but firm enough to inspire driver confidence, despite a marked degree of oversteer (the tendency of rear wheels to lose traction and skid sideways in a turn).

Mustang seemed born to race, and did so even before it went on sale. In late winter of 1963-64, Ford prepped a team of rally Mustangs to take over for the newly banned Falcon Sprints in European events. The effort was sincere enough, but the team's only major win came in the Tour de France, where Peter Proctor and Peter Harper finished one-two in class.

More success was found on the dragstrips, where 2+2s stuffed full of Ford's 427-cid big-block racked up numerous wins in NHRA's A/FX class and, less often, as "funny cars." The factory jumped into the fray for the '65 season, fielding wild "altereds" with two-inch-shorter wheelbases. And—not unexpectedly—Carroll Shelby's GT-350s tore up the tracks (and more than a few Corvettes) in SCCA B-Production-class events.

With Mustang sales roaring along as the 1966 model year approached, Ford product planners saw little reason to tamper with success. Though the '66 looked like a '65 rerun at first glance, there were a few changes.

Up front, the honeycomb grille texture was replaced by thin bars, and the thick horizontal chrome bar was discarded, leaving the galloping horse to float in its chromed rectangular frame. Mustang GTs kept the grille bar, however, with auxiliary

driving lights mounted at the ends. At the rear was a restyled fuel filler cap. Along the sides, the simulated rear-wheel scoop was decorated with three windsplits (except on GTs, 2+2s, and luxury models, which didn't have this trim). Front fender nameplates and emblems were revised, and the stock wheel covers were redesigned.

Inside alterations were more functional. For example, the original Falcon-style instrument cluster with its old-fashioned strip speedometer was replaced by the five-gauge unit with the round speedo previously reserved for the GT package. The column-mounted Rally-Pac tachometer/clock combination remained on the option list.

Changes to running gear included an upgrade of six-cylinder models from 13- to 14-inch wheels and, for all models, reworked engine mounts to reduce vibration. Engine choices remained at four: the standard 200-cid six and the three optional 289s. The already generous option list was extended to include a stereo 8-track tape player ($128) and deluxe seatbelts ($15).

Predictably, Mustang's 1966 sales were down compared to model-year '65, which was longer than usual due to the early introduction. But for comparable 12-month periods, the '66s actually ran ahead by 50,000 units. Mustang still had no direct competition and romped along at close to half a million hardtops, 70,000 convertibles, and 35,000 fastbacks.

Though it looked very much like its V-8 counterpart, the six-cylinder Mustang—which was vigorously promoted by Ford—was considerably different. Its wheels had only four lugs, while V-8 models had five. All Mustangs had standard drum brakes, but sixes had good-performing nine-inchers, V-8s 10-inchers. The six-cylinder cars also had a lighter rear axle and a slightly narrower front track, and their spring rates were somewhat lower to keep an even keel; had they used the heavier V-8

suspension, they would have appeared tail-heavy.

The Mustang six performed reasonably well for a car of its class. *Motor Trend's* automatic-equipped model ran 0-60 mph in 14.3 seconds and averaged 20 mpg on regular gas.

Existing at the other end of the performance spectrum was the Shelby Cobra GT-350, made smoother and less raw for '66. Color choices expanded, and the fastback's extra-cost fold-down rear seat became a Shelby option as well. Automatic transmission was made an option—hardly the thing to excite driving enthusiasts. However, a Paxton centrifugal supercharger was another new option, sold factory-installed for $670 or as a $430 kit. Ford claimed the blower boosted horsepower by 46 percent, to more than 400 bhp. Zero to 60 times were cut to five seconds. These were potent cars that enjoyed considerable success in 1966 Trans-Am racing and in SCAA events.

Total 1966 Shelby Mustang production was 2380, including 936 Hertz models and six specially built convertibles Carroll gave to friends. (In addition, 252 leftover '65 GT-350s were updated to 1966 specs.)

The public's enthusiasm for the whole range of Mustangs made Ford well aware that competitors were readying ponycars of their own, but this had little to do with the more substantial changes that were already in the works for the '67 Mustang. These had been initiated in mid-1964, just as the country was catching "Mustang Fever," and reflected the industry's usual three-year lead time, the ritual of annual style changes, and, to some extent, Ford's uncertainty at that point on how the original concept would "play in Peoria."

So the '67 Mustang was a bolder and brawnier model that started Ford's lithe ponycar down the path of bigger-is-better mentality, a seven-year journey that would ultimately lead Ford and Mustang back to square one.

# 1964

- President Lyndon Johnson pledges a "War Against Poverty" in his State of the Union address in January

- The Beatles conquer America following a February TV appearance on *The Ed Sullivan Show*

- Plymouth's Valiant-based Barracuda debuts as an answer to Mustang

- Pontiac unveils the Tempest-based GTO, kicking off the muscle car era

- Corvair's Monza Spyder carries a turbocharged 150-bhp flat six

- Ford officially introduces Mustang on April 17, at the New York World's Fair; 100,000 are sold in four months

- A Mustang convertible paces the Indianapolis 500

- The Mustang fastback bows on October 1; a 200-cid six is standard

- After September, Mustang's 260-cid V-8 is dropped in favor of the 289

- In the fall, Ford hand-builds a dozen Shelby Cobra prototypes based on the Mustang; by the end of the year, 88 white Mustang fastbacks have been converted

*Opposite page:* Ford Advanced Studio styling studies from the early Sixties were built at the insistence of product planner Hal Sperlich, who didn't feel the market for a small, family/work car was satisfied with Ford's new Falcon. The 2+2 Allegro (*top*) resembled the '57 Thunderbird—right down to the very small back seat area. Rear and front views of the two-seat Allegro II (*middle row*) display an exciting shape that included a simulated roll bar, a clean front end, and an aggressive rear end with exhaust pipes, bumper struts, and exhaust-pipe cutouts. *Bottom:* The Allegro convertible leaned toward a sedan-like look.

A notchback Allegro (*top*) was characterized by a formal roofline, a feature that Iacocca felt imparted a quality look. Though sedate, the car did have the long hood/short deck theme that Iacocca also favored. Roof treatments differed on some studies (*second row*); in addition, Allegro was done up as a coupe (*third row*) with fender blades on the raised rear quarter panels. Iacocca liked this rather extreme touch. From the rear, a bit of the first-generation Mustang's rear-window treatment is hinted at. Designers also took a stab at an Allegro fastback (*left*), which anticipated the Plymouth Barracuda look at the busy front end.

*Top row:* The Mustang as it was approved in the Ford Design Center courtyard by Henry Ford II, Lee Iacocca, and others. The car's two different sides offered a pair of styling choices. Of course, the right side was rejected and the left was modified by smoothing out the "hop-up" above the rear wheels and removing the bars in the rear quarter ornament (later adopted for '66). The rectangular headlamps also didn't make production, and the front bumper was made smoother. The Allegro sedan is visible behind the winning design. *Right:* A September 1962 variation on the notchback Allegro of about three months earlier. *Bottom row:* Iacocca asked the design staff for ideas for the '66 Mustang—dangerous work for the designers because more than once (but not this time) Iacocca would simply scratch the original design and go with the second.

*This page:* The first Ford to bear the Mustang nameplate was the Mustang I—appropriately named, but having almost no connection, other than badges and some styling cues, with the production car. European in look and design, the Mustang I featured an aluminum body wrapped over a tubular space frame, fitted with four-wheel independent suspension, roll bar, and a Ford of Europe Taunus-Cardinal V-4 engine/transaxle mounted between the driver and the rear wheels. It revved up interest in the Mustang name, which is exactly what Lee Iacocca wanted. The side scoops were functional, to cool the mid-mounted engine. The three-spoke steering wheel was carried for production.

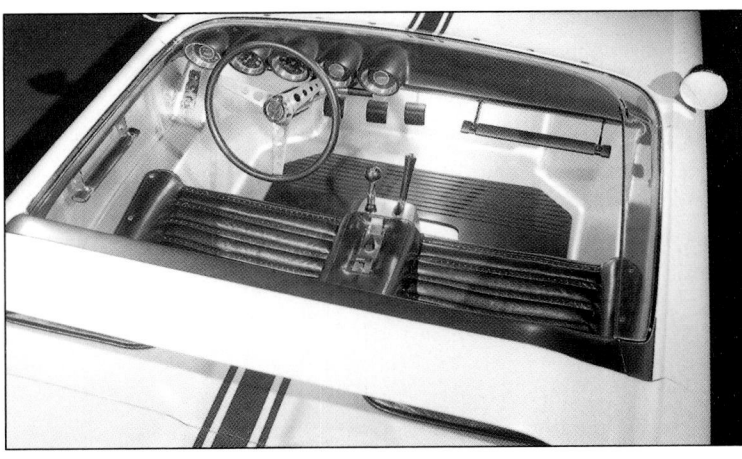

Although the Mustang design had been approved in August 1962, Engineering "feased" it for production, and Iacocca asked to see what the '66 might look like. Notice the tri-bar rear quarter ornament on the styling clay (*above*), a design element that was picked up for '66. The bright metal spear running just above the rocker panel molding was abandoned. The convertible clay (*right and below*) was firmed up, but it still showed a Cougar on the gas cap cover and grille. Because the sporty new car was basically a Falcon with new skin, the license tag says "Spec. Fal.," for "Special Falcon." The instrument panel (*below right*) was mostly Falcon, fitted (at this date, 4-5-63) with an optional console and three-spoke steering wheel with a running-horse Mustang logo and Ford Mustang name.

*This page:* The ragtop Mustang II was essentially a disguised version of the production car that would debut the following year. In 1963, Ford Design was still intent on using the name Cougar and had a list of other badges, including Torino, which appeared on the Mustang II of May 1963 (*top left*). By the car's initial display at Watkins Glen in October, the Mustang name was set, along with the running horse in the grille and front-fender badging. The removable hardtop was considered for production. Inside (*left*) were integral armrests and lights similar to those introduced in mid-1965 with the Interior Decor Group option.

*Top left:* In August 1963, Ford Design considered a complicated set of glass louvers in a strut down the middle of the fastback's roof. The struts were designed to be tipped and opened, which sounded great but wasn't very practical. *Top right:* A coupe was the prototype for a proposed vinyl roof. *Above:* For '66, Ford Design proposed to strengthen the horizontal grille bar, add inset headlights and a hood ornament, and remove the horse in the grille. Iacocca felt buyers would pay an additional $50 for a car with a hood ornament, but this doodad didn't make it to production. *Right:* The same fastback sported '66-style Shelby taillights with a horizontal bar and a flip-up rear gas cap.

The approved '66 fastback (*top left*) still had '65 wheelcovers—and a little friend, too (*top right and rows two and three*), which, although not a Mustang proposal, did have a long hood and (very) short deck. Lee Iacocca, who liked this little two-seater (executed by Ford Advanced Studio under Don DeLaRossa), preferred to view new car proposals beside other Fords in order to compare them for size and get an idea of what they would look like in Ford showrooms. *Left:* A production 1964½ Mustang. The car was sufficiently rich-looking that many people had difficulty believing its base price was just $2368.

Pre-production prototype convertibles (*top row*) and coupes (*second row*) did not carry the large horizontal grille bars that were added very late in the design process. The Sunlight Yellow 1965 convertible (*right*) dispensed with chromed rear-quarter ornamentation for a cleaner look. The car did, however, have an Accent Stripe that outlined the bodyside sculpturing in a reverse C pattern around the rear quarter's simulated scoop. The Rangoon Red convertible (*above*) carried a 289 V-8—a fact that was boldly proclaimed via fender badging.

*Top and middle:* Ford paced the Indianapolis 500 in 1953 and did not return until 1963 with the T-Bird, followed by the Mustang in 1964 and Torino in 1968. The Shelby GT-350 (*above*) debuted in January 1965. *Right, foreground to background:* Mustang I, Mustang II, production Mustang, and Shelby GT-350 Mustang.

The styled steel rims seen on this Guardsman Blue '64½ convertible (*top left*) are add-ons, and didn't make production until '65. The optional Accent Stripe (*top right*) eliminated the rear quarter ornament. The Caspian Blue '64½ convertible (*above and right*) has white vinyl buckets with long console, Rally Pac, and 4-speed.

The GT Equipment Group (*above and right*) included stripes, GT grille with integral fog lights, styled steel rims, and four-barrel carburetor.

# 1965

- Two U.S. warplanes are shot down during a combat mission over Laos

- Chevy creates the Nova Super Sport by dropping a 327-cid V-8 into its compact Nova

- The Classic-based Rambler Marlin bows; fastback styling is appealing, but the 3+3 interior misses the ponycar point

- The Mustang-based Shelby GT-350 Cobra officially debuts at Riverside Raceway on January 27

- A competition version of the Shelby GT-350 Cobra, the GT-350R, is homologated for SCCA B-production

- Success of the street-version Shelby Cobras prompts a move of Shelby American, Inc., from Venice, California, to a pair of enormous hangars at Los Angeles International Airport

- 2+2 Mustangs fitted with Ford's 427-cid big block regularly win NHRA A/FX-class races and, occasionally, "funny car" competitions

- Top NHRA racers campaigning in Mustangs include Gas Ronda, Les Ritchey, and Phil Bonner

- AC's Shelby Cobra, masterminded by ex-race driver Carroll Shelby, gains Ford's awesome 427-cid V-8

- Total "1964½"-65 Mustang model-year sales are 680,989; convertibles account for 101,945

*Top left:* In 1965 and '66, Ford dealers sold a Mustang pedal car, built by AMF, for $12.95. Later, the popular toy was marketed by Western Auto stores. *Top right:* Early Mustang ads prominently displayed the car's base price, $2368. *Middle and above:* The GT debuted in the spring of 1965 and came with a redesigned instrument panel.

*Top left:* Wheelcovers identify the '65 GT fastback. *Top right:* Chromed valve covers and an open-element air cleaner were unique to the 289 High Performance V-8. Fastbacks (*left*) came standard with rear quarter scoop deleted. Rear roof quarter vents (*above*) were functional when front air inlets were opened.

*Above and right:* Mustang enthusiasts in Australia imported more than 10,000 Mustangs into their country between 1989 and 1994. One of them was Mark Evans, who restored his 1965 200-cid I-6 fastback and converted it to right-hand drive.

*Top row:* The '65 Silver Smoke Grey convertible carries the optional 289. *Middle left:* West Texas is home for this Prairie Bronze ragtop with the playful Six. *Middle right:* A Silver Blue '65 coupe casts a luxury image with its simulated wire wheelcovers and spinners. *Left and above:* The decklid-mounted luggage rack was an optional, dealer-added accessory that cost $35 in 1965.

Ford urged owners to turn their cars into GTs with over-the-counter components, and that's exactly what Jack Dayhoff of Boulder, Colorado, did with his Wimbledon White '65 coupe (*top row*), fitted with lower-bodyside GT stripes, GT fog lamps, and barred grille. The stock 289 has Cobra valve covers and an oval air cleaner. The Rangoon Red '65 coupe with white vinyl top (*other photos*) is a factory GT with "trumpet" exhausts. The 289 is the 225-horse four barrel, the base GT engine in '65. Note that the red-and-white interior matches the red-and-white exterior. The car's original owner was a Ford salesman.

*Top left:* This Ivy Green '65 coupe with white vinyl top has a very rare accessory: fog lights, normally seen only on GT models. The 289 (*top right*) has power steering, power disc brakes, air conditioning, and factory dress-up kit with chromed air cleaner lid and valve covers. The Phoenician Yellow coupe with black vinyl top (*middle row*) has a stock 289. Mustang was the first car to capitalize on the option theme in a big way; to find one that wasn't owner-personalized is unusual. A quick glance at the blue coupe (*left*), for example, reveals V-8 fender badges and simulated wire wheelcovers.

*Above, left, and top left:* Base engine for 1964 ½ was the 170-cid I-6—not a good choice with power-robbing extras. The base 3-speed manual was non-synchronized in first gear. This convertible is the archetypal first-generation Mustang, having the original body style with the base engine and transmission, and no air, power steering, or automatic.

*Left, far left, and above:* Shelby's GT-350 Mustang had the horsepower for any amount of accessories, but its need for speed ruled out automatic, air, or other power-robbing options. Instead, Carroll Shelby put the money into Cobra-izing the 289 and modifying the suspension: Upper-front control arms were relocated and lowered, and override rear traction bars were added. Even the stripes and fancy wheels were options. Mustang "builders" have copied and embellished Shelby's GT-350 example for years.

The GT (*left*) debuted in the spring of '65 and sold strongly: 15,079 during the first half of that year. The GT got the new five-dial instrument cluster (*above*) that became standard on every 1966 model. The Interior Decor Group (with Pony seats) arrived as a separate option at the same time.

In the summer of '66, exactly 333 "High Country Special" Mustangs, in coupe, convertible, and fastback form (one example only), arrived in Denver, Colorado, on a 23-car freight train. Colors were limited to Aspen Gold, Timberline Green, and Columbine Blue, as seen on this convertible (*middle row, left, and far left*). Special brass badges affixed to the front fenders provided identification. This car has the Pony seats, Rally Pac, and console. The High Country Specials were devised by Thurlo Newell of Ford's Denver zone office, and came to market two years before the better-known California Specials.

# 1966

- American G.I.s launch a major offensive against a Viet Cong stronghold near Saigon
- General Motors apologizes to consumer advocate Ralph Nader for investigating his private life
- Dodge's fastback Charger debuts

.................................................

- Alterations to '66 Mustangs are minor, and include revised standard hubcaps, grille, and fake side vents
- Ford heavily promotes the inline-six Mustang engine
- Some '66 Mustangs have a "Pony" interior featuring ponies stampeding across the seatbacks
- Styling studies toy with the idea of a "Kammback" Mustang station wagon badged Aspen; a targa-top convertible is also considered
- A Paxton supercharger is available on the '66 Shelby GT
- Throughout the year, Hertz rents 1000 Shelby GTs at airports around the country; many are returned with competition fatigue, and Hertz cancels the program after a year
- Mustang sales for the model year dip slightly, to 607,568, and include 72,119 convertibles; with 7.1 percent of total market share, Mustang is the industry's third-best-selling nameplate

*Top:* The High Country Special was a clever way for Ford to salute the state of Colorado, where the Mustang sold in big numbers throughout the Sixties. This Columbine Blue coupe looks right at home high up in the Rockies. Collectors believe the '66 HCs were produced on one day, July 15, 1966, which corresponds to a data plate code of "15G." *Other photos:* It's hard to beat a Rangoon Red convertible with 289 V-8 power.

*Top left:* For $96 extra in 1966, Ford would paint a new Mustang in any color the customer desired, such as the Mack Truck Orange on this fastback. *Top right:* The Pony seat interior looked great with the orange exterior. *Above:* Few buyers chose the six-cylinder Sports Sprint option, which was no more than a chrome and decal dress-up option. Even the six (*above right*) could be optioned with the Rally Pac (*right*), a dual pod tach/clock strapped to the top of the steering column.

*Right:* The hardtop was by far the most popular 1966 Mustang, with 501,965 built, or an incredible 73.7 percent of the total for the extended '65 model year. Wimbledon White was the most popular color, making this Mustang the most recognized car of the postwar era. The formal rear roofline gave the original Mustang a "little Lincoln" look; in fact, in profile, the lines closely followed the 1955-1957 Continental Mark II. Mustang also capitalized on the long hood/short rear deck theme used by Lincoln to symbolize wealth and status. The front grille opening was purposely placed very high, which made the car unlike any other on the American road in the mid-Sixties.

*Other photos:* The convertible came in second in 1966 production, with 101,945 units. This ragtop is optioned out with most of the high-dollar "toys," including the GT package, styled steel wheels, Rally Pac, power top, air conditioning with "short console," simulated wood steering wheel, deluxe interior with Pony seats—even a luggage rack mounted on the decklid. Unwary buyers were sometimes surprised to discover that options and accessories could easily double the base price of a Mustang. Regardless, Ford's emphasis on options caught on with the other Detroit automakers, who eventually allowed buyers to "personalize" their cars.

This beautifully restored 1966 Mustang is a rare Silver Frost with black vinyl roof, styled steel wheels, and deluxe black interior. As good as the car looks inside and out, the real show starts when the hood is lifted to reveal a 289 with a Ford dress-up kit, much rarer than Cobra valve covers and air cleaner. This explains the chrome on the valve covers, radiator cap, master cylinder cap, dipstick, and on the low-restriction, Hi-Po-style air cleaner.

*This page:* The 1966 GT is identical to the '65 GT—from the front. That's because GTs continued to have the large bars (to hold the GT driving lights) flanking the galloping horse in the grille; on other '66 models, the bars were absent. The base GT engine was again the 225-horse 289 with hydraulic lifters and the regular-production air cleaner assembly. This GT has rare Tahoe Turquoise paint, color code "U." The deluxe interior could be mistaken for that of a '65 except that the air conditioner, still an under-dash unit, looks different with a black camera case finish and redesigned air registers. From the rear, a GT insignia on the gas cap identifies the '66 model. Trumpet exhausts routed through the rear valance on 1965 and '66 models.

Mustang's rear quarter ornaments (*above*) were restyled for '66, with three "forward thrusting bars," in Ford's words, which added to the look of "fleetness and motion." The ornaments could be deleted for $13.90 and replaced with an Accent Stripe. This convertible has the standard "simulated spoke" wheelcovers (*top*). Every '66 got a bright hood lip molding, which was introduced with the GT in mid-1965. Pony seats (*left*), so named because the backs of the buckets carried embossed images of ponies, are often misidentified as GT trim, when in fact the seats were part of the Interior Decor Group.

In 1966, Carroll Shelby's high-performance version of the Mustang was catalogued as the Shelby GT-350, whereas in 1965 it had been the Mustang GT-350. It's easy to spot a '66 by the stylish Plexiglas rear quarter windows, plus functional fiberglass rear-brake cooling scoops. The stock Magnum 500 wheels on the white GT-350 (*above and right*) are modified with spinners. At the end of the '66 model-year, Shelby-American built six GT-350 convertibles, including the yellow one below, that were not for public sale. These cars, all automatics with non-functioning rear brake scoops, were gifts from Carroll Shelby to friends and employees.

Most of the 1000 Shelby GT-350 Hertz rental cars were black with gold stripes, but a limited number were Candy Apple Red with gold stripes (*left and above*). The cars were available to Hertz Sports Car Club members in 1966.

This maroon, modified '66 (*left and above*), one of thousands of early Mustangs painted to resemble a Shelby, makes no attempt to fool anybody as to heritage. Every Shelby is backed by paperwork from Shelby-American and can be checked by the Shelby American Automobile Club. The "KC" added to the GT-350 bodyside lettering are the initials of the owner's wife.

LEAD TIMES ARE A FRUSTRATING fact of life in the auto industry. Because it takes three to six years for a car to go from drawing board to showroom, stylists and engineers often work on a new model before they know how well the public liked the one they just finished.

Mustang's instant success raised some vexing questions when developmental work on the follow-up '67 edition began in mid-1964. While planners knew it would need some changes, they didn't know precisely what those changes ought to be. Of course, changing things too much might hurt sales—but then, Ford couldn't be sure the ponycar craze wasn't just a flash in the pan.

There was also the question of how arch-rival Chevrolet would respond—if at all. For a while, General Motors design chief Bill Mitchell insisted his company had a Mustang-fighter in the beautiful second-generation 1965 Corvair. But that was only a smokescreen for the Camaro, a true Chevy ponycar being readied for '67. As Ford engineer Tom Feaheny told author Gary Witzenburg: "It was a long ways down the road before we were aware that they were coming after us."

Beyond this, "[The '67] was an opportunity to do a lot of refinement work," as Feaheny put it. "Frankly, the amount of engineering in that [first Mustang] was not as great as it could have been. . . . We really wanted to do the job right the second time around." Feaheny also noted that product planning chief Hal Sperlich wanted to "one-up the original in every

## CHAPTER 3
# 1967-68: All Deliberate Speed

respect. . . ." Finally, the mid-1964 arrival of Pontiac's GTO muscle car encouraged Ford to enlarge Mustang's engine bay for a big-block V-8. Ford figured that even a ponycar could always use more deliberate speed in the burgeoning horsepower race.

The result was a '67 Mustang that retained its predecessor's basic chassis, inner structure, and running gear, but was different most everywhere else. The big news, of course, was the planned big-inch engine: the 390 "Thunderbird Special" V-8 with four-barrel carburetor and a rousing 320 horsepower. As a Mustang option it cost $264, versus $434 for the "Hi-Po" 289 small-block. Ford recommended the 390 be teamed with new "SelectShift" Cruise-O-Matic transmission, which cost $233 with either of the top-power V-8s. SelectShift's big attraction was permitting manual hold of any of the three forward gears for maximum acceleration. Other powertrains were basically unchanged, but the 390's arrival swelled choices to no fewer than 13.

Though it certainly made for potent performance, the 390 also made for a very front-heavy Mustang (fully 58 percent of total curb weight) that understeered with abandon. Though the option

came with F70-14 Wide Oval tires to help counter that, most everyone who drove a 390 said small-block Mustangs handled better.

Big-block buyers were also well advised to order the $389 Competition Handling Package, though that meant ponying up for the GT option too. Also available with the HP small-block, the "comp" package delivered stiffer springs/ front stabilizer bar, Koni adjustable shocks, limited-slip axle, quick-ratio steering, and 15-inch wheels, all of which improved handling at the expense of ride. With that, few buyers bothered with the Competition option. Of course, the big-block's big payoff was spectacularly robust acceleration: typically 7.5 seconds 0-60 mph, 15.5 seconds at 95 mph in the standing quarter-mile, and close to 120 mph flat out.

Complementing the burly 390 was a more muscular look for all models via a lower-body reskin. Most-changed of all was the 2+2, which went from a semi-notchback to a sweeping full fastback roofline a la Ford's GT40 endurance racer. All models gained a concave back panel with separate triple taillamps, more-kicked-up rear fenders, and a longer nose bearing a bigger grille with no flanking "gills." A new, extra-cost Exterior Decor Group added thin horizontal bars to the back panel and turn-signal lights to the hood in twin dummy scoops. Combining the GT option with automatic changed front-fender badging to "GT/A."

Wheelbase was unchanged, but overall length grew two inches, width increased

The redesigned body that arrived for the 1967 model year had been in development even before the original Mustang went on sale. The changes, as seen on this '68 GT, were subtle and very much in keeping with the free-spiritedness of the car's initial design.

by 2.7 inches, and front track by 2.6 inches. That last increase was made chiefly to make room for the bulky 390, but it also improved handling. Front springs were relocated above the top cross-member, while lowered upper A-arm pivots and a raised roll center were good ideas borrowed from Carroll Shelby's GT-350. The welcome effect of all this tweaking was to reduce understeer by holding the outside front wheel more perpendicular to the road. Since the changes didn't demand higher spring rates, ride didn't suffer. New rubber suspension bushings lowered noise, vibration, and harshness.

The '67 shed another vestige of Mustang's Falcon origins with a bulky new "twin-cowl" instrument panel dominated by a pair of large, circular dials ahead of the driver. Newly optional for all models were the Tilt-Away steering wheel from recent Thunderbirds and the equally useful "Convenience Control Panel" (four warning lights above the center-mount radio).

The '67 Mustang compared quite favorably against its new rivals. It offered the widest selection of V-8s, though the Camaro with the optional 375-horsepower 396 had the edge on any other ponycar in a straight line. Mustang had less passenger and cargo room than Plymouth's handsomely reworked '67 Barracuda, rode a bit harder than the Chevy, and was noisier than Camaro or Barracuda. But none of those could match Mustang's swing-away wheel or the Mustang convertible's new articulated-glass rear window (a horizontal crease allowed it to "bend" as the top folded).

Still, Mustang's first real competition (including new corporate-cousin Mercury Cougar) pushed 1967 model-year orders some 25 percent below the '66 tally. The mainstay hardtop sustained most of the loss. But 472,121 sales wasn't bad, and

Mustang bested runner-up Camaro by more than two to one.

Carroll Shelby turned the "more Mustang" '67 fastback into a new GT-350 that convincingly one-upped Ford. There was a new fiberglass nose with two high-beam headlamps dead-center in the grille, as well as a larger hood scoop, sculptured brake cooling scoops on the sides, and two more scoops on the rear roof for interior air extraction. A modest "lip" spoiler appeared above wide taillight clusters purloined from Cougar. In all, it was a busy but arresting package.

Thanks to customer feedback and the stock Mustang's added weight, Shelby made power steering and brakes "mandatory options" for '67 (you still paid extra, but couldn't get a car without them). Interior appointments not shared with showroom Mustangs now included a racing steering wheel, additional gauges, and a functional roll bar with inertia-reel shoulder harnesses.

But that was only half of it. Typical of the man, Shelby passed on the 390 in favor of the physically similar, new 428 V-8 to create a second Shelby-Mustang, the GT-500, which promptly outsold the small-block model two to one. The GT-350 itself retained a 289 warmed to Shelby specs, but without steel-tube headers and straight-through mufflers. Actual power was thus lower despite an unchanged advertised rating.

Less muscle and weighty new fluff naturally hurt GT-350 performance. The GT-500 was predictably quicker, yet somehow disappointing. Carmakers were now deliberately understating power figures to avoid running afoul of insurance companies. Shelby's 428 was thus billed at 355 bhp, but probably had far more. *Car and Driver*, whose test car timed 6.5 seconds 0-60 mph, said that while the 428 "isn't the Le Mans winner," the GT-500 "does with ease what the old [GT-350] took brute force

to accomplish." But *Road & Track*, which got 7.2 seconds in the same sprint, said the GT-500 "simply doesn't have anything sensational to offer. . . ." Shelby had an answer to this, too: an optional 427—which *was* the Le Mans engine—rated at 390 bhp, though few were ordered.

Regular Mustangs didn't keep cutting it so well on the sales track, for the '68 models skidded to about 300,000 orders. One problem was even rougher ponycar competition with the arrival of American Motors's new Javelin and AMX. Then too, Mustang prices were higher. The '68 ragtop was up to over $2800 base list, and a few options could run it above $4000—a lot in those days.

Familiarity was another factor in Mustang's '68 sales slide, as styling was little changed. As before, crease lines ran from the upper front fenders to loop around simulated scoops ahead of the rear wheels before running forward into the lower doors. GTs now accented this with jazzy optional "C-stripes." All models wore a more deeply inset grille, with the running horse (still in a bright rectangle) now flush-mounted rather than free-standing. The horizontal grille bar was erased, leaving GT fog lamps to "float" at the outboard ends of the cavity.

The rest of the GT package was little changed. The '68 edition included dual exhausts with chrome-plated "quad" outlets, pop-open fuel cap, heavy-duty suspension (high-rate springs, shocks, and front sway bar), F70-14 whitewall tires on six-inch rims, and styled steel wheels. Aggressive Wide Oval tires were again sold separately.

Though engine choices were more numerous than ever for '68, a few were detuned to meet that year's new 50-state emissions standards. Lower compression pushed the base 200-cid six to 115 bhp, down five, while the two-barrel 289 V-8 withered from 200 to 195. But rated horses on the big 390 actually *increased,* to 335. And for the first time there was an optional six: a 250-cid unit lifted from Ford's truck line, offering 155 bhp for just $26 extra. Four-speed manual was no longer listed for six-cylinder Mustangs. The high-winding four-barrel 289 also departed, but its role as the middle V-8 was filled by a considerably changed small-block stroked out to 302 cid and a rated 230 bhp.

Topping the chart at a whopping $755 was Ford's mighty 427 big-block, with tight 10.9:1 compression and a conservative 390-bhp rating. Though restricted to Cruise-O-Matic, it was good for 0-60-mph times of around six seconds, making for the fastest showroom-stock Mustang yet. But its heaviness (which tended to overwhelm the front suspension) and formidable price precluded many sales. Incidentally, all '68 Mustangs benefited from optional power front-disc brakes with new floating calipers, which provided extra stopping ability over the previous fixed calipers with no extra pedal effort. The design was also said to promote longer brake life and, with fewer parts, to be more reliable. Ford recognized the need for front discs in big-engine Mustangs by making them a mandatory extra for cars equipped with the 390 or 427.

The 427 was hastily retired at mid-year, replaced by the 428 Cobra Jet, a huskier version of the new big-block lately offered in Thunderbirds and big Fords. For drag racing and insurance purposes, it was advertised at 335 bhp on 10.7:1 compression, but was undoubtedly much stronger.

Announced at about the same time was a fortified 302 with high-compression heads, larger valves, wilder cam timing, and a pair of four-barrel carbs. Humorously underrated at 240 bhp, it was clearly devised for the new Trans-Am road-racing series, but Ford had trouble getting it into production after getting

SCCA's okay, so only a handful of Mustangs got it. No matter: Camaro won 10 events to Mustang's three, and Chevy claimed the Manufacturers' Cup to end Ford's two-year Trans-Am reign.

Lengthening Mustang's '68 option roster was a Sports Trim Group with wood-grain dash, two-tone hood paint (also available separately), "Comfort-Weave" vinyl seat inserts, wheel lip moldings on six-cylinder models, and styled steel wheels and larger tires for V-8 cars. Other new extras included a rear-window defogger and Fingertip Speed Control. A spring/summer Sprint package offered V-8 power, GT-style C-stripes, pop-open gas cap, and full wheel covers or Wide Oval tires on styled wheels.

Appearing only for '68 was the limited-edition California Special. Sold mainly in the Golden State and styled along Shelby-Mustang lines, it was essentially a standard hardtop with a "ducktail" spoiler above Cougar-type taillights, plus mid-bodyside tape stripes and a plain grille cavity with fog lamps but no Mustang emblem.

The real Shelby Mustangs got another facelift for '68, sporting a full-width hood scoop, hood louvers, a larger grille with square running lamps (not driving lights), sequential rear turn signals, and miscellaneous trim shuffles. More significant were Shelby's first convertibles, a GT-350 and GT-500 with a built-in rollover hoop. Luxury options like air conditioning, tilt steering wheel, tinted glass, and AM/FM stereo now outnumbered performance features. But with federal emissions limits then in force, the GT-350 was switched to the new 302 and sank to a rated 250 bhp. Shelby revived a Paxton supercharger from '66 to give it about 100 more horses, but the option again found few takers.

That's because Shelby buyers still preferred big-block power. Early '68 GT-500s retained their previous 428, albeit

re-rated to 360 bhp, but some later cars got ordinary 390s because of a 428 shortage caused by an engine-plant strike. Buyers weren't told of the substitution, and it was nearly impossible to spot. Mid-model year brought some redress in the replacement GT-500KR (for "King of the Road"). Also offered in fast-back and convertible form, it carried the new Cobra Jet, basically the 428 with big-port 427 heads, larger intake manifold and exhaust system, and an estimated 40 extra horses. Shelby also tossed in wider rear brakes.

Shelby volume rose for the fourth straight year with 1968's total of 4450 units. But it would go no higher. Carroll's cars were fast turning into cushy cruisers whose once-strong performance image was only being eroded by increasingly potent showroom Mustangs. One sign of changing times was the late-1967 production shift from Los Angeles to Michigan, where stock Mustangs were converted into Shelbys. From here on, Ford alone would handle Shelby promotion, advertising—and development.

As elsewhere in Detroit, all '68 Mustangs boasted new safety features per congressional decree. Heading the long list were an energy-absorbing steering column, retracting seatbelts, standard backup lights, dual-circuit brake system, hazard warning flashers, side marker lights, and energy-absorbing seatbacks.

Mustang's '68 sales were good, though not great compared to earlier years. Some FoMoCo executives grew uneasy, aware that the car's novelty had begun to fade. But there was a reason: The ponycar market was nearing its peak barely four years after Ford opened the gate. Competitors had appeared to claim their pieces of the pie, making inroads into Mustang sales. No matter. Mustang was about to become even bolder and brasher. Sadly, it would also never be quite the same again.

# 1967

- Israel crushes Arab forces in the "Six Day War"

- The Mustang-based Mercury Cougar debuts

- General Motors introduces two contenders in the lucrative ponycar stakes: the Chevrolet Camaro and Pontiac Firebird

- Plymouth's Barracuda now has an available 280-bhp 383-cid V-8

- A 390-cid "Thunderbird Special" V-8 is now optional with Mustang

- An all-new dash helps Mustang shed a remnant of its Falcon origins

- Convertible Mustangs gain articulated rear glass

- The Shelby GT-350 Cobra gains a stretched fiberglass nose, large side scoops, rear ducktail spoiler, '67 Cougar taillight lenses, integral roll bar, and inertia-reel shoulder harnesses—the latter an industry first

- Carroll Shelby drops Ford's 428 into his Shelby Cobra and creates the GT-500; advertised bhp is 335 but is probably more; a 390-bhp version is a seldom-ordered GT-500 option

- At the Winternationals in Pomona, Ford's SOHC 427 dragster-style Super Mustang flies through the quarter mile in 8.28 seconds at 171 mph

- With 472,121 model-year sales, Mustang outsells Camaro by a two to one margin; 44,808 of those Mustangs are ragtops

To the uninitiated, the 428, dubbed the Cobra Jet when it debuted in the Mustang lineup on April 1, 1968, was no more than a bored and stroked 390, first dropped into the Mustang in '67. But Cobra Jet meant big port heads similar to the Ford 427 Low Riser, a 390 GT camshaft, a cast-iron copy of the 428 Police Interceptor intake manifold, and a 735 CFM Holley four-barrel. Rated conservatively at 335 horsepower @ 5200 rpm, with or without Ram Air, the CJ's real output was 375-400 horses.

*Top left:* This June 1966 restyle proposal, though intended for model-year 1969, undoubtedly influenced the look of the '67 Mustangs. *Top right:* The design team tackled a new fastback in October 1966. Notice the chopped top and gaudy side scoops. *Middle left:* This October 1966 wagon proposal was finished in fiberglass and set off by a complete interior. The amount of side glass is considerable for a car of this size. *Above:* Literally hundreds of designs were proposed when Ford tried to alter the best-selling new car in history. Ford Design deemed this developmental clay of a coupe "far too ugly" to make production. *Left:* This fastback from April 1965 is very close to the '67 fastback, except for the windows in the rear pillars.

*Above:* In 1968, Mustang placed second to Chevrolet's Z-28 in the Trans Am racing series. Shelby Racing prepared the #2 notchback driven by Allan Moffat and Horst Kwech. *Right:* The Mustang dash moved uptown in 1967, integrating five round pods in front of the driver. The brushed aluminum instrument panel, console (highlighted by a shifter with gear indicator lights and a sliding compartment door), and "Convenience Control Panel" with center lights were optional. *Below:* Mustang's famous running-horse logo. *Below right:* These styled steel wheels feature unique blue center caps. The design, introduced in 1965, lasted until 1967. The rocker panel molding was a $15.59 option on the coupe and convertible, but standard on the 2+2.

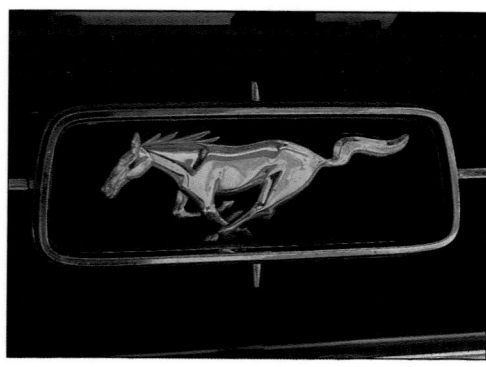

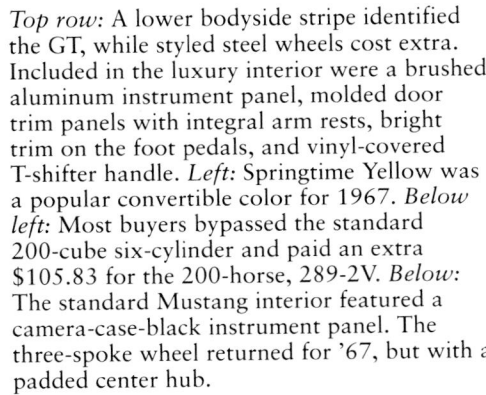

*Top row:* A lower bodyside stripe identified the GT, while styled steel wheels cost extra. Included in the luxury interior were a brushed aluminum instrument panel, molded door trim panels with integral arm rests, bright trim on the foot pedals, and vinyl-covered T-shifter handle. *Left:* Springtime Yellow was a popular convertible color for 1967. *Below left:* Most buyers bypassed the standard 200-cube six-cylinder and paid an extra $105.83 for the 200-horse, 289-2V. *Below:* The standard Mustang interior featured a camera-case-black instrument panel. The three-spoke wheel returned for '67, but with a padded center hub.

*Top row:* GTs shared their interiors with the rest of the V-8 Mustangs in 1967. However, this 1967 GTA (GT with Automatic) was ordered with the "Interior Decor Group," making it a "Luxury" model, identifiable by body number: 76B for the convertible, 65B for the hardtop, and 63B for the fastback. *Middle row:* The ribbed lower back-panel grille on this Hi-Po, Raven Black GT fastback was an option for any Mustang that had the Exterior Decor Group. *Right:* For 1967, the convertible again had the styling of the coupe.

*Top:* A vinyl-covered roof added $74.36 to the base price ($2461.46) of the '67 hardtop. This is a rare GTA model. *Middle row:* Another rarity: a 1967 High Country Special, available in fastback, convertible, and coupe. It's seen here in Aspen Gold, one of its three standard, special-order colors. Columbine Blue and Timberline Green were the other two. *Far left:* Brass badges, mounted on the front fenders, spelled out High Country Special and the model year, 1967. *Left:* The dealer who sold this HCS went to the trouble of making a key with a running-horse logo.

*Top row:* The 1968 High Country Special was strictly a coupe, based on a prototype Carroll Shelby called "Li'l Red." Hood lock buttons, blackout front grille, and driving lights give the front end a unique look. Side stripes flowed into a rear fiberglass side scoop with a High Country decal. *Above:* The rear taillights are 1965 Thunderbird, the same as those used on the '68 Shelby. *Above right:* The GT/CS interior is no different from stock, although there were proposals to inscribe "California Special" on the steering wheel. *Right:* There was no fastback GT/CS, but the GT in this body style was wild enough.

*Above and left:* This 1967 High Country Special looks like any other convertible except for its Aspen Gold paint and a unique brass badge visible just above the running-horse logo on the front fenders. Originally sold by Courtesy Ford in Littleton, Colorado, this High Country came from the factory as a Sports Sprint. *Below:* This regular-production black convertible has an attractive pinstripe; the stripe could be had in red, black, or white.

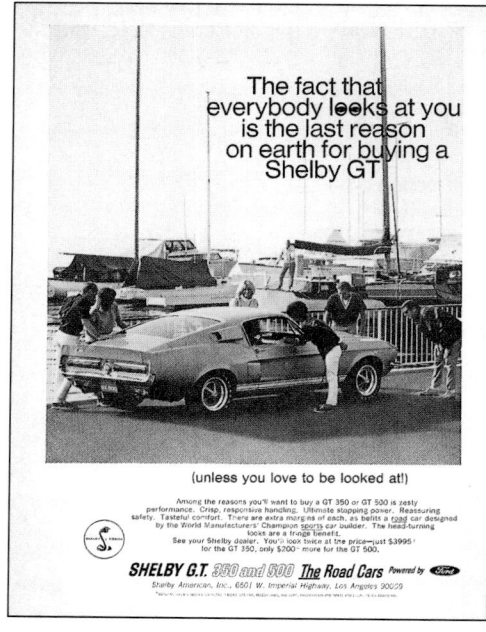

The fact that everybody looks at you is the last reason on earth for buying a Shelby GT

(unless you love to be looked at!)

Among the reasons you'll want to buy a GT 350 or GT 500 is zesty performance. Crisp, responsive handling. Ultimate stopping power. Reassuring safety. Tasteful comfort. There are extra margins of each, as befits a road car designed by the World Manufacturers' Champion sports car builder. The head-turning looks are a fringe benefit. See your Shelby dealer. You'll look twice at the price—just $3995* for the GT 350, only $200* more for the GT 500.

SHELBY G.T. 350 and 500 *The Road Cars* Powered by Ford
Shelby American, Inc., 6501 W. Imperial Highway, Los Angeles 90009

*Top left:* Some Shelby dealers discovered that the huge 5½-inch driving lights were illegal in their state. *Above left:* Taillights were pirated from a '67 Cougar. Rear lower scoops ducted air to the brakes, while the upper scoops exhausted air from the cab. *Top right:* The GT-350 came with the small-block 289, which for '67 was a 306-horse Cobra-ized version of the solid-lifter Hi-Po 289. *Left:* Shelby colors for '67 were Lime, Dark Blue, White, Dark Green, Medium Blue, and Red, seen here. Interiors were either Black or Parchment. These wheels are the optional Kelsey-Hayes, five-spoke "Mag-Stars." *Above:* Typically, attractive young people surrounded Shelby cars in magazine ads.

*This page:* Maximum heat on the street in '67 describes the GT-500, devised by Carroll Shelby as an answer to Chevy's dominant SS 396 Camaro. Shelby dropped the 428 family-sedan big-block into his GT-500 and hopped it up with a dual-quad aluminum intake topped by a pair of Holley 600s; horsepower was 355 @ 5400 rpm. Except for the model designation within the stripes and on the front fenders, a GT-500 was the spitting image, as Carroll would say, of the GT-350. Shelby was still selling his 427 AC Cobra Roadster in 1967, but as every Shelby Mustang had a "Cobra" engine, the snake emblem (*above*) became part of the marketing plan, as evidenced on the front fenders of this GT-500.

# 1968

- Martin Luther King, Jr., and Robert Kennedy are assassinated

- Because of war-related unrest at home, President Johnson announces he will not run for reelection; in the fall, Richard Nixon is elected President

- Chevy advertises this season's Z-28 Camaro as the "closest thing to a Corvette yet"

- A redesigned, "tunnelback" Dodge Charger is launched

- AMC mounts a credible challenge to Mustang with the Javelin, smartly designed by Richard Teague

..................................................

- General Motors executive vice-president Semon E. "Bunkie" Knudsen is named Ford Motor Company president in February

- Ford assumes control of the Shelby Mustangs, moving production from L.A. to Michigan

- The GT-350 now runs with a 302 small-block; bhp drops to 250

- The GT-500 retains the 428, re-rated to 360 bhp; some GT-500s get 390 V-8s, due to an engine-plant strike that halts 428 production

- Mid-year brings the Shelby Cobra GT-500 KR (King of the Road) with 428 Cobra-Jet V-8

- Shelby production peaks at 4450

- Model-year Mustang sales are 317,404, and include 25,376 convertibles—respectable, but a dramatic drop from '67

*Top:* Ford gave the '68 Mustang GT a unique look that was highlighted by striking C-shaped body stripes. Styled steel wheels with a slotted disc pattern were stock on GTs. *Above:* A well-optioned convertible could top $4000. Elimination of the horizontal grille bar allowed the GT fog lamps to "float" at the outboard ends of the big mouth cavity. *Left:* Most '68 coupes—the year's most popular Mustang—were sold with Cruise-O-Matic transmission, signaling increased buyer interest in sport and luxury.

*Top row:* Ford built 52 Cobra Jets in December of 1967 to homologate the car for Super Stock drag racing. The CJs had no fiberglass or aluminum panels because there was no need to reduce weight in the SS/E class. The radio-free, heater-delete interior of the racing CJs got a roll bar, shoulder harness, and driver seat belts. Most drivers added oil pressure and water temperature gauges to the vacated radio slots. *Above left:* The NHRA re-factored horsepower for the class to 355 (up from 335), which still gave the CJ a class-racing edge. *Above:* The 390 engine was no match for the CJ power plant, despite its 320-horse rating. *Left:* This '68 390 GT fastback, like other GTs without the 428 CJ, does not have the ram air hood scoop.

*Top row:* The '68 fastback was virtually a '67 with new side marker lights. Under the hood, the 230-horse 302-4V replaced the 289, which in 2V tune was dropped at mid-year. *Left:* Inside, more safety laws brought forth the seatback release, shoulder harness, and heavily padded two-spoke wheel. *Bottom row:* In 1968, no Mustang coupe had more pizzazz than the California Special, built exclusively for the lucrative California market. Goodies included unique side stripes and GT/CS decal, Shelby Mustang fiberglass side scoops, blackout grille with driving lights, and twist-type hood lock buttons.

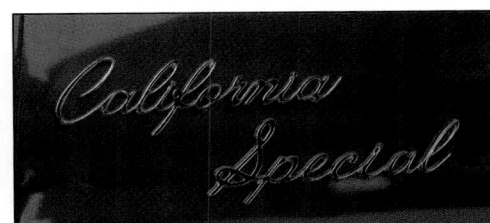

*Top left:* California Specials built before April 26, 1968, came with Marchal driving lights, while later GT/CS Mustangs came with Lucas units. *Top right:* Mustang owners often dressed up their engine compartments with Shelby Cobra-lettered oval air cleaners. *Above:* Every GT/CS was identified by script-style Mustang badges. *Below:* The 289-2V in this GT/CS is dressed up with Cobra finned aluminum valve covers. *Left and below left:* The GT/CS is often mistaken for a Shelby, which wasn't built in the coupe body style.

*Left and above:* 1968 was the last year of the "little Mustang"; the car subsequently made a decisive move into the muscle-car ranks. GT meant Grand Touring, and did not imply awesome drag-racing capability. GTs—the coupe in particular—had a neat, formal appearance. The black hood scoop was for looks, not function. A vinyl top might seem incongruous on a torquey muscle car, but it looked fine on a road-racy GT. The coupe seen here runs with a 230-horse 302-4V, the top-performing small-block V-8 in the '68 lineup. GT wheels were badged with GT insignia on newly designed styled "slotted disc" steel rims.

Front fender "Cobra Jet" emblems (*above*) revealed the presence of the 428 big-block under the hood of every GT-500 KR. The initials stood for "King of the Road," a nickname favored by Carroll Shelby and rushed into production when Shelby learned that Chevy planned to use the name on a new big-block Camaro. The '68 model year marked the first time the big-block Shelby didn't out-muscle the big-block regular production Mustang, as both had 428 CJs by mid-1968. *Right:* The Shelby was a Grand Touring luxury Mustang in 1968, available with every option from air conditioning to a tilt steering column.

*Top row: Hot Rod* magazine drag-raced a stock '68 CJ like this one to a 13.56 ET @ 106.64 mph. The CJ tach was optional. *Middle left:* Nearly every CJ had ram air in 1968½ and was coded "R"; however, very few ran with "Q"-coded Police Interceptor 428s. *Middle right:* One of the most popular special-order colors in 1967 was Playboy Pink, so named because it was the color of the car given to *Playboy* magazine's Playmate of the Year. *Left and above:* This GT convertible carries a GTA badge, indicating it left the factory with an automatic transmission.

*Top row:* Note the absence of an Accent Stripe on this 1968 390 fastback GT. For the first time, this stripe was not a part of the GT Equipment Group. The "390 GT" came with a two-bolt block, cast-iron crank, cast aluminum pistons, hydraulic cam, cast-iron intake manifold, Holley 600 carburetor, and a single-point distributor. With 427 lbs/ft of torque @ 3200 rpm, standing-start takeoffs were more like blastoffs. *Middle row:* A '68 fastback fitted with the 200-1V Six made 115 horsepower @ 3800 rpm and 190 lbs/ft of torque @ 2200 revs. Owners learned that the light front end reared like a playful pony on launch. *Right:* More dangerous than playful was Shelby's version of the Mustang, whether GT-500 big-block or high-winding small-block GT-350.

*Top row:* Shelby introduced a convertible in 1968, complete with a stylish, padded roll bar with a set of D-rings—handy for mounting a surfboard! Every interior was deluxe and featured Cobra snake emblems on the steering wheel and padded console top, plus a center console with Stewart-Warner gauges for oil and amps. *Above:* The 1968 Shelby Cobra GT-500 fastback was very expensive for its time, with a suggested retail price of $4317.39. The car had sequential taillights, unless ordered in California, where this mild gimmick was illegal. *Left:* In 1968, GT-350s and GT-500s came with pop-open rear gas caps with a snake and "Shelby Cobra." *Above left and far left:* The GT-500 KR had the same snake emblem, which was flanked by "Cobra Jet."

*Right and below:* Shelby's 1968 big-block GT-500 convertible had a 4-speed stick and standard 3.89:1 rear axle—ingredients for a terrific boulevard cruiser. Options included Selectaire air conditioning, power disc brakes, power steering, Select-O-Matic automatic transmission, even Tilt-Away steering column and a standard power top. Interior colors were limited to black or saddle *(below right).* The 428 *(bottom right)* was Ford's Police Interceptor with 410 heads. Fitted with hydraulic lifters and a Cobra aluminum intake manifold topped by a 715 CFM Holley four-barrel carburetor, the 428 developed 360 horsepower at 5400 rpm. Officially, the 1968 Shelby Mustang was cataloged as a Cobra; hence the Cobra snake emblems and nameplate on the front fender *(bottom left).*

The 1968 Shelby was more Shelby than ever. Enthusiasts loved the fiberglass rear-quarter scoops (*above*), which gathered fresh air that cooled the rear brakes. The top extractors, also fiberglass, removed hot air from the cockpit. The front end of the 1968 Shelby Cobra (*above right*) bore little resemblance to that of the Mustang on which the car was based. Scoops ran nearly the entire width of the fiberglass hood (*right and far right*), which was secured by a pair of twist-type hood lock buttons. The hood louvers exhausted hot engine air.

*Left:* Tasca Ford, a dealer from East Providence, Rhode Island, sponsored many drag cars, such as Mystery 7, driven by Bill Lawton. Tasca is best known for leading the charge to create a low-cost big-block that could stay with the 396 Rat motors from Chevrolet. The dealer's efforts culminated with the 428 Cobra Jets of 1968-1970. The folks at Tasca also ran a large over-the-counter performance parts program, and they raced what they sold. Mystery 7 (one of the early "funny cars") was so named because it was powered by a single overhead-cam 427 Ford dual-quad big-block. The engine never made production, but was "mysteriously" offered over the counter at Tasca. Mystery 7 ran the quarter-mile in about seven seconds.

*Top row:* The Shelby Cobra GT-500 KR (King of the Road) replaced the '68 GT-500 at mid-year. The King's 428 CJ was rated at 335 horsepower, but 400 was closer to the truth. The rear decklid was fiberglass and formed a flip-up rear spoiler. The unit required a set of special fiberglass "end caps" to mate with the rear fender. The rear taillight panel, also fiberglass, was painted silver, regardless of body color. Just 318 ragtop versions were built during the KR's half year of production. *Right and bottom row:* The Mach 1 show car of 1968 was one of those rare radical designs that everybody seemed to like. The production Mach 1, introduced in 1969, came very close in looks to its namesake, but had more rounded lines and lacked the rectangular headlamps (not legal then), dramatically protruding nose piece, chopped top, and (not seen here) closely snuggled quad exhausts.

*Left and above:* In the late 1980s, the 1968 model #1 Trans Am notchback was restored in Dallas, where Carroll Shelby got his first look in 20 years at the car. It carries a conventional-port 302 with Webers.

*Above:* Prepared by "Shelby Racing" and driven by Jerry Titus and Ronnie Bucknum, this blue Trans Am Mustang fastback finished first in class at the 1968 Daytona 24 Hour Trans Am. *Above left:* Shelby's first regular production convertible, seen here in white with a white top, was available as a small-block (GT-350; 404 built), a big-block (GT-500; 402 built), and as a 428 Cobra Jet big-block, (GT-500 KR; 318 built). Most Shelby buyers bought the fastback in 1968, and in the following numbers: 1140 GT-500s, 933 GT-500 KRs, and 1253 GT-350s. *Left:* The "Ed Martin Ford" 428 Cobra Jet is still competitive in class drag racing in SS/F.

PRESIDING OVER THE INTRODUC-tion of the 1969 Mustang was a new Ford Motor Company president: General Motors veteran Semon E. "Bunkie" Knudsen. Predictably, Detroit was flummoxed by the most startling executive defection since Bunkie's father, William S. Knudsen, left Ford for Chevrolet after a row with old Henry in the Twenties. Arriving with Bunkie was talented GM designer Larry Shinoda, who soon headed Ford's Special Design Center. Other management changes were rumored, and they'd happen soon enough, for Bunkie's Dearborn career would be quite short: begun in late 1968 and all over by the close of '69.

Knudsen and Shinoda were too late to influence the '69 Mustang, though their fondness for racy styling and high performance would be very evident in Ford's next restyle. Knudsen promised that "the long hood/short deck concept will continue," with "a trend toward designing cars for specific segments of the market."

The '69 Mustang lineup coincidentally reflected those words with a steed for every need, including new grand touring, luxury, and ultra-performance models. Wheelbase and the basic overall package size were not changed, but most everything else was. Design work began early, in October 1965, with first thoughts curiously aimed at a mini-Thunderbird concept. Later efforts were directed at an all-out muscle car, which was gradually toned down into a more practical shape that still looked jazzier than previous Mustangs.

## CHAPTER 4
# 1969-70: A Steed for Every Need

Dimensionally, the '69 marked a sharp departure from tradition. Overall length swelled four inches, most of it in front overhang, and the new models were slightly lower and wider. Coping with extra fuel-wasting weight was a fuel tank enlarged from 17 to 20 gallons.

Happily, interiors were more spacious. Thinner doors improved front shoulder room by 2.5 inches, and a modified frame crossmember beneath the front seat allowed a significant 2.5 inches of additional rear leg room. Trunk space grew "13 to 29 percent," according to bubbly Ford press releases, but that didn't mean much because there'd been so little room before. Outside, Mustang's familiar face gained an extra pair of headlights within the grille, the old side sculpturing was erased, rear fenders bulged more noticeably, and taillights were no longer recessed.

Taking careful aim at the likes of Firebird and Mercury Cougar was the new six- and eight-cylinder Grandé hardtop. Priced some $230 over its standard counterpart, it boasted a vinyl roof with identifying script, twin color-keyed door mirrors, wire wheel covers, two-tone

paint striping just below the belt, and bright body moldings. Dash and door panels were adorned with imitation teak trim (a good copy). Quietness was served by some 55 extra pounds of sound insulation.

More exciting was the new Mach 1 fastback. A $3139 intruder into Shelby territory, it wore simulated rear-quarter air ducts, decklid spoiler, and functional hood scoop. The last was nicknamed "The Shaker" because it stuck up from the air cleaner through a hole in the hood, where it vibrated madly. With that, plus a sweeping "SportsRoof" and NASCAR-style hood tie-downs, the Mach 1 looked every inch a performance machine. And with a standard 351-cubic-inch V-8 producing 250 horsepower, it was.

The 351 was devised to fill an obvious displacement gap in Ford's engine lineup. Descended from the original 260 small-block of 1962, it was basically a 302 with a half-inch-longer stroke. We're speaking here of the 351 "Windsor" engine, not the equally famous "Cleveland" unit. The former was named for the Canadian plant that built it starting in autumn 1968, a year before Cleveland production began (in Ohio). Despite many premium features, the Windsor would play low-tune "economy V-8" in most 1970-74 Dearborn models, leaving the performance role to the Cleveland.

The product of a $100 million investment, the Cleveland used a unique block with an integral timing chain chamber and water crossover passage at the front. Its deck was exactly one inch higher than

Mustang continued to emphasize performance for 1969-70. This '69 Shelby GT 500 convertible—one product of Ford's ongoing partnership with ex-racer Carroll Shelby—ran with a 428 Cobra Jet engine. It was fearsome on street and strip.

the 302's, while cylinder heads differed dramatically from the Windsor's in having canted valves giving wedge-type combustion chambers. In addition, its intake valves were tilted forward and the exhausts leaned back for shorter port areas and more-direct gas flow.

Bracketing these V-8s were the base 220-bhp 302 and the beefy 428 Cobra Jet, available with or without Ram-Air induction and conservatively rated at 335 bhp in either case. While the Mach 1's 351 was optional for lesser Mustangs, the "CJ" was the performance king. To put its power to the ground, Ford gave cars so equipped a special heavy-duty suspension with staggered rear shocks—one ahead of the rear axle, the other behind—to reduce wheel tramp in hard takeoffs.

Six-cylinder Mustangs weren't neglected for '69. Both the base 200- and optional 250-cid engines gained resited "center percussion" mounts that greatly improved operating smoothness.

After some last-minute styling help from Shinoda, Ford released an even more exotic Mustang—the Boss 302—in early 1969. It was conceived to beat the Camaro Z-28 in the Sports Car Club of America's Trans-American road-racing series for ponycars and compact sedans. (It might have been called Trans-Am had Pontiac not grabbed the name for its hottest '69 Firebird.) Ford had to make 1000 to qualify the Boss 302 as "production," but ended up turning out 1934 of the '69s.

Shinoda's interest in "airflow management" showed up in the Boss 302's spoilers, which were effective above 40 mph. The four-inch-deep front dam was raked to direct air around the car, while the rear spoiler was an adjustable inverted airfoil. Matte-black rear-window slats *a la* Lamborghini's Miura did nothing for airflow but looked terrific. In contrast, the functional aero aids netted a gain of perhaps 2.5 seconds per lap at

California's Riverside Raceway with no increase in power.

Of course, there *was* an increase in power—a big one. The Boss 302's special high-output (HO) small-block was said to produce 290 bhp, but actual output was estimated as high as 400. Features included big-port "Cleveland" heads, solid lifters, aluminum high-riser manifold, Holley four-barrel carb, dual-point ignition, four-bolt central main bearing caps, forged crank, and special pistons. To help prevent accidental over-revving of this fast-winding powerhouse, an ignition cutout interrupted current flow from the coil to the spark plugs at 5800-6000 rpm.

Boss 302 goodies also included ultra-stiff springs, those staggered shocks, a 4-speed gearbox pulling a shortish final drive (a Detroit "Locker" differential with choice of three ratios was optional), power brakes with big 11.3-inch-diameter front discs and heavy-duty rear drums, and F60 × 15 Polyglas boots. A Traction-Lok limited-slip differential was optional, as were Autolite "inline" four-barrel carbs on a special "Cross Boss" manifold. Ford hadn't missed a trick. Even wheel wells were radiused to accept extra-wide racing rubber.

Except for the Boss 429. This big-block brute was born of Ford's desire to run its new "semi-hemi" 429 V-8 in NASCAR stockers. Rules mandated 500 production installations but didn't specify models. As Torino was Dearborn's designated NASCAR racer, Ford sidestepped the rules by selling street 429s in the smaller Mustang. This *was* Knudsen's doing—and glorious it was.

Besides "crescent-shaped" combustion chambers, as Ford called them, the Boss 429 engine employed a thinwall block, aluminum heads, beefed-up main bearings, and a cross-drilled steel-billeted crank. There were actually two versions of this "820" powerplant: a hydraulic-lifter

"S" unit fitted to the first 279 cars, and the later "T" edition with different rods and pistons and either mechanical or hydraulic lifters. Both were nominally rated at 360 bhp in street form or 375 bhp in race trim, but as with the HO 302, those ratings were deliberately understated in order to avoid the ire of insurance companies.

The semi-hemi was too big for even the '69 Mustang's bigger engine bay, so Ford farmed out Boss 429 assembly to Kar Kraft, a low-volume specialty constructor in Brighton, Michigan. There, on a mini-assembly line, engines were stuffed into selected fastbacks, which required altering front suspension and inner fender wells, adding diagonal braces between wheelhouses and firewall (to resist body twist in hard acceleration), and moving the battery to the trunk (no room for it under the hood with the 429 installed). For good measure, tracks were widened and wheel arches flared to accommodate F60 × 15 tires on seven-inch-wide Magnum 500 wheels.

Other Boss 429 features included a big, functional hood scoop, specific front spoiler, and engine oil cooler. Power steering and brakes were standard, and Traction-Lok helped put all that torque to the pavement. (A Detroit No-Spin axle was optional.) Outside, this Boss was more subdued than either its little brother or the Mach 1: just discreet i.d. decals and a Boss 302-style rear wing.

For what amounted to a factory drag racer, the Boss 429 was surprisingly lush. Each one had the Decor Group that was optional on everyday Mustangs, plus high-back front bucket seats, a center console, and woodgrain dash trim. Ford also threw in the optional Visibility Group with lights for trunk, ashtray, and glovebox. Automatic transmission and air conditioning weren't available at all. Still, the big Boss was the costliest non-Shelby Mustang to date at $4798.

Not that either Boss was intended to make money. They were "homologation specials" built to satisfy racing authorities. *Car Life* tested both and found the little guy quicker to 60 mph—6.9 seconds versus 7.2—though it lost in the quarter-mile at 14.85 seconds/96.14 mph versus 14.09 seconds/102.85 mph. Reported top speed was 118 mph in each case. Obviously, the Boss 429 was potent, but its chassis was overwhelmed in hard acceleration. When modified for the strip, it was fearsome, but on the street it was almost a disappointment.

Not so the Boss 302, which in *Car Life's* tests turned the exact same quarter-mile time as Camaro's Z-28. *Car and Driver* pronounced the Boss 302 "the best handling Ford ever. . . . It's what the Shelby [GTs] should have been but weren't." All of which made for a peerless performance buy even at a not-inexpensive $3588.

*C/D's* reference to the Shelbys was telling, especially as the '69s weren't Carroll's work at all. They were Ford's contrivances—little more than a custom styling job on the new '69 fastback and convertible. GT-350 and GT-500 versions of each returned with a reshaped fiberglass nose and a big loop bumper/grille that combined for three extra inches in overall length. Scoops were everywhere—five NACA ducts on the hood alone—and wide reflective tape stripes ran midway along the flanks.

But the sad fact was that with more weight and stiffening emission controls, the '69 Shelbys were the tamest ever. The GT-500 was no longer "King of the Road," but retained that '68 model's 335-bhp 428 CJ, though actual horses were down 25 by most estimates. The GT-350 graduated to the new 351 Windsor, but advertised power was unchanged from its previous 302. Worse, this same engine could be had in the new Mach 1 for much less money.

Brock Yates derisively called the '69 GT-350 "a garter snake in Cobra skin." But if the magic was gone—and it was—it was only because Carroll Shelby was no longer involved with these namesake cars.

A more serious problem was sales competition from the new Mach 1, not to mention the Boss 302 and 429, which seemed purposely designed to put the Shelbys out to pasture. Of course, the Bosses were no more numerous or cheaper to build than the Shelbys. But they were "a curious duplication of effort," as Yates noted, and only dimmed what luster the Shelbys still had. "The heritage of the GT-350 is performance," Yates mused, "and it is difficult to understand why the Ford marketing experts failed to exploit its reputation." But fail they did, and Shelby model-year production fell by fully 25 percent, to 3150 units.

After seeing his car win only one Trans-Am event in 1969, Carroll Shelby retired from the car business, though not forever, as we know—and not before getting Ford to agree to end the Shelby Mustang. Thus, unsold '69s were given Boss 302 front spoilers, black hoods, and new serial numbers to become "1970" models, a little over 600 in all. With that, the Shelby Mustang was dead.

Among other Mustangs, the advent of specific luxury and performance models produced interesting results. Out of 184,000 cars sold in the first half of '69, only about 15,000 were Grandés versus nearly 46,000 Mach 1s. On cue, Ford chief John Naughton promised "heavy emphasis on performance" for what he termed the "Sizzlin' '70s."

But Mustang entered the 1970 season facing new competition from Dodge's belated Challenger and a completely redone Plymouth Barracuda, followed at mid-season by a handsome second-series Chevy Camaro/Pontiac Firebird. Little wonder, then, that Mustang's model-year volume suffered another big decline,

going from some 300,000 units to 190,727. Though this partly reflected the fast-withering demand for ponycars in general, familiarity was also to blame.

And indeed, changes for 1970 were evolutionary. All seven models returned with a tasteful facelift featuring dual headlamps and a flat-again back panel. Mechanicals changed little. New appearance options for fastbacks included Boss-type backlight louvers, an adjustable rear spoiler, and bodyside C-stripes. An optional Hurst shift linkage was also new to Mustang.

Mach 1 again wore its own grille, but now with built-in driving lamps. It also still came with the GT Equipment Group, though that package was no longer optional for other Mustangs, leaving enthusiast drivers with only the Competition Suspension.

Ford built another 6319 Boss 302s for 1970, and they would be the last, as the Boss 302 was no longer needed once the division withdrew from the Trans-Am after claiming the 1970 championship. The Boss 429 would also depart after a final 505 copies, all built during '69 with either the 820T or a new 820A engine with minor emissions-control adjustments.

The luxury Grandé hardtop and other 1970 Mustangs inherited the Mach 1's standard high-back bucket seats. Prices hadn't climbed much since the early days. The basic six-cylinder hardtop still listed at only a bit over $2700, the V-8 convertible for as little as $3126. Alas, the number of 1970 Mustang ragtops built was only about 7700. Growing buyer preference for air conditioning and closed bodies were fast conspiring to depress demand for convertibles of all kinds, Mustang's included.

Though its 1970 ponycar sales looked worrisome, Ford had big plans for '71—literally. Bunkie was about to have his day with a ponycar like no Mustang before—or, thankfully, since.

# 1969

- On July 20, Neil Armstrong and Buzz Aldrin walk on the moon

- The Cougar Eliminator is Mercury's answer to the Mustang Mach I

- A Chevy Camaro paces the Indianapolis 500

- Bunkie Knudsen is dismissed as FoMoCo president late in the year

- The Boss 302 (approximately 400 bhp) arrives early in the year

- The Boss 429 competition engine is made available to Mustang buyers for homologation purposes

- The Mach I fastback carries a functional "shaker" hood scoop; the 351-cid, 250-bhp "Windsor" V-8 is standard

- The mighty 428 Cobra Jet continues as an optional Mustang engine

- Shelby Mustangs are now built at Ford's Southfield, Michigan, plant alongside stock Mustangs

- The Shelby GT-500 carries Ford's 428; the GT-350 steps up to the 352 Windsor

- Carroll Shelby announces his retirement from race-car development and severs his relationship with Ford

- An "Apex" styling study proposes a two-seat Mustang

- Mustang model-year production is 299,824, including 14,746 convertibles

In the summer of 1966, Ford designers were asked to sketch proposals for the '69 Mustang. One of the designers was Bill Shenk, whose illustrations are seen on this page and the following. He recalled, "[T]he designs were based off some of the cues of the earlier Mustang, as far as having the eggcrate grille with the high-mounted mouth, the horse and corral, the similar headlight arrangement. The Mach 1 was to have a long hood, short deck, and the side pockets [top of the rear quarters] fitted with fake air extractors. Generally, we were trying to maintain the same flavor and feel of the early Mustang."

Shenk's fanciful drawings were done early in Mach 1 development, long before a clay had even been considered. Shenk and other Ford designers did know the Mach 1 would have to use the same chassis and platform as the base six-cylinder Mustang and would share the same overall styling with coupes and convertibles. The challenge was to re-skin the basic concept into a variety of supercar archetypes. "In those days," Shenk recalled, "we had no fuel restrictions, so it was an interesting project from that point of view. We were challenged as to how far we could go and lose the image, or how far we would back off and maintain, still, a healthy, thoroughbred look to the car." A glance at Shenk's original sketches shows that this young designer gave the car a very aggressive stance, and the production Mach 1 likewise carried over these styling notions into a well-received design.

As Ford Design looked ahead to model-year 1969, the station wagon idea (*top left*) was rendered in clay in the summer of 1966. Ford nixed the idea and decided to market the new-generation Mustang as a muscle car. A fastback (*top right*) was sent to Bonneville, where it set 295 USAC speed and endurance records on the Salt Flats. *Above:* This street-legal Boss 429 was built by Tasca Ford, a Rhode Island dealership. The car had a 494-cube Can-Am aluminum block with automatic transmission; it could run the quarter in the low 11s. Meanwhile, the red fastback (*above right*) reveals that the body style could be simultaneously sedate and sporty, even with standard wheel covers. *Right:* Amazingly, the same body shape in Boss 302 guise looked like it was ready for some Trans Am racing—at least when it had the blackout hood, side stripes, rear wing, and special wheels.

*Left:* The new 1969 Mach 1 had a drag-racing image and quickly superseded the GT, which was suggestive of road racing. Cosmetic touches were aggressive, of course, though the hood scoop was non-functional.
*Below:* Inside, the Mach 1 had the sportiest interior in the Mustang lineup, highlighted by high-back bucket seats with Comfortweave knitted vinyl inserts. The steering wheel was a deluxe, three-spoke "Rim-Blow." Engine choices started with the 351-2V (*below left*) and progressed to the 428 Super Cobra Jet with Ram Air. *Bottom left:* The Boss 429 was a fastback only. *Bottom right:* The 429 "Semi-Hemi" was shoehorned into the engine bay. Oddball valve covers allowed spark plugs top entry to the hemispherical combustion chambers below.

A "coupe with a scoop" (*right*) describes the basic no-frills '69 hardtop running with the optional 428 Super Cobra Jet with Ram Air. The standard "dog dish" hubcaps that covered the lug nuts were easily popped off for drag racing. Inside (*below*), the C-6 automatic transmission made the most sense for consistent shifts down the quarter mile. The engine bay revealed a 428 (*below right*) with "the shaker," a ram-air-cleaner assembly that protruded through a cutout in the hood and shook back and forth with the rumbling engine below. The more sedate Grandé (*bottom*) was Mustang's luxury package for 1969. All were hardtops fitted with vinyl roofs and an identifying upper-body stripe.

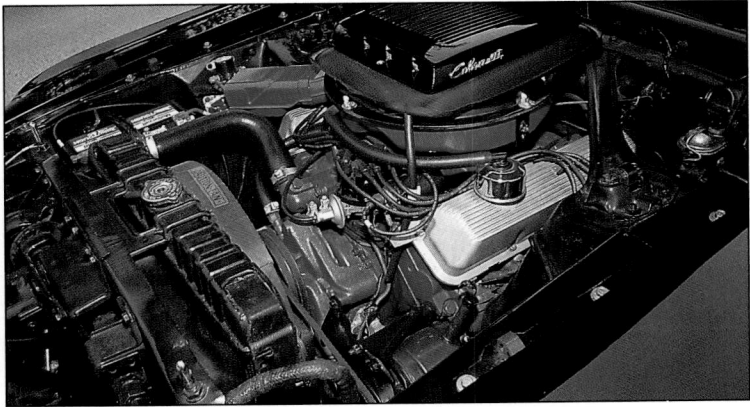

In 1969, most Mustang performance buyers who wanted a convertible or hardtop opted for the GT (*this page*). For this reason the '69 GT fastback (*top left*) is a particularly rare Mustang. Its lower-bodyside stripes were much more sedate than the beltline counterparts on the cop-baiting Mach 1. Styled steel wheels had GT center caps. The interior (*middle left*) was attractive but rather plain. At the rear (*left and second from top right*), red-outlined letters on the pop-open gas cap spelled out GT. The GT package added just $146.71 to the price of fastback, hardtop, or convertible. The GT seen here was ordered with the shaker hood scoop and 428 Cobra Jet big-block.

*Top row:* The all-new Grandé found 22,182 buyers; a huge total, considering production of all other Mustang hardtops was 128,458. Just as the Mach 1 overshadowed the GT for '69, the Grandé became more popular than the deluxe version of the Mustang hardtop, which amounted to a mere 5714 cars in 1969. *Right and below:* One of the rarest 1969 muscle Mustangs is this 428 Super Cobra Jet convertible that mixes the pleasure of open-air motoring with pavement-peeling power. (There was a bigger engine for 1969—the 429 HO—but it was available only in the fastback.) This 428 ragtop has no cubic-inch fender badges, although the shaker hood scoop for Ram Air (*below right*) provides fair warning to would-be challengers. The 428 CJ dictated a competition suspension, which included staggered rear shocks on 4-speed cars.

*Left and above left:* Mustang went to four front headlights in 1969, with two additional beams mounted at opposite ends of the traditional eggcrate grille. This fastback is a base model with added hood scoop, front spoiler, rear wing spoiler, and a very rare hood tach (*above*), which was a dealer-installed accessory. The driver could see the tach needle through the windshield without having to take his or her eyes off the road. When the 428 Cobra Jet engine was ordered without Ram Air, the non-functional scoop was adorned with 428 Cobra Jet badges (*below*), as on this Acapulco Blue Mach 1 (*below left*). The rear window louvers and rear wing spoiler were very popular Mach 1 factory options, but neither was standard with any 1969 Mustang.

*This page:* In September 1969, a Ford design group headed by Larry Shinoda proposed the "Composite Mustang" as a replacement for both the Shelby GT series and the Boss 429. The car got its name because it used the chassis of a Boss 429, the dash of a Cougar XR-7, the fiberglass fenders and hood of a Shelby GT, and the fastback body of the Mustang. It also was known as the Quarter Horse, being one-fourth of each car and, like a quarter horse, built for the quarter mile. Two of these exotics were built: the 1970 Grabber Blue example with white interior and Boss 429 engine seen here, and a Candy Apple Red example with white interior, optioned with the 429 Thunder Jet.

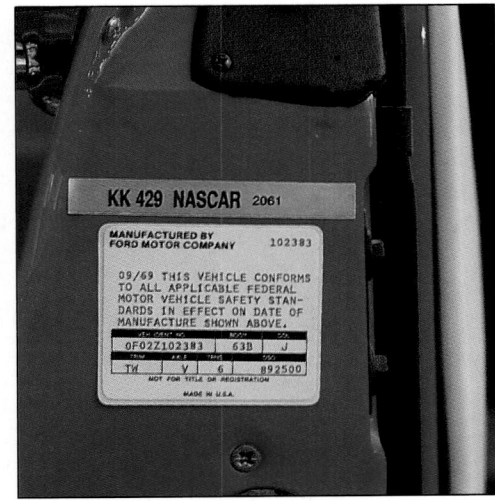

*Opposite page:* Mustang fans went crazy over the fastback body style, especially in the Mach 1 series. Incredibly, of the 299,924 1969 Mustangs produced, 134,438 were fastbacks—an astounding 45 percent of the total. Of the fastback run, 72,458, or slightly more than half, were Mach 1s. Although we have no breakdown of Cobra Jets by body style or Mach 1 series, it's interesting that Ford built 13,193 Mustangs with this big-block engine. A preponderance of CJs were ordered in the fastback, of course. Both of the red Mach 1s (*top row*) were CJs in the Mach 1 series. *Car Life* tested a 428 CJ Mach 1 and recorded a best ET of 13.90 @ 103.32 mph in the quarter. The Raven Black Mach 1 (*middle and bottom row*) came with the 390, an engine in its final year; 10,494 390 Mach 1s were ordered.

In 1969 and 1970, the Shelbys had a look almost completely distinct from the regular Mustang, thanks to a unique fiberglass front-end clip (*top*). Fiberglass side scoops ducted air to the front and rear brakes. GT-500s came with the 428 Cobra Jet (*right*), as indicated by front fender badges (*above*). The two scoops at the rear of the hood exhausted hot air from the engine bay.

Shelby-American had proposed a notchback GT-350 in 1967, but it didn't make production. However, Shelby's 1965 sale to Mexican businessman Eduardo Velasquez of a Mustang notchback with full-race 289 engine and Shelby GT-350 competition suspension suggested that a broader market existed south of the border. Velasquez raced his car successfully and ordered many parts from Shelby. Finally, in 1969, Shelby started a company called Shelby de Mexico, which modified Mustangs for sale to Ford dealers throughout Mexico. Unlike the domestic GT-350s, which were fastbacks and convertibles, the Mexican GT-350s were coupes with modified engines, add-on fiberglass parts, T-Bird taillights, and special wheels and badging.

# 1970

- During an antiwar protest at Ohio's Kent State University in May, four students are shot to death by National Guardsmen

- Ponycar sales are down in general, hurt by buyer interest in such compacts as Ford's Pinto and Maverick, Chevy's Vega, and AMC's Gremlin

- Mercury imports Ford of Europe's sporty Capri coupe

- The rebodied Plymouth Barracuda is joined by the Dodge Challenger

- Lee Iacocca is named president of Ford Motor Company

- Ford acquires a controlling interest in European design firm Ghia of Italy; Ghia designers produce a running prototype of a small, sporty car in just 53 days, helping to redirect thinking of what will eventually become the Mustang II

- The top Mach I engine for the year, the 428, is replaced by a 429 during the model run

- Ford abandons its efforts in Trans-Am, USAC, NASCAR, and international competition

- About 600 leftover '69 Shelby Cobras are sold as 1970 models

- Mustang, sans Shelby participation, comes out on top in the Trans Am race season

- Model-year Mustang production falls to 190,727, including just 7673 convertibles

The Grandé (*top and bottom*) entered the 1970 model year largely unchanged from 1969, though with a new "landau" vinyl roof, which did not cover the rear pillars or the back of the roof; a full vinyl roof was optional at extra cost. The Mach 1 (*middle*) came with a new wide rocker panel molding.

The 1970 Mustang Milano show car (*top row*) was a '70 fastback chopped to 43 inches in height, painted "Ultra Violet," and highlighted by concealed headlights and air scoops similar to those on the 1969-70 Shelby GT series. The electrically operated rear hatch was a design idea that never made production.

*Above left:* The 429 T-Bird engine almost made production in the Composite Mustang. Instead, the 429, with hemispherical Boss cylinder heads and beefed-up NASCAR bottom end, was specially fitted into the 1969-70 Boss 429 supercar. The 429 made it into the regular-production Mustang lineup for the 1971 model year, when the engine bay was finally wide enough to hold it without special modification of the front shock towers for clearance. *Left and above:* Convertible and hardtop production dropped dramatically for 1970: 7673 ragtops and 128,458 hardtops.

*Top left and top, upper right:* In 1969, American Raceways International asked Ford's Special Promotions Division to build five Mustangs with unique graphics for use as pace cars. This is the ARI Michigan International Speedway convertible pace car, a 428 SCJ convertible modified for high speed and durability. Gary Pietraniec of Dearborn Heights found and restored the car, and painted and lettered a Mustang pedal car (*top, lower right*) to match. *Above:* The yellow convertible is a rare 1970 model with a shaker hood scoop to ram air to the 351-4V Cleveland (*above left*), badged on the front fenders beneath "Mustang" script (*left*).

Ford's Boss 429 supercar (*above*) was hand-modified on a special assembly line at Kar Kraft in Brighton, Michigan. Because the 429 engine (*left*) was too wide to fit the engine bay of the stock 1969-70 Mustang, the shock towers had to be cut back for clearance.

Ford built 859 Boss 429s in 1969 and 499 in '70, and lost money on every one of them. But the company's real goal was to build the 500 cars needed to homologate the 429 Boss engine (*middle right*) for NASCAR competition, and to boost Mustang's muscle image on the street. *Remaining photos:* The special assembly line militated against the use of graphics, rear wing, and sport slats.

*Left, above left, and above:* The Boss 302, like the Mustang fastback, was virtually unchanged for 1970. The major alteration was a new striping pattern, penned by Larry Shinoda, the same designer who came up with the Boss 302 name. Every one of the cars came with a 4-speed Ford transmission, assisted by a Hurst T-handle shifter. The sport slats, rear wing spoiler, Magnum 500 wheels, hood tach, and shaker scoop for Ram Air were optional.

*Above:* The Boss 302 engine, seen here with the stock chromed air cleaner lid, came without the shaker. The engine was Ford's big-headed small-block for Trans Am competition, and had to be built for the street to make it eligible to race. Ford built a look-alike Trans Am for the street, too, and called it the Boss 302 (*right and above right*). It looked racy but production was relatively low: 1628 in 1969 and 7013 in '70.

*This page:* The Boss 302 stood out on the street, but the engine had to be revved to six grand to top out the horsepower at 290. In Trans Am tune, the powerplant carried Ford to the 1970 Manufacturer's Championship. Every Boss 302 can be documented as factory original by a look at the VIN and a glance at the fifth character, which is a "G" for the Boss 302 engine. No other Mustang came with this engine. A dealer-accessory hood tach (*above*) is seldom seen with a Boss 302.

*This page:* One of the most unusual Mustangs of 1970 was the Twister Special, ordered by the Kansas City sales district office for Ford's traveling "Total Performance Day," held Friday, November 7, 1969. The Twister Special had graphics identical to the ARI pace cars, with a Twister decal replacing the ARI logo on the rear quarter panels. All 186 cars (96 Mustangs and 90 Torinos) were to be 428 CJs, as seen here, but Ford ran low on 428s and used 351-4Vs in some of the cars.

The Mach 1 (*top row*) far exceeded the popularity of the Boss 302 (*middle row and left*) for obvious reasons. The Mach 1 came standard with a tractable 351-2V engine, with optional 351-4V and 428-4V Cobra Jet, with or without ram air. Even the 351-2V had more torque (355 lbs/ft @ 2600 rpm) than the Boss 302 (290 lbs/ft @ 4300 rpm). Mach 1 buyers could order automatic transmission, air conditioning, and other power-robbing options and accessories, while the Boss 302 was single-purpose, with a high-rpm, big-valve 302 standard with one transmission choice, the 4-speed. Automatic was unavailable with the Boss 302; likewise air and most other amenities were not available.

*This page:* Ford called it the Boss 429, but to enthusiasts it was the "Shotgun," the "Semi-Hemi," the "Blue Crescent," or the Ford "Porcupine." With its free-breathing, dry-decked aluminum heads; staggered and canted valves; semi-hemispherical combustion chambers; forged steel innards; and bulletproof four-bolt bottom end, the Boss 429 remains the most exotic of all muscle Mustangs, good for 375 horses @ 5200 rpm.

*This page:* Model-year 1970 Shelbys were actually converted 1969s, left in the system when the decision was made to drop the line altogether. Black hood stripes and black plastic front spoilers—elements lifted from the 1969 Boss 302—were the two major changes. For proper identification, the first digit of the serial number was changed from "9" to "0." Notice the snake emblem and "Shelby" logo (*top right*) on the front quarters. The Cobra name was pulled from Mustang after 1968. However, Cobra Jet badges (*center left*) continued to identify Shelby engines. Although the Shelby GT-500 had a CJ with Ram Air, the GT-500 was not the best-performing Mustang in the lineup, a distinction reserved for the dominant Boss 429. The Shelby had played out its role in the Mustang story and was dropped completely after 1970.

GIVEN TYPICAL AUTO INDUSTRY lead times, it's clear that the 1971 Mustang was shaped by events in 1968-69. And momentous events they were. Prime among them was the abrupt dismissal of Bunkie Knudsen as Ford Motor Company president after less than two years on the job. In typical corporate style, chairman Henry Ford II said little more than "things just didn't work out."

To soften the blow of Knudsen's firing, HFII appointed a presidential troika comprising R.L. Stevenson for International Operations, R.J. Hampson for Non-Automotive Operations, and Lee Iacocca for North American Operations. But that lasted only a year. Iacocca became overall president in late 1970, in part as belated recognition for having "fathered" the Mustang.

Yet the ponycar was fast losing its appeal. Mustang sales had been sliding since '67, while Chevy Camaro and Pontiac Firebird were holding ground but not gaining any. Neither was Mustang's uptown sister, the Mercury Cougar. Javelin and AMX were successes for tiny AMC, but not by Ford standards. Neither were the rebodied 1970 Plymouth Barracuda and its aptly named new Dodge Challenger stablemate. By 1971, compacts like Ford's own Pinto and Maverick, the Chevrolet Vega and Nova, and AMC's Hornet and Gremlin were cutting deeply into ponycar sales, which were down to about half of what they'd been in best-ever 1967.

Bunkie's term as president may have been short, but it was long enough for

# CHAPTER 5
# 1971-73: Big Events

him to leave his mark on the 1971 Mustang. Iacocca didn't have much to do with it because he'd been moved up from Ford Division general manager in 1965, and was thus no longer directly involved with shaping future products.

Among factors that *were* shaping future Fords was a raft of new goverment-mandated emissions standards that took effect within days of Iacocca's becoming Ford president. These called for steep cuts in hydrocarbon (HC), carbon monoxide (CO), and oxides of nitrogen (NOx) that would only be achieved with the post-1974 adoption of the catalytic converter, a sort of "afterburner" that helps lower all three pollutants by using chemicals to foster more complete combustion or formation of less harmful substances (such as changing CO to carbon dioxide).

More immediately, General Motors cut compression on its 1971 car engines to permit the use of low-lead and no-lead gas, then coming on the market as mandated emissions regulators. Ford, Chrysler, and American Motors followed suit for '72. In a related move, all U.S. makers *except* Ford quoted two sets of horsepower figures for '71: traditional SAE gross (dynamometer readings of

engines without fan drive, exhaust system, or other accessories), and more realistic SAE *net* figures (with ancillaries installed as in an actual car). Dearborn grudgingly joined in for '72.

Engineers also scrambled to meet the new mandate for bumpers that could withstand a five-mph shunt without damage to headlights or other "safety-related equipment." These would be required at the front on '73 models and both front and rear on '74s. Given existing technology, "crash bumpers" meant extra weight that hurt fuel economy, though that caused little evident concern in Detroit or Washington. After all, gas was still plentiful in 1971, and still cheap at about 50 cents a gallon. But the haste to comply with all the new rules too often showed—in ugly "battering-ram" bumpers or engines tuned so "clean" as to sputter and stall hot or cold.

If the '71 Mustang evidenced the heavy hand of Congress as much as any American car, it was a very different Mustang also because of the intercession of Ford. Ford planners had concluded that buyers were flocking to compacts because ponycars lacked interior space. Given that, the decision to make the '71 a bigger, roomier, heavier Mustang was perfectly logical in the context of the late Sixties, especially since looming federal mandates seemed almost designed to foster bigger cars.

Bigger the '71 definitely was—as big as a Mustang would ever get. A quarter-horse was now a Clydesdale. Styling work began as early as May 1967, about nine months before Knudsen arrived in

Ford's ponycar became increasingly bulky and imposing-looking during 1971-73. Potent performance was still available for those who desired it—and could afford to satisfy Mustang's thirst for fuel. This '72 Sprint model was one effort to pump sales.

Dearborn. Most clay models produced through early '68 were heavy-looking and Thunderbird-ish to the point of clumsiness. Designers eventually stripped away the flab, opting for crisp, severely creased lines married to bulging fenders and kicked-up "ducktails." By mid-June '67, the basic elements of the final production design were in place—with Knudsen's blessing.

The result was a Mustang ballooned eight inches in overall length, six inches in width, and some 600 pounds in curb weight, though wheelbase grew only an inch, to 109. The trademark long hood/short deck proportions were retained, but the car was more "styled" than ever, reflecting the tastes of Knudsen and designer Larry Shinoda (who departed Dearborn when Bunkie did). Most noticeable were an almost horizontal fastback roofline, a blunted nose, and a more acutely angled windshield with hidden wipers. The last betrayed Shinoda's GM background, as did a slim new Camaro-like dashboard.

The advent of color-keyed polyurethane bumper covers gave the '71 Mach 1 a more unified frontal appearance compared to other Mustangs, meeting the crash-bumper edict with style. The model also came with twin dummy hood scoops (optional on other models) and a specific grille with a small running horse on honeycomb mesh, flanked by horizontal parking lamps styled like driving lights. Other Mustang grilles presented the traditional large chrome-framed horse and a revived horizontal divider bar.

Those fast-tightening emissions standards took a predictable toll on Mustang's '71 engines. The Boss 302's HO V-8 was replaced by a Boss 351 Cleveland with four-barrel carburetor and 330 gross horsepower. Despite high 11:1 compression, it was more tractable than the HO, and more durable, too, since it wasn't as high-revving. On other models the base V-8 was the expected two-barrel 302, though it was down 10 horses, to 210. The little 200-cubic-inch six was dropped, while the 250 also lost 10 horses, settling for 145. Optional V-8s comprised a two-barrel 351 with 240 bhp (also off 10), a four-barrel version with 285, and a new four-barrel 429 Cobra Jet, which replaced the 428 to deliver 370 bhp with or without Ram Air induction. There was also a Super Cobra Jet boasting 375 bhp.

Though still a high-performer in standard trim, the Mach 1 could again be ordered with air conditioning ($407), automatic transmission ($238), and conveniences like tilt steering wheel, "sport deck" rear seat (a fold-down job as offered on fastback Mustangs since '65), AM/FM stereo, and intermittent wipers. Other goodies included sports interior ($130), power front disc brakes ($70), center console ($60), and instrument group ($54). In fact, liberal use of the option book could raise the $3268 base price to well over $5500. No-cost items again included high-back bucket seats, front spoiler, dual exhausts, and racing-style door mirrors.

The 429 CJ option cost $436 but was worth every penny for Mach 1 performance: 0-60 mph in 6.5 seconds, 0-75 in about 9.0 seconds, the standing quarter-mile in 14.5 seconds. With automatic and 3.25:1 rear axle, top speed was about 115 mph, fuel "economy" 10-11 mpg. "It is a decent mixture for those who want good performance and some comfort," wrote Chuck Koch in *Motor Trend*, "but it still remains a little unwieldy for city traffic."

That high-output Cleveland V-8 was the heart of a new Boss 351 fastback that ousted the Bosses 302 and 429 as the racer's Mustang. Disappointingly, though, it looked much like a Mach 1 except for name decals, special mid-flank striping, and a Boss-type front spoiler.

Koch tested one of these too, and found it handled better than the Mach 1, thanks to its standard "competition suspension" with uprated coil springs and shocks, staggered rear shocks, and a hefty stabilizer bar at each end. The Boss 351 also proved quicker than Koch's Mach 1 429, capable of 0-60 mph in 5.8 seconds and the quarter-mile in 13.8. However, a short 3.91:1 rear axle limited top speed to only about 100 mph.

Against these potent V-8s, the basic 210-bhp 302 was pretty tame. It typically delivered 10-second 0-60 times, the quarter-mile in 17.5 seconds, and only 86 mph flat out (with a 2.79:1 axle ratio and automatic). Yet this performance was acceptable for the day, as was mileage (up to 17 mpg). All things considered, the 302 remained the best all-around Mustang engine.

Viewed dispassionately, the '71 Mustang was not a bad car, though it got a lot of bad press at the time, as indeed it still does. It was larger only because buyers didn't like cramped interiors. Of course, that meant extra weight and thirst too, but with gas still so cheap, most buyers didn't have to be concerned with fuel economy (though they would be come the winter of 1973-74). And surprisingly, the '71s rode and handled better than previous Mustangs, something biased chroniclers typically ignore. Understeer was reduced, roadholding was improved, and new variable-ratio power steering provided better road feel than Mustang's fixed-ratio setup.

Of course, a good car doesn't necessarily mean good business, as Ford knew all too well. Adding to sales pressure from sporty compacts were fast-rising insurance rates on "performance" cars regardless of motive power. Whether lowly six or muscular big-block V-8, buyers paid a much higher premium to own a ponycar like Mustang instead of, say, a Maverick.

So despite its all-new design, Mustang sales sagged once more, '71 model-year production failing to reach 150,000. That includes an estimated 1800 copies of the Boss 351, which was dumped at mid-season (no need for it once Ford gave up racing). As you might guess, this is the most collectible '71 Mustang today.

There's little to do with a one-year-old design but live with it, which is what Ford did for the '72 Mustang. Even-stricter emissions limits dictated further detuning of the base 250 six, 302 V-8, and all 351s. Ironically, the big 429, another reason for the '71's size increase, was eliminated. As mentioned, Ford joined other Detroit automakers in switching from gross to net horsepower quotes. The six was thus more accurately billed at 95 bhp for '72, the 302 at 136 bhp, and the 351s at 168-275 bhp. The last figure applied to a detuned Boss 351 called 351 HO, a late addition to the option chart.

But little else changed, leaving Ford to talk mostly of new colors and fabrics. Among these was a new Sprint Decor Option featuring white paint set off by broad blue patches on hood, rockers, and back panel, plus large American-flag decals on the rear fenders. "Control and balance make it a beautiful experience," said the ads, but 1972 Mustang sales looked none too beautiful to Ford accountants, who tallied another dip: this time about 20 percent.

Back in the secret dens of Dearborn, work was winding down on a wholly new Mustang more faithful to the original ponycar spirit. Not surprisingly then, the big steeds were little changed for one more year. What did surprise Ford—pleasantly—was a slight sales gain. The ragtop scored the largest increase: a resounding 100 percent, to nearly 12,000 units. But that was only because Ford had announced that the topless Mustang would not return, the result of a pending

government mandate for rollover protection that ironically would never come to pass. While the '73 was not Mustang's "last convertible," it was Ford's final factory-built ragtop for a decade.

Mustang fared better than most '73 Detroiters in having five-mph front bumpers that stuck out only a little more than in 1971-72 and thus didn't look too bad. That apart, you had to look twice to discern a '73. As before, Mach 1 nose styling was optionally available for other models in an Exterior Decor Group. In both cases, the horizontal "sport" parking lamps were now turned vertically, a small spotter's point. Prices were little changed from '72, when they'd been cut to spark sales. The base six-cylinder hardtop listed at $2760, while the V-8 convertible topped the line at $3189. The luxury Grandé hardtop, still hanging in with standard 302 and posh appointments, stickered at $3088—$124 below its '71 figure. The '73 Mach 1, again with standard two-barrel 351 and 168 net bhp, also started at $3088.

Mechanical modifications were few. Bigger brakes appeared across the board, cars with non-power front discs were treated to larger calipers, and radial tires were a new factory option. So, too, was "dual ram induction," a special hood for cars with the two-barrel 351. It featured working dual air scoops, matte black or silver paint, decals, and twist-type hood locks, all borrowed from the Mach 1. Optional with the 302 was a two-tone hood with dummy scoops. Mustang was now the only Ford available with the HO 351. As throughout the corporate line, drivetrain choices were thinning due to the high cost of certifying each permutation for emissions compliance under the EPA's newly mandated 50,000-mile durability test.

To comply with EPA guidelines, Mustang tailpipe pollutants were now handled by crankcase ventilation and

exhaust-gas recirculation. The latter routed gases from the exhaust manifold through a vacuum valve into the carburetor, where they were diluted by the incoming fuel/air mixture. This permitted leaner carburetor settings for lower emissions.

More new federal edicts were evident elsewhere in the Mustang's design. For example, the dash got extra padding and was shorn of projections that might cause injury in a crash. Far more dubious was the "starter interlock" that prevented firing up the engine if either front-seat occupant forgot to buckle up. Though mandated for all 1972 models, this device proved so irksome (and trouble-prone) that Washington actually rescinded the requirement after 1973 in a blinding fit of rationality.

Plentiful options were as important as ever to Mustang sales, and they were hardly less numerous for '73. The optional vinyl top now came in a choice of six colors and covered the whole roof on hardtops, the front three-quarters on fastbacks. Also still available: forged aluminum wheels, "metallic glow" paint, decorative side stripes, raised-white-letter tires, and competition suspension. A useful newcomer was an electric rear-window defroster for hardtops and SportsRoofs.

In design terms, the 1971-73 models were the last in the mold of the smash-hit original. Sporty styling, performance that was at least interesting, and a long option list had all endured, but everyone knew that Mustang had veered way off the ponycar path and needed to get back on track—pronto.

It was about to do just that with a new-generation car for the brave, battered world of the Seventies. Unfortunately, the regrettably underachieving Mustang II would prove as controversial in its own way as the "Clydesdale" cars it replaced.

# 1971

- China joins the United Nations in November

- A bloody September uprising of prisoners at New York's Attica State Correctional Facility is put down by police and state troopers

- Pontiac's Firebird Formula 400 is joined by new 350 and 455 models

- AMC's Javelin gets new, humped-fender styling

- The redesigned Mustang gains 600 pounds and eight inches in overall length, though wheelbase grows by only an inch

- Increasingly stringent emissions controls banish the Boss 302's HO V-8; it's replaced by a lower-revving Boss 351 Cleveland, which is itself dropped at mid-season

- Mustang's top engine is a new four-barrel 429 Cobra Jet rated at 370 bhp

- Total model-year Mustang sales drop further, to 149,678; 6121 of those are ragtops

*Top:* An alternate front-grille proposal featuring vertical bars for the '71 Mustang would have broken with Mustang tradition. *Middle:* The approved grille design featured the time-honored horse and "corral" flanked by horizontal bars. *Right:* The approved grille for the Mach 1 was typical blackout style, but a small, center-mounted running horse was also added.

*Top:* The optional Sport wheelcovers with simulated mylar lug nuts were identical to the ones that were standard on the 1970 Mach 1. Bright front bumper guards with rubber inserts and bodyside protective moldings with color-keyed vinyl inserts were part of the "Protection Package." *Above:* Front fenders came with "Mustang" script for '71. Buyers who wanted a 4-speed transmission could not order the 302-2V (*left*), which was available only with 3-speed manual or Cruise-O-Matic. Few people ordered the manual. Most of the 302 two-barrel engines were backed by an automatic and a set of 2.79:1 or 3.00:1 rear axle gears, with or without Traction-Lok.

RAM AIR

*This page:* The 1971 Boss 351, built for one year only, came standard with NASA-style Ram Air hood scoops (*above*), front chin spoiler, Mach 1 grille, dual color-keyed racing mirrors, argent lower back panel, hood lock buttons, and wild side stripes with a Boss 351 logo. Every Boss 351 was a fastback, dubbed the SportsRoof by Ford. The two performance options visible on this Moss Green Boss are the set of 7 × 15-inch Magnum 500 wheels and the decklid rear wing spoiler. Clearly this Mustang was built for high performance.

**106**

The 1969-70 fastback came with optional "sport slats," which were not available on the '71 Boss due to the extreme slope of the "flatback" rear window (*top and above*). The high-winding, solid-lifter Boss 351 engine (*left*) was protected by an electronic rev limiter. Back panels for '71 were painted black or argent and carried the "BOSS 351" identifier.

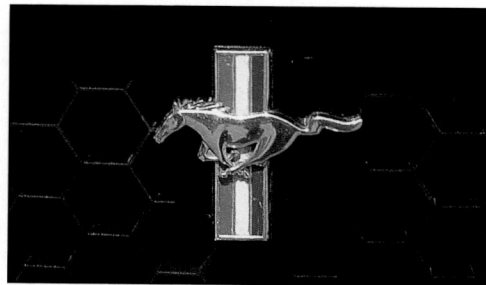

*This page:* Ford did a great job with the 1971 Mach 1, which included a new urethane, body-colored front bumper, honeycomb grille with sport lamps, dual racing mirrors, hood lock buttons, dual exhausts, and a pop-open gas cap. The vertical tri-color Mustang grille ornament (*above*) was a nice touch. Options included rear wing spoiler, side stripes, Magnum 500 wheels, and NASA-scooped hood for ram air. Bright Red with black stripes was one of the most popular color combinations.

*Top left:* Only about 50 '71 Mustang convertibles were equipped with the 429 Cobra Jet. Most buyers who hankered for the big-block purchased a fastback Mach 1 (*top right*), which came standard with the 302-2V. *Left:* A beautifully restored '71 Boss 351. *Above:* Light Pewter Metallic was a striking color choice for the Boss 351. The Boss 351 was produced for one year only, with a production run of 1806.

*Top left:* Perhaps the most unusual and least-known 1971 Mustang was the "Sports Hardtop," which Ford introduced in the spring of the year to pump up sales. The Sports Hardtop package (seen here in Grabber Green Metallic) consisted of Boss 351-style side stripes, lower-bodyside paint, a NASA-style hood with non-functional scoops, Mach 1 honeycomb grille, and a color-keyed urethane front bumper. This example has optional dual racing mirrors and 7 × 15-inch Magnum 500 chromed wheels. *Right and top right:* The Grandé continued on as sedately as before, distinguished from the base Mustang mainly by exterior trim and a pseudo-luxury interior. *Above:* The hardtop's roof pillars swept back to create a tunnel effect that embraced the rear window; Ford called this the "tunnel backlite."

Although some Mustang fans complained about the sheer size of the longer, lower, wider '71 fastbacks, its designers were enthusiastic about it. A smaller Mustang arrived for 1974, of course, but before it did development was started on a '74 model line intended to be even larger and quicker than the 1971-73 generation. In the summer of 1969, when it appeared Ford would continue to sell Mustangs on the basis of horsepower as well as styling, Ford Design threw itself into work on prototypes. A pair of Mach 1 proposals (*top left and middle left; top right and middle right*) were particularly eye-opening. Earlier ideas (not seen here) lopped eight to ten inches from the rear overhang, but the length was reinstated on later proposals. Because the design squeezed the grille, fender louvers were added in an attempt to get cooling air into the engine. None of the cooling scoops, including side openings, worked. *Left:* In February of 1972, Ford introduced a mid-year Mustang special, a "Sprint" in red, white, and blue. It was joined by similarly striped Sprint models from Maverick and Pinto.

# 1972

- President Nixon, a longtime enemy of communism, makes an official visit to China in March; in November, he wins a second term via a landslide victory over Democrat George McGovern

- In May, presidential candidate and Alabama governor George Wallace is shot and seriously wounded by would-be assassin Arthur Bremer

- The Torino Cobra is dropped

- Plymouth kills the GTX and big-block Barracuda

- Olds's 4-4-2 and Pontiac's GTO are reduced to option status

- The Firebird Trans Am gains a four-speed manual as standard

................................................................

- '72 Mustangs lose their big-block V-8s and Boss 351

- Mustang styling continues much as for 1971; Sprint Decor Option—comprised of lively fabric, colors, and wheels—is introduced to pump sales

- Lee Iacocca begins to push for a Mustang redesign; a last-minute consumer clinic in San Francisco in February suggests that buyers want to see a notchback Mustang as well as a fastback

- The Mustang Milano takes to the auto-show circuit; it's a chopped-top version of a stock '70 Mustang SportsRoof

- Model-year Mustang sales amount to 125,093, including 6401 convertibles

The Sprint package was available with the Mustang hardtop or SportsRoof (*top*), which became the "B" package with 15-inch Magnum 500 wheels and F60 × 15 tires. The "A" package had standard brushed aluminum hubcaps with trim rings. Even the plain-vanilla hardtop (*above*) made a bold statement. Surprisingly, the 109-inch wheelbase of the 1971-73 generation was a mere inch longer than that of previous Mustangs.

*This page:* Ford had planned to continue the performance theme in 1972 but had to rethink its strategy due to tough federal emissions standards that mandated lower compression ratios. The 429 CJ couldn't pass emissions without major changes and was dropped, leaving the Mustang without a big-block for the first time since 1966. The top performance V-8 was the 351 HO, a de-tuned, low-compression version of the '71 Boss 351, also dropped for '72.

**113**

A cursory look at a '72 Mustang, particularly a Mach 1 (*this page*), gave no indication that the "Total Performance" racing campaign had been scrapped after the previous model year. The '72 was the most cosmetically unchanged Mustang up to this point in the car's history, but Ford was definitely out of the big-block business, and out of the Trans Am racing series as well. No more Drag Packs were offered, and 3.90:1 and 4.11:1 gear sets went bye-bye, too. Ford had entered the "cosmetic supercar era," a term coined by *Super Stock & Drag Illustrated* magazine.

The standard Mustang gas cap (*below*) identifies this Mach 1 as a 1972 model and not a '71 (which had the pop-open cap). The standard Mach 1 engine was the 302-2V with 141 net horsepower, basically the same V-8 that produced 210 horses one year earlier. The difference was due not to the lower compression ratio (now 8.5 instead of 9.0), but the new way of rating the engines by "net" rather than "gross" figures.

*This page:* The 1972 ½ Mustang Sprint consisted of a special white body with unique blue and red hood stripes; a blue and red rear taillight board; a USA shield emblem on each rear quarter; dual color-keyed racing mirrors; and the Exterior Decor Group (honeycomb grille and color-keyed front bumper, plus hood and fender moldings). Inside, unique white vinyl buckets and trim were accented with Lambeth cloth inserts and white carpet. The Sprint saluted the Olympics in an Olympic year. Like any other Mustang, the Sprint could run with a six-cylinder or V-8, 4-speed or automatic, and have air conditioning and any other option that didn't interfere with the patriotic color and trim.

*This page:* Although the Sprint was offered to the public as a hardtop or fastback, Ford built 50 Sprint convertibles for the 1972 Cherry Day Parade in Washington, D.C. Standard-order Mustangs carried a two-digit DSO (District Special Order) code indicating the sales district where the car was originally sold. Special-order cars like the Sprint convertible had a special six-digit code, and can be documented.

# 1973

- A cease fire is declared in Vietnam, effective January 27

- In May, the U.S. Senate begins its investigation of the Watergate break-in and subsequent Nixon-administration cover-up

- An October oil embargo levied by Arab oil producers prompts talk of gas rationing in the U.S.

- Domestic auto-industry figures for horsepower, torque, and compression continue their downward slide

- Firebird hangs in with a 310-horsepower 455 V-8

- Mustang is the only Ford product to offer the division's High Output 351 V-8

- Ford announces that '73 will bring the final Mustang convertible

- Federal impact standards take effect, prompting a redesign of Mustang's front bumper

- Adjustment of Mustang's crankcase ventilation and recirculation of exhaust gases makes for leaner carburetor settings and lower emissions

- Mustang model-year sales rebound slightly, to 134,267; convertible sales almost double, to 11,853

*This page:* Touted as the "last" Ford convertible, the '73 Mustang ragtop found 11,853 buyers, up from 6401 in '72. Forged aluminum wheels were offered for this year only. Ford did a great job with the new standard blade-shaped urethane front bumper, considering that the piece had to withstand the five-mph static-impact standard set by the federal government.

A 1973 Mustang can be identified by its "crosshatch" grille. Rear bumper guards were standard; optional deluxe guards added horizontal rub strips. As on the Dark Green Metallic (*top row*) and Gold Glow (*below left*) convertibles seen here, the cars could be accented with a factory argent tape stripe identical to the one used on the '71 Boss 351. The 1973 interior (*left*) was loaded: tilt steering wheel, AM/8-track stereo, power steering, power brakes, automatic, and the Instrumentation Group, which added a tach and trip odometer along with a triple instrument pod with oil, amp, and temperature gauges mounted above the radio. *Below:* This Light Persimmon convertible is wearing the standard, but seldom seen, brushed aluminum hubcaps with trim rings. The '73 convertible was quiet and comfortable and available with a wide range of comfort and convenience options.

*Right and middle row:* Proof that the Mach 1 changed little during the 1971-73 generation is this '71 beauty, known as "Yellow Fellow" at home in Australia. It's a national show champion in that country and is 100-percent Dearborn stock except for a conversion to right-hand drive. NACA-style scoops ram fresh air to ignite 300 horsepower in the 351-4V Cleveland V-8, backed by a C-4 automatic that spins a set of 3.00:1 gears in a nine-inch nodular rear end. The rear wing spoiler stabilizes the car at high speed. Amenities include air conditioning, power steering, and a Philco Ford radio.

*Left:* The new-for-1973 stripe scheme decorates this Blue Glow SportsRoof Mach 1. The model year was the last for Mustang's optional 351, by now hanging on as a Cobra Jet, with four-bolt mains, nodular iron crank, solid lifters, magnafluxed connecting rods, and dual exhausts. Net horsepower came in at 275—an impressive figure, but a far cry from the glory days of just a few years earlier. With 35,440 sold, the Mach 1 was second only to the hardtop in 1973 model-year sales.

*Left and middle row:* This Medium Bright Yellow 1973 Mach 1 came stock with the 351-2V Ram Air engine. In 1973, Ram Air was available exclusively for the two-barrel V-8s because Ford got "caught" by the EPA trying to certify the Ram Air four-barrel with the results of the Ram Air 2V engines. Because the ploy failed, Ford missed the deadline to certify the 351 CJ with Ram Air. A plastic assembly on the underside of the hood directed air through the filter and to the engine *(below)*. *Bottom row:* A Bright Red 351 CJ convertible with an owner-added black tape stripe, which was factory-offered only with the Decor Group. That package also included the Mach 1 grille, which the owner also added. Not added were the lower-bodyside black (or argent) paint and bright moldings that would have completed the Decor Group package. The front spoiler was optional with any '73 Mustang.

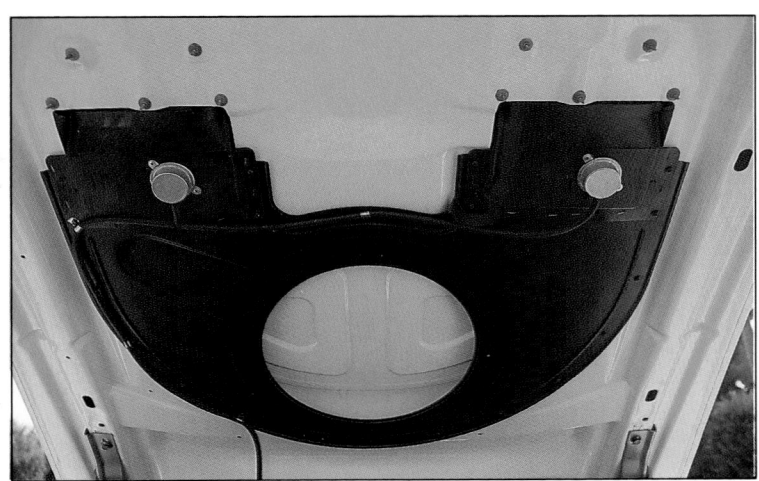

*This page*: Another Australian Mustang: This one a '73 "Reddy Teddy" "Mach One," in Aussie talk, powered by a 351-2V Cleveland, backed by a "T-Bar Automatic" (Ford C-4 SelectShift with factory T-handle) and a "Nine Inch Diff" (differential). The car has the stock forged-aluminum wheels unique to the '73s. Done up nicely in Bright Red, the Mach 1 was driven 27,000 miles by the first owner, who kept it 10 years. Now in the hands of its second owner, it's been fully restored. The car is stock except for the full conversion to right-hand drive.

In debut-year 1969, Grandé sold only enough to account for 7.4 percent of the total Mustang run; the percentage dipped slightly for 1970, then steadily rose. By 1973, Grandé production set a record with 25,274 units, the highest ever for the model, and 18.7 percent of the total Mustang production run. That works out to about one in every three hardtops sold that year. The Medium Brown Grandé (*top row*) has a standard full vinyl top. The Bright Yellow example (*above and left*) has a black vinyl top; other color choices were white, blue, brown, ginger, and avocado.

THE MUSTANG II PLAYED A VITAL role in the history of Ford's ponycar. Without it, we might not have new Mustangs today. It was certainly well timed, bowing on the eve of the 1973-74 Energy Crisis. While that was the sheerest coincidence, the oil embargo definitely spurred interest in this smaller, thriftier ponycar. The result was a smashing 385,993 first-year sales, just 10 percent shy of the '65 Mustang's record 418,812.

Impetus for the Mustang II came from the fast-growing popularity of sporty import coupes, particularly the Toyota Celica but also Ford's own British/German Capri and GM's German-built Opel Manta. While such "mini-ponycars" sold fewer than 100,000 units in 1965, they did 300,000 in '72 and were forecast to top 400,000 by '74. Mustang II's mission was to capture a big slice of this sizable new pie.

Oddly enough, the Mustang II began in the muscle-car mania of mid-1969 as a mere evolution of the big 1971-73 design. But as Lee Iacocca took over as Ford Motor Company president in 1970, the decline in ponycar demand accelerated even as the imported Capri started doing brisk business for Lincoln-Mercury. Accordingly, Iacocca ordered a series of consumer clinics to gauge prospects for a smaller, domestic sporty car. Favorable response led to two development efforts, but neither pleased Iacocca, Design vice president Gene Bordinat, or Advanced Design chief Don DeLaRossa.

Then, in November 1970, Ford acquired control of Ghia in Italy, and

# CHAPTER 6
# 1974-78: Starting Over

Iacocca asked the famed coachbuilder for a new concept. With typical dispatch, Ghia delivered a running prototype in just 53 days, a sloped-nose fastback that greatly accelerated work toward the eventual Mustang II. "The quick delivery of that real, live, drivable sample," Iacocca said later, "coalesced our thinking and gave us something tangible . . . early in the game, an experience that I had never had before in my career in the company. . . ."

With that, Iacocca staged another intramural design competition of the sort he'd used to stimulate creation of the original Mustang. Begun in August 1971, it involved the Ford and L-M production studios, Advanced Design, and the Interior Studio. All worked from concepts mandated by Iacocca: "The new Mustang must be small, with a wheelbase between 96 and 100 inches. It must be a sporty [pillared] notchback and/or fastback coupe; the convertible is dead and can be forgotten [he'd later think otherwise at Chrysler]. It must come with a 4-speed manual gearbox and a four-cylinder or small six-cylinder engine. Most important, it must be luxurious—upholstered in quality materials and carefully built."

In late November, management reviewed five full-size clays: a notchback and four fastbacks. The hands-down winner was a fastback from the Lincoln-Mercury team under Al Mueller (who painted it a bright persimmon to increase its chances). But though the design was little altered for production, it got mixed internal reviews, and some felt the derivative notchback was a hodgepodge. Actually, the notch wasn't approved for production until a bare 16 months before production start-up, saved only by favorable reaction at one last consumer clinic. At least the fastback was more practical than earlier "SportsRoof" models by dint of a European-style lift-up rear "door," a first for a Mustang and another boost to American acceptance of hatchback body styles. A *two*-seat fastback was also investigated, but was never seriously in contention.

The interior was far less involved. It was chiefly the work of Ford veteran L. David Ash, who decided to make his mockup more realistic than usual by giving it exterior sheetmetal and even four wheels. "It was a time-consuming thing to build," he said later, "but it served its purpose very well. We didn't have to go through an elaborate series of meetings to determine everything. It was all approved right here. We were on a crash basis to get it done, and it was very enthusiastically received. . . ." And why not, as it was at least partly inspired by the upscale likes of Jaguar, Rolls-Royce, and Mercedes—just the thing for what Iacocca envisioned as "a little jewel."

The all-new Mustang II of 1974-78 signaled Ford's desire to return to the manageable size of the early models. The snug dimensions and pleasing fuel efficiency were welcome, but performance was sacrificed to luxury, as on this '78 Ghia.

Unlike the massive sculptured dashboards of 1969-73, the Mustang II panel was slimmer and more straightforward. A large oblong design put all controls right ahead of the driver, as well as warning lights and instruments that included standard tachometer and ammeter. Seats were initially covered in pleated cloth, vinyl, or optional leather—all rather plush.

Dimensionally, Mustang II retained its predecessors' long hood/short deck proportions, but on a reduced scale—smaller than even the original and close to sporty imports like Toyota's Celica. Against the '73 Mustang, the "II" was no less than 20 inches shorter overall, nearly 13 inches shorter in wheelbase, four inches narrower, and a significant 400-500 pounds lighter.

At announcement time, some suggested the Mustang II was just a sportier version of the subcompact Pinto, and Ford grudgingly admitted that many components were shared. But it also claimed the '74 Pinto was upgraded to take advantage of some Mustang II parts and features.

For example, though both used the same double-A-arm front suspension, the Mustang's lower arms were attached to a rubber-mounted subframe, where Pinto's were bolted to the main structure. By carrying the rear of the engine/transmission assembly, the subframe reduced driveline vibration to the Mustang II's cabin and contributed to more precise steering and a smoother ride.

Rack-and-pinion steering was also shared, but the Mustang's was again mounted to minimize harshness. Also, its rear leaf springs were two inches longer than Pinto's, and its shock absorbers were staggered, as in previous high-performance Mustangs. Damping was computer-matched to equipment and weight. The Ghia notchback, for example, got softish settings, while the

optional competition suspension had the stiffest springs, plus a thicker front anti-roll bar.

Iacocca's final design brief made no provision for a V-8, a first for a Mustang—and no bulky inline-six, either. Initial engine choices thus came down to a 2.3-liter (140-cubic-inch) single-overhead-cam four and a 2.8-liter (171-cid) enlargement of the German Capri's overhead-valve V-6.

Sometimes called the "Lima" engine after the Lima, Ohio, plant that built it, the 2.3 was the first American engine based on metric dimensions. That wasn't surprising. Originally designed for some of Ford's larger European cars, it was a bigger version of Pinto's 2.0-liter four. The V-6 was strictly a European design, and even sold in U.S. Capris from 1972 on (upsized from 2.6 liters/155 cid). However, Ford switched it from siamesed to separate exhaust ports for improved performance and thermal efficiency. Standard in the Mach 1 hatchback and optional elsewhere, the V-6 was supplied by Ford's West German subsidiary in Cologne.

Mustang II's manual gearbox was basically the 4-speed unit from the British Ford Cortina as used in the Pinto, but strengthened to handle Mustang's more potent engines. Automatic, of course, was optional: a light-duty version of 4-speed Cruise-O-Matic. Standard vacuum-assisted brakes comprised 9.3-inch front discs and 9 × 1.75-inch rear drums.

Mustang IIs, including the new top-line Ghia notchback (replacing Grandé as the luxury model), exhibited predictably "American" ride and handling. The Mach 1 was more capable and entertaining with its V-6, radial tires, and optional competition suspension. No early Mustang II was truly peppy. The car was heavy for its size—curb weight was a porky 2650-2900 pounds—so a V-6 with 4-speed would do 0-60 mph in a

lackluster 13-14 seconds and reach only about 100 mph.

As if to prepare buyers for this reduced performance, Ford redesigned Mustang's trademark running-horse emblem into a less-muscular steed that seemed to be trotting instead of galloping. That symbolism went largely unnoticed, but not the car itself, as its terrific first-year sales attested. Icing the cake, Mustang II won *Motor Trend* magazine's 1974 "Car of the Year" award.

The Mustang II would run five years without major change. Four-cylinder and V-6 notchback and fastback, Ghia notchback, and the Mach 1 were cataloged throughout, and all offered numerous options per Mustang tradition. Aside from air conditioning and various radios and tape players, the '74 roster included a vinyl top for notchbacks, a tilt/takeout sunroof, and forged aluminum wheels.

Ghia options were expanded for 1975 to include a $454 flip-up glass "moon-roof" and a Silver Luxury Package with Cranberry-color crushed-velour upholstery, Silver paint, and vinyl top—and, depressingly, a standup hood ornament. At the same time, the Ghia's rear-quarter glass was slimmed down into "opera" windows, another period styling fad. Also new for '75 was an optional "extended-range" (17-gallon) fuel tank. This betrayed the fact that even the smallest Fords of that day were rather thirsty. Mid-model year brought "MPG" models with improved fuel efficiency. Though the MPGs soon vanished, their catalytic converter did not.

The biggest news for '75 was the return of the small-block V-8—Ford's answer to enthusiast pleas for better performance. Offered optionally through '78, this was the familiar 302 tuned for 122 net horsepower (139 bhp after '75). Cooling requirements dictated larger grille eggcrates, a change applied to all models regardless of engine after '74.

Other manufacturers were bound to follow Ford's lead, and for 1975 the Mustang II had strong new competition in the Monza 2+2, derived from Chevy's subcompact Vega. Monza's optional 4.3-liter (262-cid) V-8 seemed no match for Mustang's "5.0," and in straightline acceleration it wasn't. Yet *Road & Track's* editors clearly preferred the Chevy with its fresh, Ferrari-like styling, plus comfort, ride, handling, and fuel economy that were all judged superior to the Ford's.

Of course, such reports hardly helped sales, and Mustang II volume dropped more than 50 percent for 1975. But it would drop no more, holding at about 190,000 units annually through 1978. If not exactly a torrid pace, this was a lot more encouraging—not to mention profitable—than the weakened tempo of 1971-73.

In further pursuit of sport—or whatever interpretation of it still allowed by the government—Ford trotted out the Cobra II for 1976. Initially priced at $312, this was a trim option for hatchbacks comprising sports steering wheel, remote-control door mirrors, brushed-aluminum dash and door appliqués, black-finish grille, styled steel wheels, radial tires, flip-out rear-quarter windows with louvered covers, front air dam, rear spoiler, and simulated hood air scoop. Requisite model i.d. and/or badges appeared on rocker panels, grille, tail, and front fenders. All '76 Cobra IIs were white with blue tape striping on rockers, hood, roof, and tail; other color combinations were added for '77. It was flashy, but a mere echo of the late, great Shelby Mustangs it strained to emulate. Incidentally, when ordered on a Mach 1, the package created the amusing official designation Mustang II Mach 1 Cobra II.

No less subtle was the Stallion, another all-show option (also offered in slightly different form on '76 Pintos and Mav-

ericks). Again for fastbacks only, it delivered acres of black paint with silver accents, forged aluminum wheels, and snorting horse's-head front-fender decals. One other change for '76 involved the Ghia moonroof, which was now optional for any Mustang II and available with either silver or brown tint.

A new option for '77 Ghias was the "Sports Appearance Group." Offered only with black or tan paint, it included a color-keyed console, three-spoke sports steering wheel, cast aluminum wheels with chamois-color spokes, and a decklid luggage rack with hold-down straps and bright buckles. Wheel choices for all models now included "lacy spoke" aluminum rims with chrome or white-painted spokes. A new T-top roof with twin lift-off glass panels arrived for fastbacks only.

Still available (at $160-$400) was the useful Rallye Equipment Package for V-6 and V-8 models. This grouped the firm competition suspension with Traction-Lok limited-slip differential, an "extra-cooling" package, and chrome-tipped dual exhausts. Buyers also got larger raised-white-letter tires, color-keyed remote door mirrors, a leather-rim steering wheel, and a quartz digital clock.

Which brings up the fact that although Mustang II was "less ponycar," it was no less a Mustang in offering so many options. Among those not already mentioned: anti-theft alarm (about $75), electric rear-window defroster ($60-$75), flip-out rear-quarter windows for fastbacks ($30), fold-down rear seat for notchbacks (around $60; standard on fastbacks), center console ($65), and the usual power assists. The competition suspension added only $25-$60 depending on model and year.

For 1978, Ford offered more "paint-on performance" in the King Cobra option. Like the Cobra II, which continued, it was strictly for fastbacks, but even more

outlandish. A gigantic snake decal covered the hood, and tape stripes were emblazoned everywhere else. "King Cobra" was written in large letters on each door, on the deep front air dam, and on the standard rear spoiler. Black paint was used to finish the grille, window moldings, headlamp bezels, and wiper arms. Also included were the 302 V-8, power steering, the aforementioned Rallye Package, and Goodrich 70-series T/A radial tires. That was the least Ford could to do to back up the boastful styling. And in fairness, the King Cobra's 17-second quarter-mile time was "high performance" by 1978 standards.

At the other end of the scale, the '78 Ghia offered lush new "Wilshire" cloth upholstery, while the standard notchback could be ordered with a Fashion Accessory Package comprising door pockets, striped fabric upholstery, lighted vanity mirror, and a four-way manual driver's seat—all clearly aimed at women buyers.

Otherwise, the '78s were much like earlier Mustang IIs. Sales were still holding up: 192,000 for the model year, second only to debut '74. They might have been higher, but low inventory prompted some '78s to be delivered to dealers early and registered as 1977 models.

The Mustang II is neither well-loved nor fondly remembered today. Its styling—once regarded as fresh and lively—has not aged gracefully, and enthusiasts find the car a depressing reminder of the trials and tribulations that made most Seventies automobiles so dull. But it has significance in bridging the gap between the last of the traditional models and the exciting new third generation that would carry Mustang through an even more difficult and challenging age.

We can thus be grateful for the Mustang II. You may not like it, but it kept Ford's ponycar alive through some very rough times, and for that it deserves a certain respect.

# 1974

- Doomed to impeachment for his role in the Watergate cover-up, Richard Nixon resigns the presidency on August 8; his successor is Vice-President Gerald Ford

- The gasoline crisis worsens; lines at service stations commonly stretch for blocks

- Mercury Cougar says goodbye to sportiness and embraces luxury

- Camaro's Z28 is temporarily dropped at the end of the year

- This is the final year for the AMC Javelin, Plymouth Barracuda, Dodge Challenger, and Pontiac GTO

..................................................

- The downsized, wholly redesigned Mustang II is in showrooms during the 1973-74 energy crisis, a propitious marketing moment

- The familiar long hood/short deck profile is retained, but the package is smaller than even the original 1964½ model

- The initial Mustang II offers a four and a six, but not a V-8—a first for Mustang; the 2.3-liter four is America's first mass-produced engine built to metric measurements

- Mustang convertibles disappear, and will not return until '83

- The Mustang logo is redesigned

- Mustang's upmarket model is now called Ghia

- The Mustang II sells a robust 385,993 units during the model year

*Top:* This early Ford Design concept for the second-generation Mustang II was not elegant enough to suit Lee Iacocca—hardly surprising, since early Mustang II designs were based on Ford's utilitarian Pinto. *Middle:* Ford pondered the feasibility of a two-seat Mustang by comparing a tape drawing with a clay model. *Above:* The first approved Mustang II shape was a fastback (*left*), which was later modeled into a companion pillared coupe (*right*).

Mustang II...
the sporty, personal way to Free Wheel...

*Left:* The show car selected by Ford to promote the new 1974 Mustang II was the "Sportiva II," which featured a targa-style open top and integral roll bar. *Above:* Mustang II returned to the car's roots with a high-mounted grille fitted with a running horse and simulated driving lights. *Below:* The production Mustang II, seen here in Ghia trim, had an elegant shape—perhaps *too* elegant. Ominously, the base engine was now a four-cylinder; a V-6 was optional and there was no available V-8 at all.

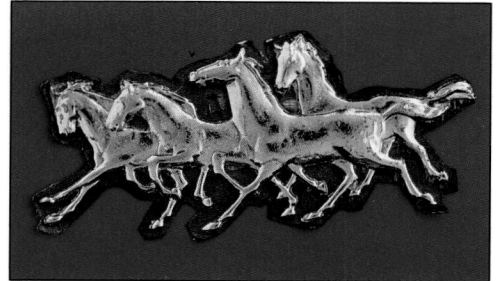

Mustang II

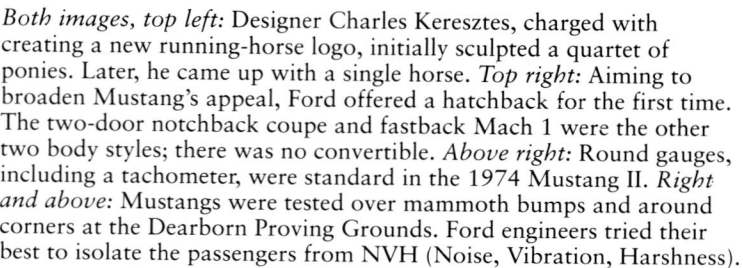

*Both images, top left:* Designer Charles Keresztes, charged with creating a new running-horse logo, initially sculpted a quartet of ponies. Later, he came up with a single horse. *Top right:* Aiming to broaden Mustang's appeal, Ford offered a hatchback for the first time. The two-door notchback coupe and fastback Mach 1 were the other two body styles; there was no convertible. *Above right:* Round gauges, including a tachometer, were standard in the 1974 Mustang II. *Right and above:* Mustangs were tested over mammoth bumps and around corners at the Dearborn Proving Grounds. Ford engineers tried their best to isolate the passengers from NVH (Noise, Vibration, Harshness).

The '74 Mach 1 (*top left*) was available only as a two-door fastback, while the luxurious Ghia (*top right*) was limited to a two-door notchback coupe. The standard-series Mustang, however, could be ordered as either the three-door fastback hatchback (*above left*), or the two-door hardtop (*left*). The engine of choice for the Mach 1 was the V-6, but the rest of the lineup came stock with the new 2.3-liter four-cylinder (*above*), which was the first metric engine designed, developed, and made in the United States. Built at Ford's Lima, Ohio, engine plant, this four was the lowest-rated engine ever installed in the Mustang, with 88 horsepower @ 5000 rpm.

*Top row:* Mustang II's interior seating continued with the popular standard bucket seats, divided by the center transmission hump or an optional console. Mustang II upholstery was buttoned-and-tucked in squares for a luxury look. The steering wheel design seen here did not make production. *Bottom right and bottom middle:* Ford did not anticipate the Arab oil embargo that hit just as the Mustang II debuted in late 1973, but advertisements drove home the point that the car was the "right car at the right time." Millions of people who now looked for economy instead of high performance were attracted to the little Mustang II's miserly way with fuel. Even better, Ford had not abandoned the Mustang's familiar styling cues (*right and below*).

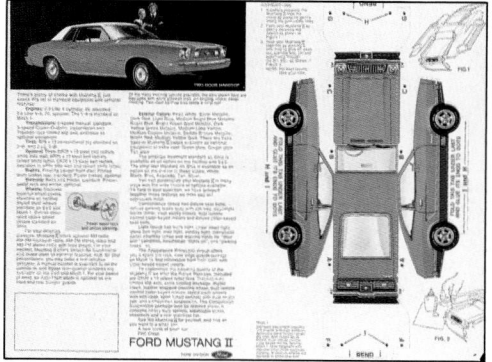

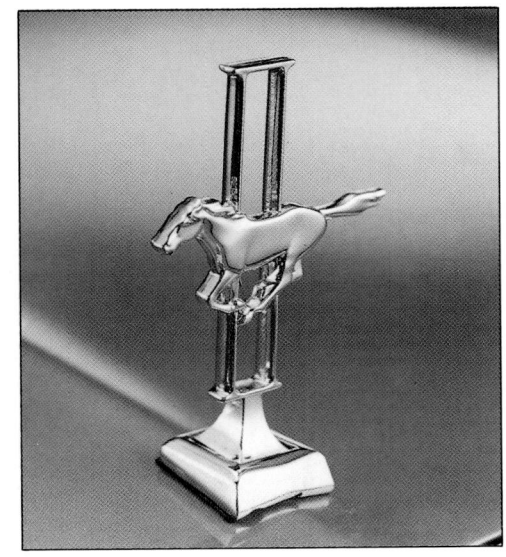

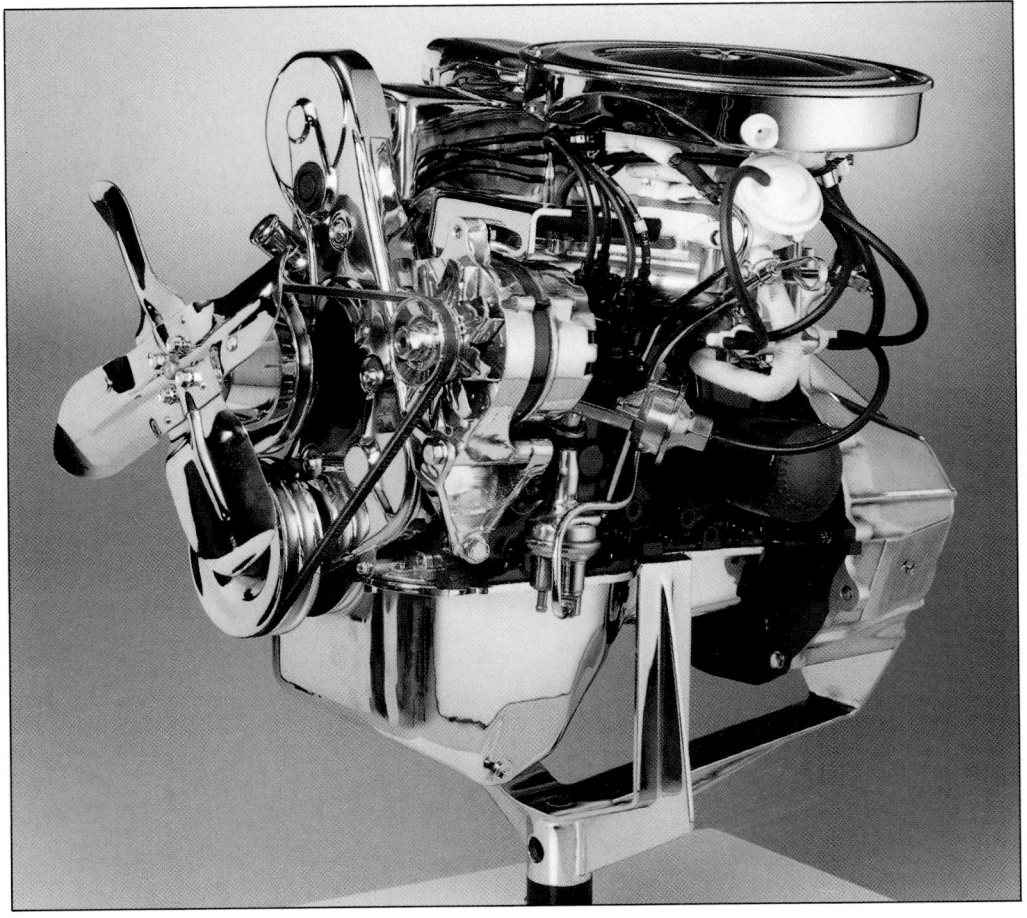

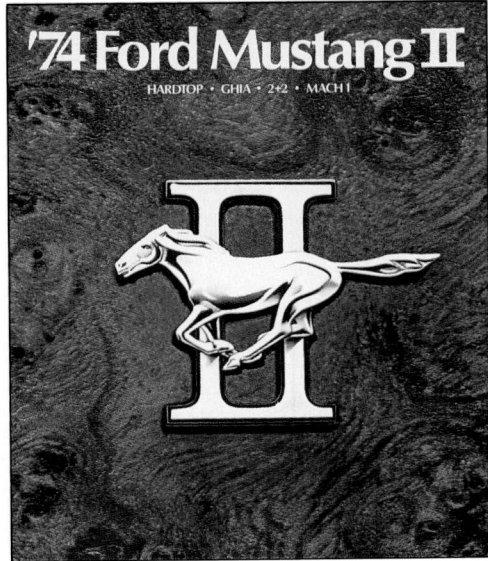

Top left: The new Mustang interior was genteel rather than aggressive. Top right: The Mustang II hood ornament consisted of a running horse striding over a Roman numeral II. Above: The catalog featured a burled walnut look; clearly, luxury had become an important selling point. Left: In the early Seventies, 20 miles per gallon on the highway was excellent fuel economy, which is what Ford advertised for their brand-new, overhead-cam four-cylinder, which displaced 2.3 liters (about 140 cubic inches).

## 1975

- Saigon falls to Communist forces on April 30

- *Jaws* gives summertime moviegoers plenty to scream about

- The Big Three automakers offer buyer rebates for the first time

- As sales of domestic cars decline, Big Three workers are laid off in droves; some plants are closed

- Mercury introduces the restyled Capri II at mid-year

- Chevy introduces the sporty Vega-based Monza 2+2 fastback/hatchback

---

- Mustang's V-8 engine option returns with a 302 small-block, detuned to 122 net horsepower

- Styling remains unchanged except for a larger grille opening

- A new Ghia "Silver Luxury Group" package offers Silver Metallic paint, silver vinyl half-top, Cranberry velour interior, and other pseudo-luxury trim

- Mustang sales drop from the '74 level by over 50 percent, to 188,575

*Top:* Two new features for 1975 were an optional moonroof and a stand-up hood ornament, the first ever for a factory Mustang. *Middle:* The Ghia could be had with a new "Silver Luxury Group" that included Silver metallic paint, silver half-vinyl roof, hood ornament, body stripes, and silver moldings. The interior was shocking: Cranberry velour seats with color-keyed headliner, sun visors, and console. *Above:* The Mach 1 ran with a 302-2V, available only with automatic transmission.

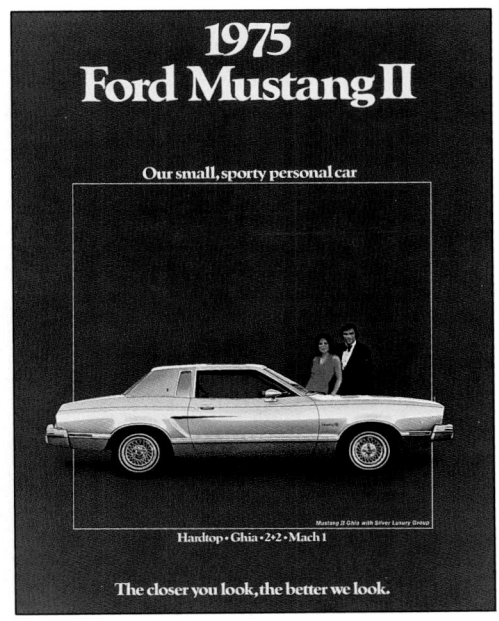

In the middle of the 1975 model year, Ford introduced a plainer Ghia (*top left*) that didn't have the fancy hood ornament. However, the Ghia continued to be identified by its unique opera window, which was pictured inside the Mustang II sales brochure (*above*) alongside a 1957 "porthole" Thunderbird. The cover featured the Silver Ghia, the flagship of the lineup, and a bargain at just $151 over the cost of the standard Ghia. The 1975 model lineup continued as in '74 with the notchback coupe, Ghia, 2+2, and Mach 1. Not listed in the brochure was a mid-year introduction, the MPG (Miles Per Gallon) model, a four-cylinder notchback that managed 26 to 28 miles per gallon on the highway, helped by a catalytic converter and a new solid-state ignition. *Left:* The '75 Mustang's grille encompassed a larger area for a bolder appearance. That was all well and good, but Mustang II production sagged in 1975, to 188,575, down dramatically from the 385,993 cars sold during the 1974 season.

# 1976

- The United States celebrates its bicentennial on July 4; in November, former Georgia governor Jimmy Carter is elected president

- Sales of domestic cars increase by 22 percent, but American Motors is sinking fast

- Front disc brakes are now standard on all American cars, as per federal edict

- Firebird's top engine is a 200-bhp 455 V-8

- Chevy brings back the Z28 Camaro as a mid-year option package; handling, not acceleration, is emphasized

- Ford workers strike in September, halting production for 28 days

- Horsepower of Mustang's 302 V-8 increases from 122 (net) to 139

- A cosmetic Cobra II package debuts, comprising sport steering wheel, front air dam, nonfunctional hood scoop, and other add-ons; colors are restricted to white with blue tape stripes on rockers, hood, rooftop, and tail

- Another all-show, no-go option package, the Stallion, is offered

- Mustang's option list expands to include crushed velour upholstery, flip-up glass moonroof, and stand-up hood ornament

- 187,567 Mustangs are sold during the model year

Model-year 1976 brought no changes to the basic Mustang lineup. The bread-and-butter two-door hardtop (*top*) poked along with the overhead-cam four-cylinder engine. Ford built 78,508 of this body style. *Middle and above:* A tape-and-stripe job for 1976 was dubbed the Stallion, available in a range of colors but most often seen in black and silver, and usually as a fastback.

The pseudo-performance Cobra II (*this page*) was the brainchild of Jim Wangers, who had dreamed up the original Pontiac GTO in 1964. The Cobra II looked sporty but got mixed reactions. It was available with the four-cylinder, V-6, or V-8. Wangers's Motortown company made and installed the Cobra II parts off-site, not far from Dearborn Assembly. As in the Sixties, the Cobra-ized Mustang came with such extras as an over-the-roof LeMans stripe, a black grille with Cobra snake emblem, simulated hood scoop, front and rear spoilers, and lower-bodyside stripes. Unique louvers over the flip-out rear-quarter windows gave the car a snakeskin appearance. The 302-2V (*below left*) developed a mere 140 horsepower, but could at least be ordered with a four-speed stick and sporty bucket-seat interior (*below*).

*Right:* Firestone steel-belted P195/70R13 raised-white-letter tires, forged aluminum wheels, and the front spoiler first seen on the 1976 Cobra II were proof that Ford wanted cosmetic performance, if not the real thing. *Below:* Even the basic coupe could wear styled steel wheels. *Bottom row:* Ford still lacked a convertible model in '75. One way to get back into droptop motoring was the T-top, so named because the roof formed the letter T when the two glass roof panels were removed. The car seen here toured the show-car circuit in 1976.

- A.J. Foyt wins the Indianapolis 500 for a record fourth time
- Elvis Presley and Groucho Marx pass away in August
- Imported-car sales hit the two-million mark for the first time
- GM offers downsized cars; Ford and Chrysler must stick with their big models for the time being

---

- The Cobra II package adds black body/gold tape stripe color option
- A bit more than a quarter of the year's Mustangs are ordered with the 302 V-8, up from 17.6 percent in '76
- The Stallion package is replaced by a Rallye Appearance Package featuring black paint with subtle gold accents
- The Rallye Package tweaks performance and handling with a Traction-Lok limited-slip differential
- In the main, alterations to the year's Mustangs are minor; inside, *faux* wood accents abandon a burled-walnut look for simulated pecan grain

The 1977 Mustang was another carryover, though the fastback (*top*) came standard with a blackout grille, front spoiler (which could be deleted), styled steel wheels, and raised-white-letter tires. The 2+2 (*middle*) came with optional twin, removable roof hatches. This car has the optional "Lacy" spoke aluminum wheels. *Above:* The T-top's glass panels could be stored in the trunk.

*Top row:* Ford promoted black fastbacks in an ad that quoted Henry Ford's famous line from his 1912 Model T days: "Any customer can have a car painted any color he wants so long as it is black." *Above and right:* Meanwhile, Ford continued to add more colors to the Cobra II line, including white with green stripes and white with red stripes, to join white with blue stripes, blue with white stripes, and black with gold stripes—Stripe City! The Cobra II found sufficient buyers to prompt Ford to move production from Jim Wangers's Motortown job shop to the Ford assembly line, where workers added the Cobra stripes, scoops, spoilers, and Cobra logo. The "V" emblem on the front fenders of this car let the world know that underhood was the 302—but still a two-barrel (the last Mustang four-barrel V-8 had shown up for model-year 1973).

*Above:* The black-and-gold 1977 Cobra IIs looked sharp and were reminiscent of the Hertz GT-350 H Shelbys that had been painted Hertz Rent-A-Car colors in 1966. As in 1976, the standard engine for the '77 Cobra II was the base four-cylinder, backed by a 4-speed manual transmission. The V-6 was optional, but the V-8 was the most popular choice. However, customers could not buy the 4-speed manual with the 302-2V in the state of California, due to that state's tough emissions standards. *Left:* A Stallion package was designed for 1977 but never made production. Ford replaced it with a Rallye Appearance Package on the 2+2, which included blackout trim on wiper arms, door handles, lock cylinders, antenna, sport mirrors, grille (minus horse emblem), and front spoiler. Bodies were Black or Polar White.

# 1978

- Sadat, Begin, and Carter meet in a historic summit at Camp David
- More than 900 followers of self-styled messiah Jim Jones follow their leader into death in a mass suicide in Guyana
- Domestic-car sales increase to just under nine million units, giving Detroit its third-best year ever

---

- FoMoCo president Lee Iacocca—spiritual father of the Mustang—is fired by chairman Henry Ford II and quickly snags a new job as head of struggling Chrysler Corporation
- Paint-on performance reaches its zenith with the gaudy King Cobra fastback package, which includes an enormous cobra decal on the hood
- Model-year Mustang sales bounce back, to 192,410

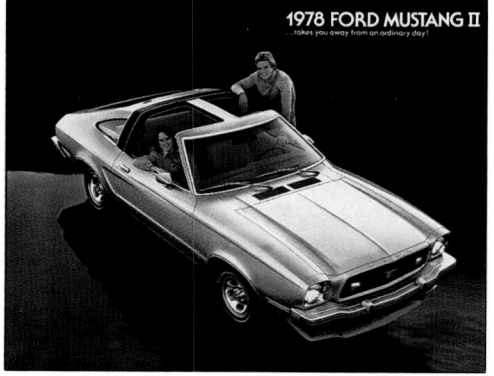

Top and above: For 1978, the "ultimate" Mustang was the wildly colorful King Cobra. With such a name, there could be no base four or optional V-6. Instead, the 302-2V was standard, as were 4-speed floor shift, power front disc brakes, power steering, raised-white-letter radial tires, and the Rallye Package, which added extra cooling capacity, heavy-duty springs, adjustable shock absorbers, rear stabilizer bar, and dual sport mirrors. T-tops were optional. *Left:* Ford called its "T-Roof" a convertible, and if it fell somewhat short of that definition, it did offer open-air motoring.

The gaudy King Cobra overshadowed the Cobra II (*left*), which was bolder looking for 1978 thanks to huge side stripes. The notchback seen in the foreground has the optional sunroof, which could be flipped up or removed and stowed in the trunk. For the '78 notchback (*middle row*), Mustang designed a Fashion Accessory Package for women that consisted of a driver's-side illuminated visor vanity mirror, four-way adjustable driver's seat, map pockets, striped-cloth seat inserts, and illuminated entry system. As with any Mustang hardtop, the 2.3-liter four was standard, but the V-6 and V-8 were optional. Another special was the Ghia with the Sports Group package (*bottom row*), featuring black, blue, or chamois body paint and a chamois or black vinyl half-roof. Pinstripes and protective side moldings with vinyl inserts completed the package.

*Top row:* Eight Monroe Handler Mustangs—one metal prototype and seven fiberglass replicas—were built in 1978 in Los Angeles at Creative Car Craft. With a big whale-tail rear spoiler and front fender flares, the cars resembled the "Kemp Cobra" IMSA GT road racer of the time and were a back-door way for Ford to return to real performance after Henry Ford II's non-racing edict, imposed after the discontinuation of the Shelby Cobras. The steel car had a 351 Jack Roush motor, while the fiberglass replicas were powered with stock 302s. *Left and bottom row:* The '78 Ghia was offered only as a two-door hardtop. The base four was standard, with optional V-6 or, as on this car, the 302 V-8. Variable-ratio power steering was introduced for '78, along with an optional aluminum steering wheel.

*Above and top row:* The King Cobra had plenty of bark, but the de-tuned 302 couldn't summon much bite. *Right:* Encouraged by the successful 1976 Cobra II contract, Jim Wangers and his Motortown shop looked at Charlie Kemp's IMSA Cobra racer and came up with a wild street version. The concept made more sense than the King Cobra because it was inspired directly by racing. However, Henry Ford II was content to continue building tape-and-stripe Mustangs while Ford and the rest of the Detroit automakers struggled to meet increasingly tough emissions standards and new CAFE (Corporate Average Fuel Economy) numbers. The only solace in all of this was that "real" Mustang performance would soon return.

**A**FTER FIVE YEARS OF SUCCESS with the Mustang II, Ford reworked it for 1979 (leaving off the Roman numeral). But where the II never inspired much passion, this new Mustang did. And why not? Like the original, it was "right" in most every way. Even the running-horse logo looked like its '65 self. So perhaps it's no surprise that the '79 design would run fully 15 model years—and sell well in every one, sometimes impressively so.

As with previous Mustangs, the '79's final shape was selected from proposals by competing in-house teams, this time the Ford and Lincoln-Mercury studios, Advanced Design, and Ford's Ghia operation in Italy. All worked from the same dimensional "hard points." Now, however, quarter-scale clay models were tested many hours in the wind tunnel. Reason: Aerodynamics was increasingly recognized (actually rediscovered from Thirties streamlining) as vital to improved fuel economy, a matter of considerable importance following the 1973-74 gasoline shortage.

Congress had already written something called CAFE—"Corporate Average Fuel Economy"—mandating specific mpg targets effective with 1978 models. In brief, all cars sold by a given maker had to average so many EPA miles per gallon each year—initially 19 mpg, rising to 27.5 mpg by 1985. Companies whose "fleet average" fell below a target would be fined for each 0.1 mpg deviation—multiplied by *total* sales for that model year. Obviously, failure to comply could be costly, though a maker could earn

# CHAPTER 7
# 1979-81: Back on Track

"credits" that could be carried forward or backward to another year. Though controversial, CAFE achieved its intent of spurring Detroit to develop thriftier cars. Adding new urgency to the effort was a second energy crisis triggered in late 1979 by the overthrow of the Iranian shah.

Detroit was still reeling from the first energy crunch when work began on the Mustang II's successor in mid-1975. Ultimately, Ford decided to use the basic platform of the evolving "Fox" compacts (the new 1978 Ford Fairmont/Mercury Zephyr twins), but with wheelbase cut 5.1 inches (to 100.4). Curb weight was pegged at a svelte 2700 pounds. Like the original Mustang but unlike the II, the two-door notchback was styled first and a three-door hatchback evolved from it. Of the full-size proposals shown to management, the winner came from a team headed by Jack Telnack, then executive director of Ford's North American Light Truck and Car Design. Four trim levels would be offered: standard, Sport Option, Ghia, and Cobra. The last stood apart with black-finish greenhouse trim and rocker panels, color-keyed body moldings, an optional snake decal for the hood, and sportier cabin decor.

Improved aerodynamics was a major design goal, and Telnack's group achieved drag coefficients of 0.44 for the hatchback and 0.46 for the notchback. "[Aerodynamics is] probably the most cost-effective way to improve corporate average fuel economy," he said. "We know that a 10-percent [reduction] in drag can result in a five-percent improvement in fuel economy at a steady-state 50 mph . . . really worthwhile stuff for us to go after." Of course, those drag numbers were good for '79, but would soon seem mediocre against even more slippery cars from Ford and others.

In profile, the '79 Mustang was a "three-box wedge," with the hood sloped down over the air cleaner from a high cowl. Though the design dictated unique inner front-fender aprons and radiator supports, the expense was approved for the sake of aerodynamics and fuel economy, which also prompted a slight lip on decklids and a small spoiler integrated with the front bumper.

Body engineering was aimed at minimizing weight to maximize both mileage and performance, so plastics, aluminum, and lighter high-strength/low-alloy steel were used extensively. A significant new plastics technology appeared in color-keyed bumper covers of soft urethane made by the reaction-injection molding (RIM) process. Thinner but stronger glass saved still more pounds. With all this, the '79 was some 200 pounds lighter than a comparable Mustang II, despite being slightly larger in every dimension.

Model-year 1979 brought clean, crisp lines and—hallelujah!—a renewed emphasis on performance.
The 302 V-8 was bumped up to 140 horsepower, and a turbocharged inline-four (powering the '79
hatchback seen here) cranked out a pleasing 131 bhp.

Interior design received equal care. Though still a "2+2," the '79 Mustang boasted 14-16 cubic feet more in total interior volume, 2-4 cubic feet more cargo space, and noticeably more room for shoulders and hips. Higher-quality fabrics and plastics were specified, as were standard tach, trip odometer, ammeter, and oil pressure gauge.

Like past Mustangs, the '79 was designed for the broadest possible market appeal, so several suspension "levels" were deemed necessary. The basic hardware was Fairmont/Zephyr, which meant modified MacPherson-strut geometry in front instead of conventional upper A-arms. Unlike similar setups still used in many cars, the coil spring did not wrap around the strut but sat between a lower arm and the body, thus eliminating the need for a costly spring compressor when replacing shocks. A front anti-roll bar was standard.

Rear geometry was a "four-bar link" arrangement, also with coil springs—lighter and more compact than Mustang II's leaf-sprung Hotchkiss design. Some models added a rear anti-roll bar that served more for lateral location than controlling sway, because the roll center was effectively lower than in the Mustang II.

Planners finally settled on standard, "handling," and "special" suspensions, each designed around specific tires. The basic setup was tuned for conventional bias-plys, the "handling" package for regular radials. The special package employed Michelin's sticky new TRX radials, whose 390-mm diameter required metric-size forged aluminum wheels. This setup gave the tightest handling with the stiffest damping, a 1.12-inch front stabilizer bar, and a rear bar. Mustang II's variable-ratio rack-and-pinion steering was retained for all models.

An intriguing new power choice was a turbocharged version of the base 2.3-liter "Lima" four, with 131 net horsepower against only 88 for the unblown unit. Though old-hat now, turbos were pretty exotic in 1979, let alone on a mass-market American car. To prevent possible engine damage, maximum boost was limited to six psi by a "wastegate" relief valve that allowed the driving exhaust gases to bypass the turbo once that pressure was reached.

Carryover engines weren't neglected. The venerable 302 V-8 gained a new low-restriction exhaust, more lightweight components, and a sturdier accessory-drive V-belt. The German-made V-6 was in short supply, so the old 200 inline-six was brought back to replace it late in the model run. The V-8 and both sixes could be optionally teamed with a new 4-speed gearbox—the standard 3-speed manual with a longer-striding overdrive gear tacked on. Ford's proven Cruise-O-Matic remained optional as well.

Per Mustang tradition, the performance of any '79 depended on drivetrain. The V-8 was a dragster engine for that day, clocking 0-60 in about nine seconds. The V-6 4-speed was still in the 13-14-second range, while a like-equipped turbo four did the trip in about 12-12.5 seconds.

Press reaction varied with powertrain. Some critics felt the V-8 was out of step with gas prices again on the rise, but the turbo four garnered plenty of "buff book" attention. Said *Road & Track's* John Dinkel: "The TRX turbo would seem to be an enthusiast's delight. I just hope that the design compromises dictated by costs, and the fact that Ford couldn't start with a completely clean sheet of paper, don't wreck that dream. . . . There's no doubt the new Mustang has the potential to be the best sport coupe Ford has ever built, but in some respects [it] is as enigmatic as its predecessor."

Speaking of enigmas, a month after the new Mustang's June 1978 press preview, Lee Iacocca was fired as Ford Motor Company president. The official reason was early retirement (on October 15, his 54th birthday), but many insiders suspected he'd be dumped sometime before Henry Ford II retired as CEO in 1980 and as chairman in '82. As usual, HFII didn't say much. Neither did Iacocca—at first. Later he declared, "You just surmise that [HFII] doesn't want strong guys around." But Chrysler Corporation needed them badly, so after 32 years with Ford, Iacocca signed on in Highland Park as president, then chairman, vowing to pull that company out of its latest financial quagmire.

Back in Dearborn, the venerable 302 was debored to 255 cid as Mustang's sole V-8 option for 1980. Though it appeared an amazingly fast response to "Energy Crisis II," it was planned long before in light of CAFE. Though it was some help to economy, performance naturally suffered.

Mustang sales also suffered. The reason was not styling, which changed only in detail, but the market, which changed drastically. In the strong overall climate of '79, Ford's new ponycar scored a substantial sales gain, reaching just over 332,000. But with a new Middle East crisis, Mustang suffered as much as any Detroit car in 1980, plunging to 241,000 units.

On the brighter side, Ford had finagled Mustang's selection as 1979 Indy 500 pace car, so a replica was a natural mid-year addition. Ford sold some 11,000 of them with both turbo four and V-8 power, then applied their special styling features—except the regalia decals, thank goodness—to the 1980 Cobra. Those touches included a slat grille, bigger front and rear spoilers, integral foglamps, and a non-functioning hood scoop. Still built around the turbo four and TRX suspension, the Cobra option added $1482 to a hatchback's sticker price (versus the previous $1173). The hood-mounted snake decal remained a separate extra at $88.

Elsewhere, high-back vinyl bucket seats and color-keyed interior and door trim became standard linewide, as did brighter halogen headlights (replacing conventional tungsten sealed-beams). Hatchbacks now came with the Sport Option at no charge, which meant styled sport wheels with trim rings, black rocker and window moldings, wide bodyside moldings, and sports steering wheel. Ghia remained the luxury Mustang, boasting low-back vinyl buckets with headrests, door map pockets, thicker carpeting, passenger-assist grips, and its own interior light package.

A surprising new 1980 option was genuine Recaro front seats, as used on the '79 Pace Car Replica. With its infinitely variable backrest recliners and adjustable thigh and lumbar supports, Mustang now rivaled costly European cars for seat comfort.

Save the smaller V-8, Mustang's 1980 drivetrain chart was a photocopy of the late '79 lineup. Both fours again had a conventional 4-speed manual transmission as standard. The six, still rated at a modest 85 bhp (versus 109 for the departed V-6), came with the manual overdrive unit. Cruise-O-Matic remained the only choice with the V-8 and was optional elsewhere.

In model years, Mustang turned sweet 16 in 1980, yet remained no less a ponycar than it was in '65. But despite striking similarities in certain "vital statistics," the latest Mustang was quite different from Ford's first ponycar. For example, it had a bigger back seat despite a 7.6-inch-shorter wheelbase, so Dearborn had evidently learned something about space utilization in 16 years. Though burdened by all manner of government-mandated safety features, the newest generation was scarcely heavier than the first, so Ford had apparently learned

something about weight control too. Of course, the 200-cid six and 255 V-8 were both rooted in 1965 engines, yet had become measurably cleaner and more fuel-efficient. In short, Mustang had come full circle—and then some: a nimble, handsome, and versatile sporty car once more, but with styling, features, and powertrains astutely designed for vastly changed times.

Though "Total Performance" was a distant memory in 1980, Ford gave hints it was itching to do it again, with Mustang leading the way. One such teaser was the Mustang IMSA, a racy "concept car" powered by a much-modified turbo four. In name and appearance, it strongly implied that Ford was thinking about a return to competition in general, and the International Motor Sports Association GT series in particular.

Then, in September 1980, Ford announced formation of Special Vehicle Operations (SVO) under Michael Kranefuss, who'd been serving as competition director for Ford Europe. SVO's mission was to devise "a series of limited-production performance cars and develop their image through motorsport." It quickly got down to business with a turbo Mustang for Porsche pilot Klaus Ludwig to run in selected 1981 IMSA GT events. Other Mustangs receiving direct factory help included a Trans-Am car for Dennis Mecham and an IMSA Kelly American Challenge racer for Lyn St. James.

As if to signal its imminent return to competition, Ford introduced the McLaren Mustang in late 1980. The work of Todd Gerstenberger and Harry Wykes, it looked somewhat like the IMSA concept—and was more easily adaptable to race duty. It also carried a turbo four, but with a new variable-boost control providing a maximum pressure range of 5-11 psi versus a fixed 5 psi. Horsepower at 10 psi was rated at 175, a considerable jump over the stock mill's typical 131-

bhp estimate (Ford never released an official rating for the engine). A $25,000 price tag and virtual hand construction limited McLaren production to only 250, including the prototype.

But all this muscle-flexing was too late to affect the 1981 Mustang, which saw few changes. Reclining backrests were added to the standard bucket seats, interior trim was upgraded, and options were expanded via power windows and a T-bar roof with twin lift-off glass panels. The turbo four was now limited to the manual transmission.

A 5-speed overdrive manual had been announced as an option for both Mustang fours in mid-1980 and became more widely available for '81. This pulled a shorter, 3.45:1 final drive (versus the 4-speeder's 3.08:1 cog) for better off-the-line snap. The overdrive fifth was geared at 0.82:1 for economical highway cruising. It was just what the base Mustang needed.

Except for one thing. As Consumer Guide® noted at the time: "Our biggest objections to the 5-speed are its linkage—stiff, yet vague—and its shift pattern . . . [with fifth] awkwardly located at the bottom of the dogleg to the right of and opposite fourth. . . . Why Ford did it this way is a mystery, but it makes getting into or out of fifth real work. Our guess is that the engineers wanted to prevent inexperienced drivers from accidentally engaging overdrive and needlessly lugging the engine, as well as to prevent confusion with the often-used third. If so, they've succeeded admirably." Ford argued the U-shaped shift motion would better emphasize the economy benefits of the overdrive fifth. Whatever the reason, it just didn't work.

But even this annoyance would soon be forgotten. Performance was about to make an unexpected comeback in embattled Detroit. *Not* unexpectedly, Mustang would show the way.

# 1979

- The American-backed Shah of Iran flees his throne and is replaced by fundamentalist Ayatollah Khomeini

- Deadly radiation leaks from Pennsylvania's Three Mile Island nuclear plant

- Double-digit inflation and a stagnant U.S. economy lead to "stagflation"; new-car sales slump as prices rise

- A second energy crisis, triggered by political upheaval in Iran, hits hard at U.S. gas pumps

- Cash-strapped Chrysler Corporation asks the federal government for a $1 billion loan

- Henry Ford II resigns as FoMoCo chief but continues as chairman

- The crisp-looking, all-new fifth-generation Mustang debuts; it rides a shortened "Fox" platform used by the Ford Fairmont/ Mercury Zephyr twins

- Mustang makes calculated use of plastic, aluminum, and alloys to limit weight and meet government CAFE standards, now at 19 mpg

- This year's Cobra package offers a turbocharged 2.3-liter four rated at 140 bhp

- Mustang paces this year's Indianapolis 500; an Indy Pace Car replica is offered to the public

- Mustang model-year sales are 332,025, up nearly 140,000 over '78

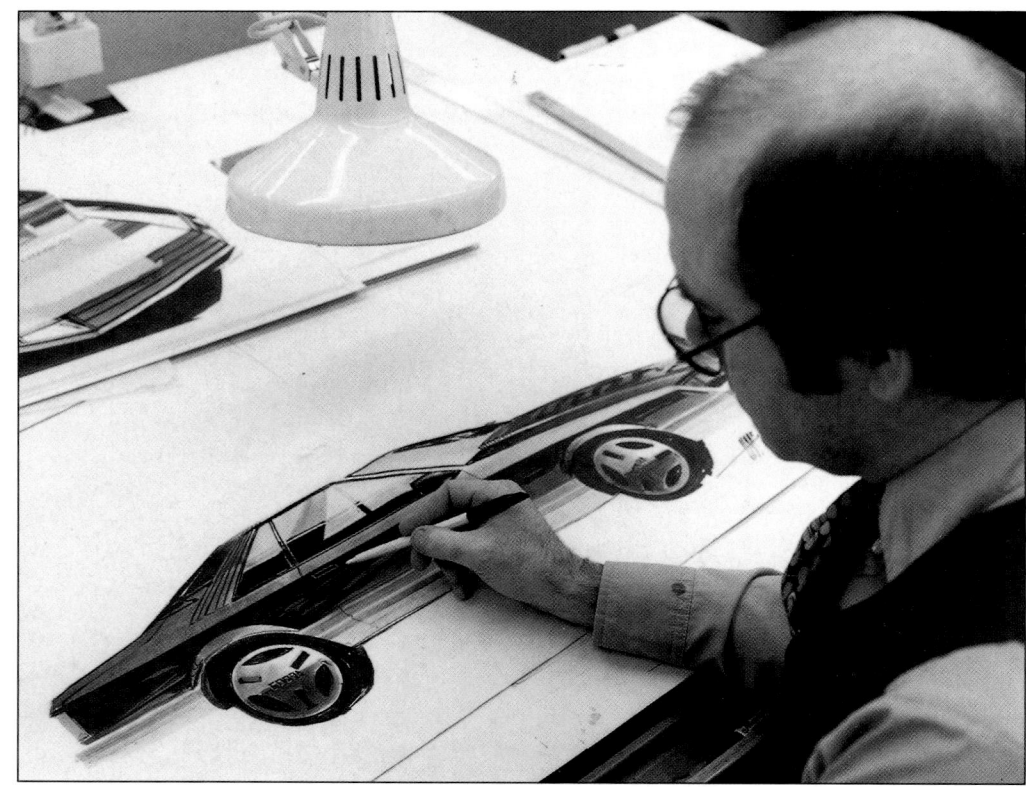

*Opposite page, top:* Designers began sketching the third-generation Mustang, seen here in Cobra guise, in the summer of 1975. *Opposite page, bottom:* Pre-production Design exec Dave Rees views early Mustang sketches by Light Car Design Manager Fritz Mayhew (*pointing*). *This page, above:* Already, designers knew the car would share platforms with the Ford Fairmont, a family sedan that had actually been designed with the Mustang in mind. This advance planning is what made the 1979 Mustang the best ever, design-wise. *Above right:* Fritz Mayhew, Jack Telnack (executive director of Ford North American Light Truck and Car Design), and Dave Rees discuss the new-generation 1979 Mustang as it takes shape at the Design Center in Dearborn. *Right:* Telnack, seen here with the approved 1979 design, returned to Ford Design in April 1975, following a stint as vice president of design at Ford of Europe. His studio, under the leadership of Don DeLaRossa, proposed a '79 Mustang that was radically different from two other Design Center studios in Dearborn and a third studio in Turin, Italy. Telnack's clay modelers did the coupe first and the fastback second; their work was approved in September 1976.

*Opposite page, top:* The third-generation Mustang was offered as a two-door sedan (*shown*) and three-door hatchback. Although the design dispensed with most of the car's traditional styling cues, it was very well received. *Opposite page, bottom:* Mustang purists were startled to discover that Ford had dropped the beloved running horse from the grille. Even the distinctive, center-mounted rear gas cap was gone, now placed behind a fuel-filler door on the passenger side of the car. *This page, above:* The totally new '79 had clean, aerodynamic lines and a European flair. The Turbo model, seen here in Cobra trim, boasted 0-50 mph times of 7.1 seconds with its 131-horse, turbocharged 140-cid four-cylinder. *Right:* Ford pushed the performance theme for 1979 models, but with an emphasis on handling rather than horsepower. The standard, normally aspirated four-cylinder pumped out a yawning 88 horses, the V-6 was rated at 109, the I-6 at 85, and the 302-2V at a meager 140 horses.

*Opposite page, top:* The new TRX suspension option was available for any Mustang in 1979. It was set off by a gorgeous set of forged-aluminum metric wheels that mounted Michelin TRX P190/65R × 390 "ultra-low profile" radial tires. A rear stabilizer bar was also part of the package. *Opposite page, bottom left:* Like the platform upon which the car was based, the dash was Fairmont-derived, with added "tech" touches that included a standard 8000-rpm tach and round gauges for oil pressure, fuel, amps, and water temperature, each fitted with the appropriate international symbol. The speedo was calibrated for miles and kilometers. *Opposite page, bottom right:* Because this car did not have the TRX option, the loaded tire did not stay perpendicular during track tests. *This page:* The Cobra option added $1173 to the base price of the three-door hatchback, which didn't include the hood decal but did include the TRX suspension and Cobra identification. Available engines were the turbocharged four or the 302-2V. Although the Cobra was the top-performing Mustang in the '79 lineup, its giddyap was lukewarm compared with top Mustangs of the late Sixties and early Seventies.

Opposite page: Lee Iacocca continued to favor formal rear rooflines—evident in the all-new 1979 Mustang notchback. The best-selling body style was technically not a hardtop but a sedan because of the supporting side pillars. The public loved this shape, as indicated by the 213,017 cars sold. Economy was still a major issue with buyers (long lines at service stations returned in '79) and a Mustang with the base four was a sporty way to get many miles per gallon. *This page, above and right:* Hardcore enthusiasts still clamored for performance after a drought of nearly a decade. To Ford and most of the rest of Detroit, the only way out appeared to be little fours turbocharged for high output when a heavy foot dictated. The continentally styled '79 Mustang dropped the cosmetic supercar looks of the '78 Cobra II and King Cobra, but took aim at the very popular "screaming chicken" hood decal on Firebird's Trans Am with a huge snake decal made optional for the Cobra. *Bottom right:* The Cobra had flair, but the Indy Pace Car Replica was even more eye-opening on the street. About 11,000 were sold with orange, red, and black graphics, front and rear spoilers, sunroof, and the buyer's choice of a turbo four or 302 V-8.

*Above:* The "2.3" front-fender badge on this notchback (also referred to as the coupe) identifies the 2.3-liter base inline-four. One liter equals about 60 cubic inches, so this Mustang 2.3 displaced approximately 140 cubes. The inline-four was not a hopeless powerplant by any means, but at 88 horsepower it was no road-burner, either. That was fine with Ford because the 2.3 was part of a corporate strategy to ensure the '79 Mustang's appeal to the broadest possible range of buyers. V-8 oomph was available for those who wanted it, while less aggressive drivers, or those on a budget, could opt for the four-cylinder and still enjoy a sporty-looking car. Whatever the engine, the '79 was lighter than its predecessor, thanks to Ford's concerted use of plastics, low-alloy steel, and aluminum. *Right:* Although the ad line "A whole new breed" seen on this brochure emphasized the freshness of the '79 Mustang lineup, the ethereal horse (plus a full moon, no less) subtly reiterated the "timelessness" of the all-American appeal that had made Mustang an enormous success 14 years earlier. The approach apparently worked, as over 369,000 '79 Mustang sales topped the '78 total by more than 177,000 units.

1979 FORD
MUSTANG
A whole new breed.

# 1980

- Ronald Reagan is elected to the presidency in a landslide over incumbent Jimmy Carter

- John Lennon is shot and killed by a deranged fan

- Nearly 27 percent of new cars sold in the U.S. are imports; all four major American carmakers finish the year in the red

- Lee Iacocca secures federal loan guarantees for Chrysler

........................................................

- Ford Motor Company reports a record $595 million loss for the third quarter; Henry Ford II resigns as FoMoCo chairman

- Mustang's Cobra package includes front and rear spoilers, integral fog lamps, non-functional hood scoop, and TRX suspension

- Recaro front buckets are a new Mustang option

- Mustang's IMSA (International Motor Sports Association) concept car tours the auto-show circuit; it's powered by a 2.3-liter turbo four

- The Special Vehicle Operations (SVO) department is inaugurated in the fall to develop limited-production performance cars

- A $25,000 McLaren Mustang debuts late in the year; its tweaked turbo four delivers a potent 175 bhp

- Public preoccupation with the price of gas contributes to a steep drop in Mustang sales for the model year, to 241,064

*This page:* The Cobra gained a more aggressive look for 1980: a reworked grille with horizontal louvers; a non-functional, rear-facing hood scoop; a front air dam with integral fog lamps; and new tape stripes. The car also picked up Cobra decals on the rear-quarter windows, dual black sport mirrors, bright tailpipe extensions, and a restyled rear decklid spoiler.

*Top:* The 1980 notchback, or coupe, was a virtual carryover from 1979, save for a hardly noticeable aerodynamic revision to the rear decklid. This coupe has the optional Exterior Accent Group. The base four boasted a 23-percent gain in fuel economy. *Above and right:* The turbocharger was available without the Cobra package for either the notchback or (*seen here*) the hatchback. Standard on this body style were black protective side moldings that "wrapped" into bumper rub strips, both set off by dual argent inserts.

*This page:* Despite the boost in image given by the new grille, front air dam, and rear decklid spoiler on the '80 Cobra, Ford replaced the optional 302 with a 255, which was essentially the same engine with a lightened block and internal parts, and bore reduced to 3.68 inches from 4.00. Clearly, Ford's promotional push was reserved for the turbo, which now topped the V-8 in horsepower—131 versus 117.

*Above:* The standard Cobra engine was the 2.3-liter turbo four; the 4.2-liter V-8, teamed with the 4-speed manual or 3-speed automatic, was optional. TRX tires continued and rode on metric forged-aluminum wheels. *Right:* A leather and vinyl-trim seat option was available on the Ghia (*shown*) as well as the Cobra and other 1980 Mustangs with the Interior Accent Group.

*Top left:* Mustang was strictly a four seater: two people in a pair of standard front buckets and two presumably smaller ones on the bench seat in the rear. *Middle left:* The rear seat remained upright on the notchback but folded down on the three-door. *Above:* The four-cylinder engine was an 88-horse 2.3-liter that came standard with a 4-speed manual gearbox. A shortage of the optional, German-built V-6 prompted Ford to bring back its own inline-six in late 1979. *Left:* An optional, leather-wrapped, three-spoke steering wheel was a mild nod to performance days of old.

*Opposite page, top:* The Sport Option for the '80 Mustang included black window frames and rocker panel moldings, plus "wrap-around" bodyside moldings with dual argent stripe inserts. *Opposite page, bottom:* Ford had not offered a convertible since 1973, but because aftermarket shops were custom-building new Mustang convertibles, Ford was reconsidering its position on the body style. In the interim, buyers could select the $625 Carriage Roof option—in black, white, blue, or brown—that mimicked the look of a top-up convertible. *This page:* Although the running horse had vanished from the grille, the hood badge did have the running-horse logo. Dual, rectangular halogen headlights were standard.

Top: There were many ways a buyer could "build" a Mustang to suit his or her tastes. This hatchback ran with the turbocharged four-cylinder. Although not a Cobra, the car's optional red/black Accent Tape Stripe and metric forged-aluminum wheels provided a hot look. *Above:* Notchback Mustangs found 152,540 buyers in 1980; of that number 23,647 were in Ghia trim. *Right:* The Cobra package increased the hatchback price by $1482—more than the $1173 it cost in 1979.

# 1981

- On March 30, President Reagan is seriously wounded by would-be assassin John Hinckley

- England's Prince Charles weds Lady Diana Spencer on July 29

- High inflation brings big automotive price hikes

- Ford replaces Pinto with the Escort, which sells strongly

- A 5-speed overdrive manual gearbox is available for the base Mustang; in all, the ponycar offers three optional engines and seven optional transmissions

- A T-roof with removable, tinted glass panels is a new option

- A dozen restored 1966 Mustang convertibles are converted to Shelby GT-350 trim, with Carroll Shelby's blessing, and sell out at $40,000 apiece

- Mustang model-year output is 162,593, the lowest since 1977

*This page:* The biggest splash for 1981 was the $916 T-top roof option (*bottom car*), which was also marketed as a T-roof convertible. A $228 "flip-up open air roof" (*top car*) was again offered as an option for the notchback and hatchback body styles. The flip-up roof could be opened for ventilation or removed completely and stashed in a storage bag. Similarly, one or both T-top panels could be removed and stowed. The hatchback and T-top coupe seen here are fitted with the standard Turbine wheel covers. The standard coupe (*middle car*) has the optional styled steel wheels with trim rings.

*Top row:* The Cobra was little changed for 1981. When ordered with the turbocharged four, the package cost $1588; buyers who opted for the 255-2V V-8 could knock off another $346 and save $65 more by deleting the tape stripe. *Above:* The Ghia was offered for one last model year in 1981, seen here with the Carriage Roof option. Available in coupe or hatchback, the Ghia added dual black remote-control side mirrors, bodyside pinstripes, and Turbine wheel covers (optioned here with wires). *Right:* The utility coupe boasted 23 mpg in city driving and 34 mpg on the highway with the base inline 2.3-liter four and new 5-speed with 0.82:1 overdrive gear.

*This page:* The base four-cylinder engine still had an 88-horsepower rating, the same as in 1980, but managed a decent kick away from a traffic light with its new 5-speed manual transmission, which came with a 3.45:1 rear axle gear, compared to a 3.08:1 in the four-cylinder/4-speed manual. Once launched, the Mustang was a blast to drive on the open road, especially with the T-top roof panels removed, which (short of a custom conversion) was as close as Mustang got to a convertible in 1981. Ford was doing its best to put the fun of driving back into the Mustang. If that couldn't be accomplished with big-block, big-elephant motors, the engineers would go for gearing, open-air roofs, TRX handling suspensions, Cobra packages, and plenty of add-on doodads. Slowly but steadily, the third-generation Mustang was returning to a level of performance that had once excited millions of enthusiasts.

DETROIT CAUTIOUSLY RETURNED to performance for 1982. Though the decisions involved were made before the oil-crisis doldrums of 1980-81, events made the revival seem almost prescient. A gas shortage was becoming a gas glut, the economy began to recover, and car buyers began buying again.

More important for this story, Ford Motor Company had weathered a serious financial crisis while ushering in two outstanding leaders to take over for Henry Ford II. Stockholders must have applauded the 1980 appointment of Philip Caldwell as chairman and the equally experienced Donald Petersen as president. For enthusiasts, Petersen was wonderful news: a knowledgeable "car guy" who loved fast, agile machines that looked great. His enthusiasm would spur a host of dramatic new Dearborn products. Meanwhile, he instructed stylists and engineers to give existing models some of the old "Total Performance" flair that had worked sales magic in the Sixties. Not surprisingly, Mustang was one of the first Fords to reap the benefits.

They appeared for 1982 in a reborn GT packing the most potent Ford small-block in recent memory. This was a new High-Output 302 that delivered a healthy 157 net horsepower via a special camshaft (adapted from a marine version of the long-running V-8), larger two-barrel carb, bigger and smoother exhaust, and low-restriction twin-inlet air cleaner. Teamed exclusively with a 4-speed overdrive manual transmission, it made for the fastest Mustang in years. Claimed

## CHAPTER 8
# 1982-86: Galloping On

0-60-mph acceleration was below eight seconds, but most magazines got closer to seven.

Looking much like the Cobra package it replaced, the '82 GT came as a hatchback with top-grade TRX suspension, front and rear spoilers, fog lamps, blackout trim, a console, and other goodies, all for a reasonable introductory price of $8308. Although the HO was optional for other models at $402 with the TRX suspension or $452 without, GTs undoubtedly accounted for the bulk of sales. Incidentally, the tame 4.2-liter V-8 was available as a $57 GT credit option, but attracted few orders.

Otherwise, there was little new for '82. Below the GT were hatchbacks and notchbacks newly badged L, GL, and GLX in ascending order of price and luxury. A larger gas tank, wider wheels and tires, and a remote-control left-door mirror were newly standard across the board. After compiling a poor reliability record, the turbo four was withdrawn, though just temporarily. Other drivetrains continued, but the 4.2-liter V-8's "mandatory option" automatic got a fuel-saving lockup torque converter effective in all forward gears, a device fast-spreading throughout Detroit.

Though 1982 brought hot new GM competition in a smaller, third-generation Chevy Camaro/Pontiac Firebird, Mustang managed fairly well for a three-year-old design. Model-year production totaled about 130,500 against some 179,000 Camaros and 116,000 Firebirds.

With their 5.0-liter V-8s, tuned chassis, and racy styling, the Mustang GT, Camaro Z28, and Firebird Trans Am made a natural "buff book" comparison test. The GM cars won points for style and handling, but Mustang was usually judged better overall. And it was discernibly quicker. *Car and Driver* reported a 0-60 time of 8.1 seconds, versus 8.6 for the fuel-injected V-8 Camaro with automatic, and a comparatively sluggish 10.6 for the carbureted V-8 Firebird with a 4-speed.

Of course, the GT wasn't perfect. Consumer Guide® criticized its power steering as too vague and light, and traction was compromised much of the time by a stiff rear end and 240 lbs/ft of V-8 torque.

Seeking handling parity with its GM rivals, the 1983 GT offered 220/55-390 Michelin TRX tires as a new option and gained a larger rear anti-roll bar, softer rear springs, stiffer front-control-arm bushings, and revised shock valving. Higher-effort power steering was also included for better high-speed control. Speaking of speed, the HO was boosted to 175 bhp via a four-barrel carb, aluminum intake manifold, high-flow air cleaner, enlarged exhaust passages, and minor valvetrain tweaks. Even better, it

While many of Mustang's competitors had disappeared by the mid-Seventies, the original ponycar carried on into the Eighties with only Camaro and Firebird to challenge it on the street. This hunky '86 GT ragtop came standard with a 200-horse 302 V-8.

now mated to Borg-Warner's new T-5 close-ratio 5-speed gearbox, as in the Camaro/Firebird, which answered gripes about poor gear-spacing on the wide-ratio 4-speed it replaced. All this plus a shorter final drive made for even faster takeoffs.

There were other drivetrain shuffles too. The 4.2-liter V-8 was dropped and the 200-cid straight six gave way to Ford's new lightweight "Essex" V-6, a 3.8-liter (232-cid) overhead-valve design with two-barrel carburetor and 105 bhp. The 2.3-liter four, again standard for non-GTs, went from two-barrel to single-barrel carburetion for the sake of economy and received long-reach spark plugs for faster combustion, reduced emissions, and improved part-throttle response. Though these changes boosted alleged horsepower to 93, the rating would fall back to 88 bhp for '84.

All Mustangs looked faster for '83, thanks to a mild facelift announced by a rounded nose that reduced air drag by 2.5 percent. Blue Ford ovals replaced running-horse emblems, and manual-shift models sported an upshift indicator that signaled when to select the next higher gear for better mileage—useful, if hardly in the free-spirited Mustang tradition.

The most glamorous '83 development was the first Mustang convertible in 10 years. Available only as a GLX with any powertrain except four-cylinder/automatic, it was a factory job, not an out-of-house conversion like some other reborn ragtops of the period. With standard power top, roll-down rear side windows, and tempered-glass back window, it added another dash of excitement to an already impressive Mustang line.

That line was further expanded at mid-'83 with a Turbo GT hatchback powered by a newly reengineered version of the hyperaspirated 2.3 "Lima" four (also used in the slick new Thunderbird Turbo Coupe). Significant changes from the '81

engine involved switching to Bosch port electronic fuel injection and repositioning the turbocharger so it would "blow through" the induction system rather than "draw down" from it. Ford's latest EEC-IV electronic engine control system governed injector timing, idle speed, wastegate, and emissions control. Other upgrades included forged-aluminum pistons, new high-temperature valves, lighter flywheel, die-cast aluminum rocker cover, and engine oil cooler. With the recommended premium unleaded fuel, this new Turbo packed 145 bhp—only five better than the previous version, but still better than the "1 horsepower per cubic inch" ideal.

Aside from nameplates, the Turbo GT was a visual twin to the V-8 version. Blackout trim, beefy Goodyear Eagle performance radials, aluminum wheels, sport bucket seats, and 5-speed manual gearbox were standard on both, and suspension was tuned to suit each engine. With the same advertised power as Chevy's base Z28, the Turbo GT could run 0-60 mph in well under 10 seconds and the standing quarter-mile in about 16 seconds, while returning 25 mpg overall.

Even so, the improved turbo Mustang proved no more popular than its 1979-81 predecessor. It was not available with air conditioning or automatic—a big drawback for most buyers—and it cost $250 *more* than a comparable V-8 GT—which could hit 60 in near six seconds flat. All this, plus a late introduction and restricted availability, held Turbo GT sales to a paltry 483 for the model year. As they say, "There's no substitute for cubic inches."

Still, the turbo four was further massaged for yet another new performance Mustang, the 1984 SVO. Named for and engineered by Ford's Special Vehicle Operations department, this exotic new hatchback sported an air-to-air intercooler and electronically variable boost

control allowing up to 14 psi, then said to be the highest pressure of any production turbo engine. These and other changes produced a remarkable 175 bhp, plus 10 percent more torque. A cockpit switch "tuned" the engine's electronics to the grade of fuel being used, and special dampers resisted drivetrain rocking under full power. Getting that power to the ground were a 5-speed manual gearbox with Hurst linkage and Traction-Lok limited-slip differential.

Chassis revisions began with junking the stock rear drums in favor of beefy discs to match enlarged front disc brakes. Big 16 × 7-inch "aero-style" cast-aluminum wheels carried meaty V-rated European Goodyear NCT radials, later switched to Eagle GT50s with unidirectional "gatorback" tread. Spring rates and bushings were much stiffened, premium adjustable Koni shocks replaced stock hardware, the front anti-roll bar was thickened, a rear bar was added, and power steering was changed from variable-ratio to fast fixed-ratio gearing.

Setting SVO apart from lesser Mustangs were a distinctive "biplane" rear spoiler made of polycarbonate plastic, a unique nose with an air intake below the bumper and a small slot above, a large hood scoop to feed the intercooler, and dual square headlamps instead of smaller quads. A deep front air dam incorporated standard fog lamps, and small fairings at the leading edges of the rear wheel openings helped smooth airflow around the fat tires. Driver-oriented cabin accoutrements included a left footrest and multi-adjustable seats borrowed from the T-Bird Turbo Coupe. Also standard were an electric rear-window defroster, AM/FM stereo with amplified speaker system, leather-rim tilt steering wheel, and Mustang's familiar graphic warning monitor. There were only five major options: air, power windows, cassette player, flip-up glass sunroof, and leather upholstery.

The SVO was the best-balanced high-performance Mustang ever. Handling was near-neutral, cornering flat and undramatic. Steering was direct and properly weighted, braking swift and sure. And performance was exhilarating: 0-60 mph in about 7.5 seconds, the quarter-mile in just under 16 seconds at around 90 mph. Top speed was close to 135 mph. But in the end, this was just another sophisticated screamer that "buff books" liked and buyers didn't. At over $16,000, the SVO looked too costly when a V-8 GT delivered for a whopping $6000 less. Sales thus totaled only 4508 for the '84 model year, though Ford had the capability to build nearly four times that many.

Between them, the V-8 and SVO killed off the Turbo GT after some 3000 hatchbacks and about 600 convertibles were built for 1983-84. All early-'84 GTs—V-8s and turbos—were '83 reruns except for a split rear seatback (as adopted for most hatchbacks that year). The Turbo GT ragtop arrived in December '83, when all GTs received staggered rear shocks, integral fog lamps, and a restyled rear spoiler.

Also new for '84: a base-trim three-door to complement the two-door model; GL and GLX equipment combined into a single LX trim level; and new GT and LX convertibles. There was also a second 302 V-8, with throttle-body fuel injection (TBI) and 10 fewer horses than the HO. It was reserved for non-GTs with optional automatic, which was now either a 3-speed or Ford's new corporate 4-speed overdrive unit—another CAFE-inspired development. The V-6 option also got TBI and went up to 120 bhp; the 3-speed autobox was the only transmission choice. Per widening industry practice, stickshift models received a starter interlock that required the driver to fully depress the clutch pedal before the engine would fire up.

Mustang reached the ripe old age of 20 in 1984, and Ford celebrated with 5000 specials called GT-350—actually a GT trim option distinguished by "Shelby White" paint and maroon stripes. It was a nice remembrance, but Dearborn's lawyers forgot to talk to Mr. Shelby, who claimed he owned "GT-350" and was promised Ford wouldn't use it without his okay. Carroll, now working again with his old friend Lee Iacocca at Chrysler, promptly sued Ford for copyright infringement. Sometimes it just doesn't pay to be sentimental.

A good barometer of the general market, Mustang sales bottomed out at just under 121,000 for 1983 before rebounding to near 142,000 for '84 and 156,000-plus for '85. In contrast, Camaro/Firebird volume began trending down, and would be below Mustang's by 1987.

In fact, Mustang had become an uncommonly good sporty-car value. The '85 base-price range ran from just $6885 for the LX notchback to $13,585 for the GT ragtop and $14,521 for the slow-selling SVO. Though much higher than '79 stickers in raw dollars, those figures looked mighty attractive against Japanese sporty coupes that were starting to gallop in price but couldn't match Mustang for performance or charisma.

Those qualities were further enhanced for '85. Low-friction roller tappets and a new high-performance camshaft muscled up the carbureted HO V-8 by an impressive 35 bhp, to 210. Similar changes boosted the injected version to 180 bhp. Both 302s again teamed only with the 5-speed manual, which got revised gearing and a redesigned linkage. Rounding out GT improvements were beefier P225/60VR15 "Gatorbacks" on seven-inch-wide aluminum wheels, as on the SVO, plus gas-pressurized front shocks and an extra pair of rear shocks to control axle tramp.

Elsewhere, the cheap L models were canceled, and SVO-type nose styling was applied to remaining '85s. The SVO itself returned at mid-year with flush headlights (newly allowed by the government), plus an air-to-air intercooler that puffed up its turbo four by 30 bhp, to 205. The intercooler also appeared on a revived Turbo GT that quickly vanished again after minuscule sales. Still, Mustang lost none of its overall appeal, and attracted about 15,000 additional buyers for the model year.

Sales surged to nearly 224,500 for 1986, a decade high achieved with few changes. The main one was adoption of sequential port injection for a single 302 V-8 rated at 200 bhp and available with either the 5-speed manual or 4-speed automatic. The rear axle was strengthened to handle the V-8 torque that now peaked at a strong 285 lbs/ft, and the SVO's fluid-filled engine mounts were added to all V-8 and V-6 models. Ford's continuing concern for Mustang owners was evident in a longer corrosion warranty, more sound-deadening, and a more convenient single-key locking system.

The inevitable yearly price increases were evident, too, but fairly modest. The notchback LX was up to $7295, the GT convertible to $14,220. The SVO was costlier than ever at $15,272, and its days were numbered. With sales always far below even Ford's modest projections, it was too unprofitable to sustain, so '86 was its swan song. Respective 1984-86 production was 4508, 1954, and 3382 units—9844 in all.

Though it ranks among the least successful of modern Mustangs from a commercial standpoint, the SVO demonstrated the versatility and staying power of the 1979-based design. And there was still more excitement to come as the original ponycar galloped toward its milestone 25th birthday.

**173**

# 1982

- Britain goes to war following Argentina's seizure of the Falkland Islands

- Princess Grace of Monaco, the former Grace Kelly, dies in a freak auto accident

- High interest rates scare American banks away from auto loans

- Gas prices begin to fall, adversely affecting sales of small cars and those with diesel engines

- Camaro and Firebird get aggressive, angular restyles

- John Z. DeLorean's Belfast auto company slips into receivership

- Mustang's new High Output (HO) 5.0-liter 302 V-8 puts out 157 horsepower; the tamer 4.2-liter V-8 enters its final year

- The 5.0 V-8 is standard on GL, GLX, and GT models

- A limited-edition Mustang convertible is introduced at mid-year

- Standard wheels grow to 14 inches in a bid for enhanced fuel efficiency

- Two Image Mustangs are built by Marketing Corp. of America; one tours with the Ford Motorcraft show, the other is sold to a private collector

- Mustang model-year production is 130,418

*Left:* Performance was back big time as the '82 GT debuted in late 1981, backed by a factory commitment to organized racing. The Team Miller Mustang GT that won Brainerd and Sears Point IMSA races in 1981 had been powered by a 560-horse, 1.7-liter four-cylinder. *Middle row and bottom:* Meanwhile, the Mustang GT was strictly a 302-2V. In a surprising move, Ford simply dropped its turbo four—for a while. The GT looked brawny with its low-slung air dam and spoiler. It stunned car magazines with 0-60 times of less than eight seconds. *Autoweek* figured this performance phenomenon would last just one year and urged people to buy before the 302 HO GT was gone for good.

*Opposite page, top:* Mercury's Capri was a Mustang in all but name and trim. The RS series was to the Capri what the GT was to the Mustang, as both were optioned with the hot 302 HO. *Opposite page, middle:* Notice the 5.0 badges on the '82 Mustang GT (identical to those on the RS Cougar) and the grille, greatly influenced by the previous year's Cobra. *Opposite page, bottom:* To accompany the 1982 introduction of the Mustang GT, Ford put a Mustang convertible on the auto show circuit and announced it would be available in late summer with the 5.0 HO. However, production was delayed until the '83 model year.

A perennial reason for Mustang's success was its wide variety of choices, which really exploded in 1982. The GT (*top left*) satisfied the power-hungry as no Mustang had since the 429 Cobra Jet-equipped Mach 1 of 1971. The T-top (*top right*) continued in coupe and hatchback form. Convertible lovers were teased with prototype ragtops (*above*). The GLX model came with a four-spoke steering wheel with woodgrain inserts (*above right*). The notchback (*right*) was offered in three trim levels: L, GL, and GLX. The four-cylinder carried on as the standard engine, but production of the highly publicized 302 rose sharply—to five times that of the comparatively tame 1981 V-8.

# 1 9 8 3

- More than 200 American Marines in Beirut, Lebanon, are killed by an Islamic terrorist who drives an explosive-laden truck into Marine headquarters

- U.S. troops expel Cuban agitators from the island nation of Grenada

- Astronaut/physicist Sally Ride is the first American woman in space

- Chrysler pays off its $1.2 billion federally guaranteed loan seven years early

- General Motors and Toyota announce a joint venture to develop a subcompact car

- A minor facelift, the first since 1979, brings Mustang a more rounded nose and restyled taillights

- Mustang fields a convertible for the first time in a decade; it's available in GT or GLX trim

- Horsepower of the HO V-8 is increased to 175 bhp, from 157

- The 220-cid straight-six is replaced by a 3.8-liter, 105-bhp "Essex" V-6

- Turbo GT hatchbacks and convertibles bow at mid-season, powered by the 2.3-liter Lima turbo four

- Model-year Mustang production slips to 120,873, including 23,438 convertibles

*Top:* When a convertible Mustang returned for 1983, it came standard in the GLX series with the V-6 engine and optional with the 5.0, as seen here. It wasn't available as a GT until June 1983. *Above:* Early '83 GTs had T-tops.

**177**

*Above:* For 1983, Mustang got a smaller grille that was widest at the top. *Top right:* In GT trim, the smaller grille was met by a hood stripe that extended over a big scoop and back to the cowl. The new GT produced 175 horsepower @ 4200 rpm—enough to make Mustang the hottest car made in America. *Right:* Even in non-GT trim, the Mustang convertible looked great for '83. *Below:* The GLX convertible's sporty interior came with a standard 4-speed gearbox (5-speed optional) when the 5.0 was ordered. V-6s had automatic. *Below right:* The 5.0 came with a single exhaust with dual outlets in 1983.

*Left:* Ford called the '83 GT "The Boss" and "One Hot Piece Of American Steel"; it completely replaced the Cobra model. *Middle row:* A convertible without fender badges carried the standard V-6; the normally aspirated four-cylinder was not available in this body style. *Bottom left:* The rarest '83 GT was the turbo four, fitted with a turbocharged 145-horse 2.3-liter shared with Thunderbird's Turbo Coupe. *Below right:* Although the '83 convertible was considered a stock factory model, its construction was farmed out to Cars & Concepts in Brighton, Michigan. Ford advertised it as available on a limited basis.

*Top left:* This Medium Yellow coupe is a GL, existing midway in luxury between the base L and the GLX. *Top right:* Bright Red was a popular color for the '83 GT. *Above:* A much less popular color was Silver Metallic, one of fourteen hues offered for the model year. *Above right:* The 302 in High Output tune featured an aluminum-intake manifold, topped with a 600-cfm Holley carb and a dual snorkel, "460" air cleaner. Inside, the 302 had a roller timing chain and a Marine cam with more duration and lift than the one used for '82. *Right:* New taillights for '83 were said to have a European flair.

*Top:* The base L-model Mustang was available as a notchback only. Ford sold 33,201 notchbacks for the model year. *Above left:* The 23,438 Mustang convertibles sold in 1983 accounted for nearly one in every five Mustangs. Just 993 of these ragtops were GTs. *Above:* Buyers were intrigued by early glimpses of the SVO, a turbocharged four set to debut for the '84 model year. So special was the SVO that it came with a unique steering wheel and shifter boot. *Left:* Mustang GLX models had bright remote-control mirrors and bright rocker panel moldings. A contrary trim scheme was used on the GL, which had black mirrors and black moldings.

# 1984

- Democratic presidential nominee Walter Mondale selects a woman, Rep. Geraldine Ferraro, as his running mate; in November, President Ronald Reagan easily wins reelection

- The Soviet Union boycotts the summer Olympic games in Los Angeles

- India's prime minister, Indira Gandhi, is gunned down by members of her personal security force

........................................................

- 5000 copies of the 20th Anniversary Mustang are produced, with "Shelby White" paint and GT-350 designation; Carroll Shelby, no longer associated with FoMoCo, responds with a copyright infringement suit

- The SVO Mustang rolls into the marketplace with a hopped-up version of the turbo four that produces 175 bhp

- A second 302 V-8, with throttle-body fuel injection (TBI) and 165 bhp, joins the 175-bhp HO V-8

- The TBI-juiced V-6 increases to 120 bhp

- Mustang's Turbo GT is discontinued

- Ford enters into cooperative product planning with Mazda to develop a sixth-generation, front-drive Mustang, to be introduced in the late Eighties

- Mustang model-year production ticks upward, to 141,480, including 17,600 droptops

Despite the big rise in V-8 Mustang sales and the popularity of the 5.0 HO GTs, Ford felt the 302 V-8, now over 20 years old, was dated. The future, Ford reasoned, was with the turbocharged four-cylinder. This thinking resulted in a special high-performance, single-purpose SVO Mustang (*top*), powered by a turbo 2.3-liter four (*above*) that produced 175 horsepower via an intercooler, tuned-port fuel injection, and 14-psi turbo boost.

*Top row:* Based only on the three-door Mustang, the SVO came with a "grille-less" front fascia with integral fog lamps. Special 16 × 7-inch cast-aluminum wheels mounted Goodyear European NCT P225/50VR-16 black sidewall tires. An off-center functional scoop made the SVO's front end unique in the year's Mustang lineup. *Above left:* Rear-wheel "spats" directed airflow around the SVO's wheel wells for improved aerodynamics. *Above:* The three-spoke SVO steering wheel allowed easy viewing of round gauges that included an 8000-rpm tach and a 0-18 psi boost gauge. The 5-speed came with a special Hurst linkage and leather-wrapped knob and lever. *Left:* SVOs came standard with a polycarbonate dual-wing rear spoiler.

*Top left:* The classic running-horse logo was part of the 20th Anniversary Special. *Top right:* Ford added inappropriate GT-350 rocker panel stripes and logo to the anniversary Mustang GT, raising the ire of Carroll Shelby, who successfully sued Ford for trademark infringement. *Above:* Of 5260 20th Anniversary Special GTs built in 1984, all but about 500 had the 302 HO V-8; the rest had the turbocharged four. *Above right:* Convertible production hit 17,600 in 1984. *Right:* Late in the '85 model year, Ford promised a 205-horse 302 HO, but the engine did not make production and the GT continued to be powered by the 175-horse 302, a carryover from 1984.

# 1985

- Japanese Prime Minister Yasuhiro Nakasone urges the Japanese to buy foreign goods
- French and American explorers locate the sunken wreckage of the *Titanic*
- President Reagan and Soviet president Gorbachev meet in Geneva
- Horsepower continues to rise industry-wide
- Domestic and import car sales set records

.....................................................

- Low-end "L" Mustangs are canceled; models are limited to LX and GT
- The Turbo GT is revived, only to vanish following minuscule sales
- Mustang's aggressive turbo four SVO gains a horsepower boost at mid-year, to 205
- Nearly one third of the year's Mustangs are ordered with V-8s
- Mustang sales rise again for the model year, to 156,514, including 15,110 convertibles

A new front fascia (with integral air dam and fog lamps on GT and LX models) and revised front grille opening made the '85 Mustang (*top*) look much different from the '84. Also new for the GT were charcoal hood paint and tape stripes, and standard 15 × 7-inch cast aluminum wheels. The '85 model year was the last for the carbureted 302 (*right*), which developed 210 horsepower @ 4400 rpm with a new roller cam, new stainless steel exhaust manifolds, and dual exhausts (another first for the 302 HO) with a Y-pipe with 2.25-inch inlet and outlet.

*Top:* The slow-selling turbo four was dropped from the GT option list after 1984, leaving the 302 as the only engine. The '85 GT was available as a convertible or three-door hatchback, but not in the formal-roof, two-door body style. *Above:* GT styling was smart and clean. *Right:* For the first time, Ford molded the GT insignia into the bodyside moldings. The four-barrel 302 HO with 210 horsepower was available only with the 5-speed manual. GT buyers who opted for automatic transmission had to order the tamer 302 EFI (Electronic Fuel Injection).

*Top row:* In 1984, Ford's Ghia studio in Italy built a high-performance, Ferguson four-wheel-drive Mustang powered by an SVO turbo four. It looked similar to the later Probe, which was originally conceived as a front-wheel-drive, Mazda-platformed Mustang. *Left:* This '85 Mustang with a world class 5-speed and other heavy-duty features was built for police duty. The car eventually wound up in private hands and was run as a drag racer. *Bottom row:* Except for the new flush aero headlights, the appearance of the 1985 SVO was carried over from 1984. However, halfway through the model year the 2.3-liter turbo four gained 30 horsepower, to 205, and more torque across a wider band; a reconfigured turbocharger and internal upgrades did the trick.

*Top:* The front end of the '85 GT was inspired by the previous year's SVO. Ford revised most exterior trim from black to a softer charcoal shade. *Above:* With automatic transmission, the 302 HO was not carbureted but EFI, with 165 horsepower at a rather low 3800 rpm. The EFI was sometimes called CFI, for Central Fuel Injection, because fuel was injected into the intake manifold in a central location, or throttle body. *Right:* GTs came with the very desirable articulated sport seats for 1985, and the console was standard in every Mustang for the first time.

*Top row:* This 1985 GT window-stickered for $13,200 brand new, but the original owner bought it for the cash price of $10,800. *Middle row:* To help settle the live rear axle, Ford engineered new quadra-shocks to take the place of traction bars. Tires were upgraded to P225/60VR-15 Goodyear Eagles, mounted on 15 × 7-inch cast-aluminum, styled road wheels, standard on the GT. *Left:* The 302 produced 35 more horses and 25 more lbs/ft of torque than in '84. *Above:* The new GT had round gauges that were easy to see through the three-spoke steering wheel.

*Above:* The Mustang SVO was a tough car to sell because it was priced $4000 to $6000 above the torquier, more powerful GT. *Top right:* The 2.3-liter SVO turbo four bristled with technological wizardry, such as electronic engine management of fuel injection, boost, and ignition timing. *Above right:* Inside, Hurst reworked the shift linkage on the Borg-Warner T-5 for smoother throws. Combined with reduced clutch pedal effort and faster steering (15.0:1 compared to 20.0:1 in '84), the SVO of 1985½ was a much-improved driver. *Right:* Standard power disc brakes front and rear made for great braking: 140 feet from 60 mph to zero. Meanwhile, the turbo SVO could accelerate to 60 in the low-seven-second range and run the quarter-mile in the low 15s at about 90 mph. When the turbo spooled up, the car gave a forceful whine and pushed the driver back into the seat.

# 1986

- The space shuttle *Challenger* explodes 74 seconds after liftoff, killing all aboard

- A Soviet nuclear reactor at Chernobyl malfunctions and releases deadly radiation

- Death takes auto designer Raymond Loewy and legendary film stars James Cagney and Cary Grant

- FoMoCo earns a record $3.3-billion profit, its earnings topping GM's for the first time since 1924

- Donald Petersen is named FoMoCo chairman

- Ford launches the mid-size Ford Taurus and similar Mercury Sable

- Mustang offers a single, revised 302-cid V-8, now rated at 200 bhp; torque is a potent 285 lbs/ft

- This year's SVO has a Hurst 5-speed and four-wheel disc brakes

- A throttle-body-injected V-6 rated at 120 bhp is standard with LX convertibles and optional on other models

- Sound deadening is improved

- High performance plus plentiful gasoline contribute to a dramatic increase in model-year sales, to 224,410, including 10,273 convertibles

*This page:* On the outside, the 1986 GT looked like a continuation of '85. Minor appearance changes to all models included recessed rectangular headlights and a Ford oval on the panel above the grille. Taillights were equally divided by a horizontal bar. There were major changes under the skin, starting with the sequential-port-injected 302 HO, now optional for manual and automatic transmissions, and a new 8.8-inch rear axle.

*Top:* The LX was available as a two-door sedan and a three-door hatchback. It could be had with the 5.0 HO, and many were ordered just that way. Not simply lighter and cheaper than a GT, the 5.0 LX was an interesting "sleeper" on the street because it had no stripes or badging other than the "5.0" to warn challengers that a 302 HO lurked under the hood. *Middle row:* The 5.0 LX sedan was favored by many police departments as a pursuit vehicle. *Right:* Although the interior was not spacious, it was large enough to hold the equipment an officer might need.

*This page:* The Mustang convertible found new life when it returned for 1983 after a 10-year hiatus. Production remained strong for 1986 at 22,946, almost equal to the 23,438 sold in '83. Articulated front sport seats (*top right*) were standard on the GT. LX and GT convertibles came with a luggage rack (*above left*) that carried the high-mount brake lamp, a new safety requirement in '86. *Above:* Quick-ratio power steering made the GT fun to drive. Note the spartan, angular dash. *Left:* The new sequential-port 302 HO boasted "high swirl" cylinder heads with shrouded valves; though interesting, the setup offered no performance advantage.

TO PARAPHRASE AN OLD SAW, the more things stay the same, the harder they can be to change. Such was the paradox facing Ford in the early Eighties as it considered Mustang's future.

On one hand, the vintage-'79 generation was selling respectably, and the reborn GT was as fast as most anything in Detroit. But as good as this Mustang was, it was clearly a car of Ford's past, and one that looked dated next to newer sporty cars. Then again, nostalgia was still a big part of its appeal, even for younger people who hadn't been around for "Mustang Mania" in the Sixties. Still, Ford was worried about what would happen to sales should the market suddenly reverse again, or if competing automakers came up with a powerful challenge. With all this, Ford reasoned, a new-generation Mustang ought to appear by 1987, if not sooner.

Work toward that car began in early 1982 as project SN8 (SN for "sporty, North America"). Under the circumstances, management predictably favored a smaller, lighter ponycar like the old Mustang II or European Capri, but with aero styling, front-wheel drive for maximum space inside, and high-efficiency four-cylinder engines instead of a thirsty, low-tech V-8. Yet early proposals designed to those requirements did not pan out well enough to suit Ford execs, so just a year into the program Ford turned to longtime Japanese partner Mazda, whose small-car expertise was at least equal to Ford's own.

## CHAPTER 9
# 1987-93: False Start, Fine Finish

Mazda was then planning the next version of its front-drive 626 coupe, one of Mustang's new-wave rivals. Dearborn figured to save money and get a better new ponycar by joining in. The result would be two cars, each with its own styling and sales network but sharing almost everything else. The idea became even more attractive when Mazda decided to set up a plant in Flat Rock, Michigan, near Ford's historic River Rouge factory, and to make part of its output available to Ford.

It seemed a match made in heaven. Ford would get a new Mustang for far less money than if they had developed it alone. Mazda also liked the economics, but especially the deal's "politically correct" image. With "Japan Inc." taking big chunks out of Detroit's sales hide, Congress was threatening protectionist legislation that the Japanese hoped to forestall by setting up U.S. "transplant" operations like Flat Rock.

But Ford hadn't counted on the outrage of Mustang loyalists once word of the plan leaked out. A *Japanese* Mustang? No way! And besides, enthusiasts cried, front drive is for dinky econoboxes, not *real* cars. Ford listened and released the erstwhile "626 Mustang"

(which Mazda sold as the MX-6) as the 1989 Probe (named for a recent series of aerodynamic show cars). The decision was a wise one. Though capable and spirited in turbocharged GT form, the Probe was too "foreign" to pass as a ponycar—an American invention, after all—even if it did have Ford styling.

Fortunately for die-hard Mustangers, rising sales in a recovering market encouraged Dearborn to rejuvenate the old warrior and keep it soldiering on until a "proper" replacement was ready. Thus did the most fully overhauled Mustang in eight years arrive for 1987. The slow-selling SVO was history (as was Mercury's Mustang, the Capri, which also hadn't sold as expected since its '79 reincarnation), but LX and GT notchbacks, hatchbacks, and convertibles all returned. Though the basic 1979 shape was still recognizable, it was slicker than ever, with a smoother nose, flush headlamps, black instead of chrome body trim, and, except on convertibles, rear side glass pulled out flush with surrounding sheetmetal. Besides a more contemporary look, these tweaks reduced drag coefficients to as low as 0.36.

As before, the LX was more restrained than the GT. Its grille, for instance, was a simple slot with a horizontal bar bearing a small Ford oval. Below was a body-color bumper with integral spoiler and wide, black rubstrips that wrapped around as bodyside protection moldings to a color-keyed rear bumper. GTs wore sculpted rocker-panel skirts that looked like the add-ons they were, plus dummy

The Mustang Mach III toured the auto-show circuit in 1993 and whetted the public's appetite for performance. The two-seater's hairy, 450-horse V-8 would not see production, but the slippery body was predictive of the all-new Mustang that would bow for '94.

scoops ahead of the rear wheels, a prominent spoiler on the hatchback, and busy "cheese grater" taillamps. At least the grille-less front was attractively aggressive, with a wide "mouth" intake in a forward-jutting airdam, flanked by round fog lamps.

Because instrument panels are among the costliest components for a carmaker to change, the '87 Mustang's brand-new one suggested that the present generation might hang on for more than a few years (as indeed it would). The design could have been mistaken for a Mazda creation. The right side was cut away on top to form a useful package shelf and lend a greater sense of interior spaciousness. On the left was an upright instrument pod with side-mount rocker switches for lights, hazard flasher, and rear-window defroster. Column stalks again controlled wipers and turn indicators, while cruise-control buttons were conveniently placed in the steering wheel. Dropping down from the center of the dash was a broad console carrying convenient rotary climate controls.

The most noteworthy mechanical alterations involved the venerable small-block V-8—no surprise, as it was now way ahead of the 2.3-liter four in customer preference. A return to freer-breathing, pre-1986 cylinder heads and other induction changes added 25 horses for a total of 225, thus matching the top Chevy Camaro/Pontiac Firebird option, a 5.7-liter Corvette mill. Torque was up too: now a mighty 300 lbs/ft. The GT retained the 5.0-liter 302 as standard, and also received larger front disc brakes and a recalibrated suspension.

Meanwhile, the lowly four shed its dull one-barrel carburetor for multi-point electronic fuel injection, but was hardly more potent at 90 bhp and 130 lbs/ft of torque. At least it now teamed with standard 5-speed manual or optional 4-speed automatic transmissions (as op-

posed to the previous 4-speed stick and 3-speed slushbox), which helped maximize what performance it could muster. A big surprise was the deletion of the 3.8 V-6 option, leaving a huge power and performance gap between the four and V-8.

And it did, only a lot of those V-8s were sold in LX trim as an $1885 package that included the GT's uprated chassis and rolling stock. In fact, demand for 5.0-liter LXs proved so strong that Ford actually ran short of engines, telling buyers that if they wanted a V-8 Mustang, they'd have to take a GT. This news did not go over well with every would-be buyer. For some, the facelifted GT seemed either ugly, outlandish, or both, which must have dismayed Jack Telnack, who had been named overall Ford Design chief in mid-1987. Others simply preferred their V-8 in the quieter-looking LX because that car was less likely to be noticed by the law.

Regardless, the newly fortified small-block provided blistering performance reminiscent of the good old days: 0-60 mph, for instance, now required slightly *less* than six seconds. Obviously, technology was allowing Ford (and others) to accomplish what had once been achieved only with cubic inches. For example, to match 225 net horsepower in, say, a '72 Mustang, buyers had to order an optional 351 V-8 offering 168-275 net bhp. Yet the '87 small-block was thriftier and smoother-running, needed less upkeep, and was more reliable.

Progress often carries a price, of course, but Mustang remained an exception. "Though far from perfect—or perfected—the Mustang GT is put together well enough and offers a ton of go for your dough," Consumer Guide® observed in *Auto Test 1987*. "Despite a full option load—air, premium sound system, cruise control, and power windows, door locks, and mirrors—our test

car [a hatchback] came to $14,352, which is an exceptional value when IROC-Z Camaros, Toyota Supras, and Nissan 300ZXs can go for $5000 more."

Of course, a better car doesn't guarantee better sales, so despite the extensive updates, Mustang volume crumbled by more than 65,000 units for 1987. Still, 159,000 total sales was good going, all things considered. (One problem was tax reform, which took effect on January 1, 1987, and initiated a phased-in elimination of the time-honored deduction of interest on car loans.) The GT's facelift was costly at some $200 million (though that included upgrading the Dearborn assembly plant), but would be quickly amortized.

And indeed, Mustang's sole alteration for 1988 was a higher-capacity standard battery for LX models. For '89, Ford belatedly recognized customer preferences by making the LX V-8 package a distinct model trio labeled LX 5.0L Sport and throwing in the GT's multi-adjustable sports seats. The only other change of consequence was moving the convertible's power windows from the option list to the standard-feature roster. Despite so few changes, 1988 sales bounded past 211,000, and the '89s sold almost as well at nearly 210,000 units.

But wait: 1989 was Mustang's 25th birthday year. Time for a commemorative special, right? Well, yes and no. Rumors abounded that factory-favored tuner Jack Roush was cooking up a hot GT with a 300-horsepower *351* V-8, plus all the handling ingredients to go with it, but development delays and fuel-economy mandates left the proposal stone-cold dead. Instead, 3800 special Emerald Green V-8 LX convertibles were issued starting in mid-January *1990*—appropriate, as Ford still regarded the first Mustang as a '65 model, not a "1964½." It was a pretty meek observance for such a milestone, but better than nothing.

With a new federal rule for "passive restraints" now in force, Mustang complied for 1990 with a driver-side air bag mounted in the steering wheel. Unfortunately, the air bag eliminated the tilt-wheel option. Door map pockets and clearcoat paint became standard, while options expanded with leather interior trim, as featured on the commemorative convertibles. Prices were as attractive as ever: under $9500 for a four-cylinder LX two-door and less than $19,000 for the top-line GT convertible. Even so, recession-era production plunged nearly 50 percent, to near 128,000.

Sales dropped to just under 99,000 for 1991, the lowest Mustang figure anyone could remember. Changes were again few. The anemic four was boosted to 105 bhp via a new eight-plug cylinder head, but only rental-car fleet managers really cared. Ragtops gained a redesigned power roof that folded closer to the body for a tidier look, and automatic-transmission cars met yet another new federal edict with an interlock that required a push on the brake pedal before the shifter would move out of Park. Prices rose a bit, with the base LX two-door going to just above $10,000, but V-8 convertibles again stickered below $20,000.

Only detail changes occurred for '92, when Mustang recorded an all-time yearly sales low of just 79,280 units. LXs were tidied up with color-keyed bodyside moldings and bumper rubstrips. And wonder of wonders, those old favorites, whitewall tires and wire-wheel covers, vanished from the options list.

The economy started to perk up by model-year 1993. So did Mustang sales, which rebounded to around 114,200. In a way, this shouldn't have happened. For one thing, GM had a swoopy new fourth-generation Camaro/Firebird, and the top power option for those cars was the Corvette's latest 5.7-liter LT1 V-8, detuned from 300 horses to a still-formidable 275.

Worse, having admitted to literally overrating output of the Mustang V-8, Ford adjusted outputs down to 205 bhp and 275 lbs/ft of torque. Meanwhile, industry spies reported that work was fast winding up on the new Mustang that enthusiasts had been anticipating for at least five years. The prospect surely moved many old fans to buy a '93.

Ford provided its own incentive with a hot hatchback that might have appeared with 25th Anniversary badges. But it wore the Cobra name and snake insignia of Carroll Shelby's legendary Sixties sports cars, mainly so Ford could keep its legal claim to both from expiring for want of use. *Road & Track* called this Cobra the "best of an aging breed," and by most any measure it was. Developed by Dearborn's new Special Vehicle Team (SVT, the successor to SVO), it generated 245 horsepower with a 302 V-8 carrying special big-port "GT40" heads, tuned-runner intake manifold, revised cam, and other muscle-building improvements. Torque, a stout 285 lbs/ft, was delivered by a beefier—and mandatory—5-speed manual gearbox, and was controlled in corners by massive 245/45ZR17 Goodyear Eagle performance radials. Also on hand, or rather underfoot, were rear disc brakes instead of drums—the first time since the SVO that Mustang had them—plus more "balanced" suspension tuning that seemed to go against conventional wisdom with *softer* springs, shocks, and bushings and a *smaller* front stabilizer bar. Interior furnishings were everyday GT, but the exterior was almost LX-modest. Spotter's points included a neater nose, taillamps borrowed from the late SVO model, handsome seven-blade alloy wheels—and the return of the good old running horse to the grille. An oversized rear spoiler was the one arguably jarring note to this speedy, sophisticated package.

Did we say speedy? Try 5.9 seconds 0-60 mph, according to *R&T*, whose test

Cobra also clocked an impressive 14.5 seconds at 98 mph in the standing quarter-mile and less than 16 seconds from 0 to *100* mph. If this wasn't Sixties performance reborn, it was certainly enough for the New Austerity Nineties. As for sophisticated, *Car and Driver's* Don Schroeder termed the Cobra "a nicer-riding, more supple car [than the GT]. Although it can feel less buttoned down . . . the Cobra makes better use of its tires and rewards coordinated hands and feet with clearly higher limits and cornering speeds. . . ."

Nevertheless, cynics viewed the Cobra as just a ploy to keep Ford's old ponycar from being completely eclipsed by GM's new ones. Indeed, *Motor Trend* called it a "shake-and-bake bridge to '94." Still, this Cobra was not only a grand send-off for an aging design, but an eloquent testimony to that design's stamina and versatility. And with only some 5000 built, the '93 Cobra will be a coveted collectible of this long-lived Mustang breed.

The most collectible of all, though, is likely to be the Cobra R-model, which saw just 107 copies. As on an earlier Shelby model, the "R" meant racing. Alterations to the basic Cobra included much bigger front brakes, competition-caliber cooling system and suspension tuning, appropriately bigger wheels and tires, and added structural reinforcements. Omitting the stock Cobra's back seat, air conditioning, and most power accessories reduced curb weight by 60 pounds—not much on the street but enough to make a crucial difference on the track. Ford sold every R-model for the full $25,692 sticker price, versus about $20,000 for a "regular" Cobra, itself a bona fide bargain.

After this flurry of excitement—and after staying so much the same through so many changes—it was time for Mustang to move on at last. An all-new ponycar was on its way.

# 1987

- The stock market plummets a record 508 points on October 19
- Metropolitan Los Angeles is rocked by a severe earthquake
- AMC is purchased by Chrysler
- Camaro offers a convertible for the first time in 18 years, plus an optional Corvette-based engine

- Henry Ford II succumbs to pneumonia at age 70
- Ford Motor Company earns $4.6 billion net profit, the most ever for an automaker
- Although still essentially the 1979 design, the '87 Mustang is heavily restyled, with a new "aero-look" body and revised instrument panel
- The 5.0-liter V-8 now cranks out a whopping 225 bhp and 300 lbs/ft of torque
- The 3.8-liter V-6 is no longer available
- Mustang's base four-cylinder sheds its one-barrel carb for multi-point electronic fuel injection; horsepower remains modest, at 90
- GT models add a Traction-Lok axle
- The SVO Mustang enters its final model year, doomed by pallid sales
- The HO V-8 now produces 180 bhp, an increase of five
- Mustang production slips again, to 159,145; 20,328 are convertibles

*Top:* The no-frills 5.0 LX was available for 1987 as a two-door coupe or (*seen here*) a three-door hatchback. The V-6 had been dropped. *Middle row:* The GT was available as a three-door hatchback or a convertible. Fluted taillight panels gave away the GT package from the rear. *Above:* The instrument panel was brand new, highlighted by pod-mounted switches and a two-spoke steering wheel.

*This page:* For 1987, Ford Design styled the GT for an "increased differential" from the rest of the Mustang lineup. The GT's unique side appearance had flared rocker panel moldings incorporating "Mustang GT," integrated "spats" at the rear wheel wells, rear fender extensions, and brand-new 16-spoke 15 × 7-inch cast aluminum wheels. The front end had a lower air dam with fog lamps and twin air scoops. The rear fascia, with a louvered taillight panel, had either a rear spoiler (hatchback only) or a rear luggage rack; each incorporated the high-mount stop light.

After undergoing major restyling for '87, the Mustang retained its familiar shape but came away with a longer hood, a new grille, and aero headlamps. The convertible (*top row*) benefited mightily from the restyle, especially with the aero look given by the GT side skirts and unique front and rear ends. The all-new interior (*above*) had long armrests, a reworked console, a redesigned instrument panel, and GT seats with power-operated lumbar support. Ford Engineering retuned the 302 HO (*above right*) for 225 horsepower (220 with automatic) with higher-flow cylinder heads, bigger intake runners, and a larger throttle body. *Right:* The LX had a base four-cylinder with fuel injection for the first time.

*This page*: The Mustang GT was easily the most popular performance car in America in the 1980s, and for good reason. It was hot and it was affordable. General Motors called it "The Box" and privately bemoaned the fact that this restyled Mustang outsold their swoopy Firebirds and Camaros. The 302 (*above*) produced gobs of torque at low rpm: 300 lbs/ft @ 3000 revs, which would light up the rear tires on launch and propel the 5.0 to sub-15-second ETs in the quarter. Rear side glass was flush with the sheetmetal, which made the car look more modern than in the past.

# 1988

- Panamanian dictator Manuel Noriega is indicted by the U.S. Justice Department on drug charges

- A terrorist bomb destroys a Pan Am jetliner above Lockerbie, Scotland

- Chrysler profits drop for the fourth straight year, but the Big Three earn a record total profit of $11.2 billion

..................................................

- When the public objects loudly to the planned replacement of Mustang by a front-drive sport coupe co-developed by Ford and Mazda, Mustang soldiers on and the joint effort is released by Ford in May as the 1989 Probe (and by Mazda as the MX-6)

- Only one change is made to '88 Mustangs: a 540-amp battery for the LX, replacing a 460-amp unit

- Mustang model-year production rebounds, to 211,225; 39,223 are droptops

Mustang saw just one change for model-year 1988: The 540-amp/hour heavy-duty battery was made standard. Otherwise, the '88 is indistinguishable from the '87. *Top two photos:* Aero skirts were exclusive to the GT package. *Third photo from top:* LX models came standard with the GT suspension. This one carries 5.0 badges. *Right:* The basic Mustang sedan ran with a 90-horsepower inline-four.

*Left and top left:* For every available color on the GT, Ford charted a lower-body paint. This was part of the GT "differential," although a monotone treatment was also available in five colors. *Top right:* The 5.0 badges on the front fenders were punctuated with a red decimal point. *Above left:* With an investment in an all-new interior, Ford was obviously committed to selling their so-called "dated" Fox-platform Mustang for many more years. *Above:* For 1988, most 5.0-liter Mustangs retained their speed-density fuel-injection systems, though models shipped to California got a new mass-airflow metering system that would be used on 5.0-liter engines nationwide the following year.

# 1989

- The tentative Chinese democracy movement reaches a bloody climax when protesters clash with tank troops at Tienanmen Square

- East Germany opens its borders, allowing its citizens to travel freely to West Germany

- Chevy reclaims the number-one sales spot, bumping Ford to second

- FoMoCo vice-chairman Harold Poling warns against excess capacity worldwide and predicts 20-percent overproduction

- Ford introduces the Taurus SHO (Super High Output), powered by a potent Yamaha-engineered 220-bhp V-6

- Ford spends $200 million to upgrade the Mustang assembly plant in Dearborn, Michigan

- Rumors of a 25th Anniversary commemorative Mustang come to nothing; the model year brings the "birth" of the six-millionth Mustang

- Mustang's GT suspension has gas-pressurized hydraulic struts, front stabilizer bar, and variable-rate coil springs

- The LX V-8 package option becomes a distinct model called LX 5.0 Sport

- Production holds nearly steady, at 209,769; convertibles account for 42,244 units

*Top row:* The GT had a curb weight of approximately 3100 pounds and could accelerate from 0-60 mph in about 6.5 seconds. Still, there's no question GM's Camaro Z28 and Firebird Trans Am were more sophisticated and had more stylish bodies. *Left:* The basic Mustang shape was boxy and had been around since 1979. The automotive press wasn't wrong when it called the car "long in the tooth," but the things Ford did to that boxy shape were flat amazing: aero rocker panels, rear wing spoiler, and front air dam with fog lights. When all was said and done, the GT (*below*) looked almost like a new-generation car. Mainly, however, it was the performance that mattered, and what you can't hear on these pages is the glorious noise that issued from the dual exhausts.

*Opposite page, top:* In 1989, Ford introduced the LX 5.0L as a separate series, available in convertible, hatchback, and two-door coupe. Although this new series lacked GT scoops and spoilers, it did have the GT's articulated sports seats and seat trim (except on the sedan), 10-hole cast aluminum wheels, GT handling suspension, Traction-Lok axle, 75-amp alternator, and dual exhausts. *Opposite page, middle and bottom:* The 1989 GT was a carryover from 1988, available in hatchback and convertible form.

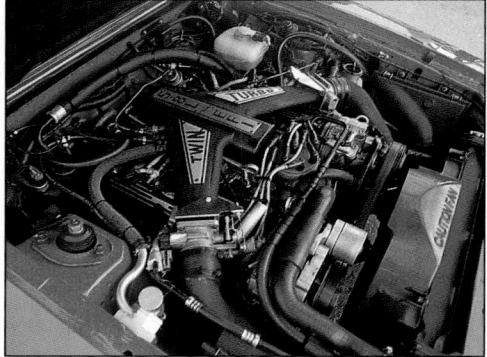

*Above:* Ford contracted Jack Roush to build a 25th Anniversary Ford Mustang in 1989½, but the car did not make production. Notice the running horse on the front fascia—an apt reminder of the car's heritage. *Top right:* The engine in Roush's prototype was a 5.8-liter EFI Twin Turbo with a specially fabricated intake—in plainer terms, a 351 V-8 with 380 horsepower @ 5000 rpm. *Above right:* Inside, Roush's 25th Anniversary special was a stock GT. *Right:* The LX 5.0 became a separate series in 1989, and could be had with any body style: convertible, three-door hatchback, or two-door coupe.

*This page:* "Power in the Hands of a Few" was the marketing slogan for Steve Saleen's "Saleen Mustang," first built in 1984. In Shelby fashion, Saleen "race-bred" Mustangs for pure driving pleasure. Notice the Saleen Mustang racing stripes on the lower body, the front bumper molding, and the urethane air dam (*top left*). Door panels (*top right*) were customized. The Saleen's 302 HO (*above*) was stock internally, but the engine bay was reinforced with a strut tower brace, and the exhausts were straight duals. Interior appointments (*above right*) included a three-spoke leather-covered Momo steering wheel, a Hurst quick-ratio shifter, and a 170-mph speedometer. At the rear (*right*), Saleen provided a Saleen Autosport Competition wing.

# 1990

- The long-hoped-for unification of East and West Germany becomes a reality
- Iraqi troops invade Kuwait and overthrow the government; in response, the United Nations begins a massive buildup of troops and materiel
- Domestic auto sales of 14.1 million cars and trucks are the worst since 1983

- Ford reclaims the number-one sales spot from Chevy
- Mustang gains a standard driver-side air bag
- January brings 3800 copies of a commemorative Mustang, an Emerald Green V-8 LX convertible
- Mustang experiences a big drop in model-year production, to 128,189, with 26,958 ragtops

One of the best-looking and most unusual police Mustangs ever built was the now-famous Seal Beach Saleen 5.0 LX hatchback of 1990. Notice the Saleen windshield graphic (*top*), large Saleen Autosport rear wing (*middle*), and Saleen Flo-Fit seats (*right*). The Seal Beach PD took this car to shows in Southern California, notably the annual "Fabulous Fords Forever" event sponsored by Ford Motor Company at Knott's Berry Farm in Buena Park. In April 1994, Seal Beach trailered the car to Charlotte, North Carolina, for the 30th anniversary celebration of the Mustang. There, the car was put on special display and offered for sale by sealed bid. Please note that the police officer was *not* part of the deal.

*Top row:* From the outside, a 1990 Mustang looked like an '89. However, Ford added clearcoat paint as an option and made a driver-side air bag standard. The LX three-door hatchback with the 5.0-liter V-8 was a GT in all but name and cop-baiting graphics. The rear wing with integral rear brake light was unique to the LX hatchback. *Left:* The LX 5.0 continued as a specific model, seen here in convertible guise and with a rear luggage rack (rather than a spoiler) to carry the rear brake lamp. *Bottom row:* The most popular GT was the hatchback, which was not too flashy in monotone Black with stock "turbine"-style wheels.

# 1991

- The Union of Soviet Socialist Republics (USSR) is dissolved following an unsuccessful attempt by Communist hard-liners to topple President Gorbachev

- The Persian Gulf War, a UN response to Iraq's 1990 invasion of Kuwait, begins in the air on January 16; the UN ground campaign begins on February 23 and is brought to a successful conclusion four days later

- The GM-financed Saturn debuts as the first new American car make in 30 years

- Rising sales of nearly new "program cars" used in rental fleets cut into new-car sales

- The lowest-priced Mustang tops $10,000 for the first time

- Mustang's base 2.3-liter inline-four gains 17 horsepower and is now rated at 105 bhp

- The GT shares a 225-bhp 5.0-liter V-8 with the LX 5.0L Sport model

- Front disc/rear drum brakes continue on all Mustangs

- Mustang model-year production falls further, to 90,460; 22,018 are convertibles

*Top:* The Ford Probe, seen here in GT trim, would have replaced the Mustang had there not been a public uproar and letter-writing campaign directed at Ford. *Middle and above:* Ford worried that the Probe would steal sales from Mustang, but this was not the case, probably because the latter offered rear-wheel drive and a big V-8, while the former was a four- or six-cylinder with front-wheel drive—in essence, two very different machines.

*Left:* Sixteen-inch, five-spoke aluminum star wheels (new for '91) came with the classic running horse atop the red/white/blue tri-bar. *Below left:* The "clamshell armrest," standard on all Mustangs since 1987, carried on for '91. *Below:* Buttons for cruise control were conveniently positioned on the steering wheel, which, from 1990, was fitted with an air bag. *Bottom left:* The 5.0 continued to produce 225 horsepower. *Bottom right:* The hatchback's rear seats folded down to make a huge cargo area.

*Top row:* Most convertible buyers went for the GT package, seen here in Bright Red, or the LX 5.0. The wildest available body color was probably Wild Strawberry Metallic. *Above:* Medium Red was a more subdued hue. Tires were widened in 1991 to P225/55/ZR-16 and were "all-season performance" on the LX 5.0L. GTs had tires of the same size, but the all-weather tread was optional. *Right:* Ford upgraded the 2.3-liter four-cylinder with twin plug heads and distributor-less ignition, upping horsepower from 88 to 105 in an attempt to spur sales of the base engine. Few people noticed.

*Left:* If a 1988-1993 Mustang didn't have 5.0L badges on its front quarters, it was a four-cylinder, because the 3.8-liter V-6 had been dropped in 1987. *Below left:* The front of the '91 LX 5.0L was identical to that of the base four-cylinder. *Below:* The combination of a 5.0-liter V-8 and rear-wheel drive gave the Mustang sales leadership in the ponycar class. It offered more bang for the buck than any other car in the world. *Bottom left:* Unlike the Corvette and other two-seat sports cars, the Mustang positioned the driver high for great visibility and easy entry and exit. *Bottom right:* The tail of the LX 5.0L was subdued; even the hatchback's unique spoiler was integral with the decklid.

*Right:* GTs were unmistakable in 1991 thanks to the front air dam with fog lights. *Below:* With the proliferation of 5.0 Mustangs in the 1980s, the aftermarket built up a huge selection of parts for the Ford small-block, which rivaled and perhaps surpassed the Chevy small-block in popularity. *Below right:* The base GT convertible listed for $19,864 and topped 20 grand with just a few options. *Bottom left:* The all-season black sidewall tires that were standard on the LX were optional on the GT. *Bottom right:* The louvered taillight panel was unique to the GT.

# 1992

- Arkansas governor Bill Clinton is elected president, defeating incumbent George Bush
- Los Angeles is rocked by rioting following the acquittal of four white police officers tried for the 1991 beating of a black motorist

---

- Ford Taurus edges out Honda Accord as the best-selling car in the U.S.
- Mustang is altered only in details: optional four-way power driver's seat; color-keyed bodyside molding and bumper rub strips for the LX model; a new dome lamp; cancellation of wire wheel covers and white sidewall tires
- Mustang sales dip slightly, to 85,515, with 13,835 convertibles

*Above:* The 1992 Mustang GT was essentially unchanged from '91, and available as a hatchback and a convertible. *Below:* The '92 LX 5.0L series was available in all three Mustang body styles: the two-door coupe, three-door hatchback, and convertible. LX models came with color-keyed bodyside moldings and bumper rub strips. On the inside, all 1992 Mustangs got a new dome light and a four-way power driver's seat.

# 1993

- American-based Middle Eastern terrorists explode a titanic bomb in the parking garage of New York's World Trade Center

- Chicago Bulls star Michael Jordan stuns the sports world by announcing his retirement from basketball

- Recession and unemployment continue; demand for used cars remains strong

- GM's ponycars, Chevy Camaro and Pontiac Firebird, gain swoopy new sheetmetal and ergonomically improved cockpits; the Camaro Z28 and Firebird Formula and Trans Am crank out 275 bhp with detuned Corvette engines

........................................................

- Mustang introduces a limited-edition, high-performance Cobra edition at the end of the year; it has a beefed-up suspension and disc brakes front and rear

- Ford's revised method of rating horsepower downrates the GT's 5.0-liter V-8 to 205, from 225; the Cobra's modified 5.0 is rated at 245

- A compact disc player is a new option

- The dramatic Mustang Mach III roadster displays its carbon-fiber body and 4.6-liter 460-bhp V-8 at major auto shows

- Despite sporting a basic design dating back to 1979, Mustang generates an impressive sales increase for '93, to 114,228; of these, 26,598 are convertibles

*Opposite page:* Ford brought back the Cobra nameplate for 1993, which had been replaced in '82 with the GT. This resurrection was much more than a badging job, as it included a 302 HO pumped with 20 more horsepower (via larger intake and exhaust ports, big valves, new intake manifold, and 65mm throttle body), a T5 transmission with heavy-duty clutch and driveshaft, 7.5 × 17-inch aluminum wheels with Goodyear P245/45ZR-17 tires, specific rear-wing spoiler, and a more compliant suspension. *Above:* Meanwhile, the GT returned—and at $2500 less than the better-performing Cobra. *Right:* In the last week of February 1993, Ford put into production this "White Monochromatic Package," available only on 5.0 LX convertibles. The white leather upholstery had ponies embroidered on the front headrests, and a unique rear spoiler took the place of the luggage rack.

*Top row:* The 1993½ Cobra was limited to 5000 copies. It featured a special grille opening with a unique running horse. Final production figures were 4993 (1784 in Red, 1355 in Teal, and 1854 in Black) and 107 R-models (racing models). The moldings that extended the rocker panels gave the car a streamlined look without using the GT's aero panels. *Above:* The '93 GT was a carryover of the '92 edition. Ford advertised a more powerful standard AM/FM radio, plus an optional compact disc player and premium radio-cassette player. *Above right:* The convertible was also a carryover from '92. *Right:* The "Yellow Package" on the LX 5.0L cost an extra $1488 and included chromed wheels, white or black leather interior with pony-embroidered front headrests, black floormats with running horses, a unique rear spoiler replacing the stock luggage rack, and Yellow paint.

*Left:* In 1992, two years before the fourth-generation Mustang would be ready, and coinciding with the introduction of the fourth-generation Camaro/Firebird, the people on Team Mustang put together a Mach III concept car with carbon fiber body panels sculpted to recreate the long hood, short rear deck, and grille-mounted running horse of the 1965 original. *Below left:* Power came from a supercharged, 450-horse, 4.6-liter, four-valve modular V-8 that pushed the Mach III to 60 mph in less than 4.5 seconds. *Below:* A dual cockpit theme was another nod to the original '65. The steering wheel was three-spoked (as it was in 1965), but this one was genuine wood by Nardi. *Bottom left:* Tires were 19-inch Goodyears on spoked wheels. *Bottom right:* The Mach III's rounded rear end carried two sets of triple tail lenses.

Amostly new Mustang rode in for 1994 on a tidal wave of anticipation and nostalgia. Announcement ads pictured it with the classic '65, declaring, "It is what is was." Yet believe it or not, the '94 almost *wasn't*.

Actually, this "reborn" Mustang was conceived somewhat reluctantly in the aftermath of the 1989 Probe. As noted in Chapter Nine, that front-drive, Mazda-based car was originally planned to replace the vintage '79-generation Mustang, an idea that generated howls of protest from Mustang fans once word got out. A chastened FoMoCo gave the front-driver another name, scored an instant hit, and kept the old Mustang going. But though the ruckus soon died down, it taught a valuable lesson: Ponycar buyers still wanted *real* ponycars, not fancy Japanese compacts.

In the wake of that stinging surprise, Mustang planning floundered for almost two years, and not without cause. For one thing, sales of the Chevy Camaro and Pontiac Firebird were sinking fast, leading some in Dearborn to consider the unthinkable: that another new Mustang might not ever be needed. Even if it was, Ford had other pending projects that promised to bring in far more money (the new Explorer sport-utility, for instance). Besides, the newly refurbished old Mustang was selling as well as ever, so why rush?

Finally, the impetus to create a new Mustang came from General Motors, which had been considering a front-wheel-drive Camaro/Firebird for several

## CHAPTER 10
# 1994-99: Driving Toward the Millennium

years—as Ford well knew from published "spy" reports. In the end, of course, GM decided on a redesigned rear-drive concept for 1993. Once GM's intentions were known, Ford's corporate pride demanded an aggressive reply, and work was authorized on a new Mustang, as project SN95.

During the course of unusually intensive customer clinics—what Ford coyly referred to as "gallop polls"—it became clear Mustang fans wanted modern styling with overtones of the '65 original; plus a cheap, easily serviced V-8, rear-drive, a low base price, and plenty of options.

A lean, "team concept" mindset was by this time gospel in Detroit, so Dearborn established a Mustang team under the aegis of Will Boddie, Ford's director for small and mid-size cars. The group worked with a surprisingly modest budget: just $700 million for the complete program, in marked contrast to the $3 billion that had been allocated for the trendsetting 1986 Ford Taurus. And of that $700 million, only $200 million was earmarked for the car itself. At 36 months, the project deadline was equally

urgent and tight.

A "retro" echo of earlier Mustang programs was sounded by the trio of SN95 mockups considered for production styling. All carried the familiar styling cues: a running horse in the grille, simulated side scoops ahead of the rear wheels, triple-element taillamps, and, of course, long hood/short deck proportions. But they also shared a smooth, muscular, slightly wedgy shape in Ford's now-customary "aero" idiom. The differences in the proposals were mainly of degree. The tamest was the "Bruce Jenner," described as a "trim, athletic" design that nevertheless scored low in clinics for looking too "soft." At the other extreme was "Rambo," an aggressively exaggerated version that failed for that reason. This left the in-between "Arnold Schwarzenegger" to win the day in consumer polls, after which it received only detail changes before production.

Interior designers, too, strove for a "classic Mustang" feel (naturally being mindful of the myriad federal safety regulations that had come into existence since the Sixties). What emerged was the familiar 2+2 cockpit with a center console, front bucket seats, and a tiny rear bench. Dominating all was a dramatically sculptured "twin-cowl" instrument panel that flowed smoothly around into the inner door panels.

Body engineers increased stiffness without undue weight gain—just one advantage of computer analysis. Although limited time and money didn't

A gorgeous, nostalgic redesign for 1994 thrilled Mustang fans—and dealers, too, for sales of the indefatigable ponycar soundly trounced those of rivals Chevy Camaro and Pontiac Firebird. By any measure, Mustang entered its fourth decade in great form.

allow a new chassis for SN95, engineers created a smartly modified platform called "Fox-4 (the number denoting model-year 1994). Steering and suspension were left basically as they'd been since 1979, but new closed-section roof members; a hefty, inverted U-member installed between the B-pillars; and on ragtops a stout underbody X-brace, allowed slightly softer damping for a smoother ride. Wheelbase gained three-quarters of an inch, front caster pitch was enhanced to increase directional stability, and tracks were widened at each end—on base models by a whopping 3.7 inches in front.

Larger rolling stock was also specified: Base models now came on 6.5×15-inch steel rims wearing 206/65 Eagle GA touring tires, which could also mount on optional three-spoke, 7.5-inch-wide alloys. GTs were treated to 7.5×16-inch five-spoke alloys with high speed Z-rated P255/55 all-season tires; 8×17-inch five-spoke wheels were optional.

Brake upgrades encompassed larger front discs, newly standard rear discs, a bigger booster, and Bosch anti-lock control as a first-time option.

The four-cylinder engine was banished, replaced by a 3.8-liter V-6, installed longitudinally and developing 145 horsepower and 215 pounds/feet of torque. The V-8, in the form of the familiar 302 small block uprated to 215 horses, was reserved exclusively for GT models. Torque, at 285 pounds/feet, was unchanged. As before, both engines teamed with 5-speed manual or optional 4-speed automatic transmissions.

A Corvette-style removable hardtop was announced as a $1545 option for Mustang convertibles. A manageable 80 pounds, the fiberglass hardtop gave the convertible the same slantback roof profile as the Mustang coupe. However, last-minute glitches delayed production of the hardtop until 1995, the only year

it was built. Only 499 were made.

Because the '94 Mustang GT gave away 60 horsepower to the 275-bhp Camaro Z28 and Pontiac Formula and Trans Am Firebirds, buff-book reviews of the new car were mixed. (Even a 302 massaged to 240 horses by Ford's Special Vehicle Team and installed in limited-production Cobras fell short of the GM ponycars by 35 horses.) While road-testers rightly lauded the Mustang's many improvements, drawbacks were not ignored. "The carryover power may challenge the loyalty of some . . . fans," mused *Car and Driver,* "[but] with substantial improvements in braking and body structure, the Mustang [GT still] offers tremendous performance for the dollar."

As if to prove the point, *C/D*'s 5-speed coupe ran the 0-60 sprint in just 6.1 seconds, and the standing quarter-mile in 14.9 seconds at 93 mph—not bad for an engine then well into middle age. The automatic version was no slouch, either: *Consumer Guide*™'s test coupe ran 0-60 in a brisk 7.4 seconds.

Yet even that performance still left the GT way behind its GM rivals. As *Road & Track* noted, "A 60-horsepower shortfall is a lot of horsepower." Ford shot back that Mustang was aimed at those who valued overall finesse above simple acceleration.

If Mustang was no lock in a drag race, it won the '94 sales race with ease, besting Camaro by about 30 percent, and outselling Firebird three-to-one. Mustang sales increased 61 percent over 1993, itself a strong sales year.

The robust sales were not completely surprising—after all, Mustang fans who participated in concumer clincis had helped to design the car. As a thank-you, Ford hosted several regional parties for Mustang clubs on Sunday, April 17, 1994—by no coincidence 30 years to the day since the smashing debut of the

beloved original Mustang.

But the celebration didn't stop there. Again recalling 1964 activities, Ford arranged to have the '94 Mustang (actually, a special Cobra convertible) named Indy 500 pace car. Sure enough, Dearborn wasn't conceding the power issue entirely to GM, and 5000 new-design Cobras—a planned 4000 coupes and 1000 ragtops (the latter offered as replica Pace Cars)—had been trickling off the line since February.

Another effort of Ford's Special Vehicle Team, the '94 Cobras arrived with a smoother front fascia; unique low-profile rear spoiler; 17-inch, five-spoke chrome wheels wearing gumball P245/45ZR Eagle GS-C tires, discreet snake i.d. on the front fenders, and a leather-lined interior with striking, white-faced gauges.

Underneath were bigger brakes with twin front calipers and standard ABS, a GT suspension again made slightly softer for "controlled compliance" handling, and a 302 massaged to give 240 horsepower—still 35 horses shy of a box-stock Z28 Camaro.

For 1995, Mustang carried on with no major changes, though the car's build quality and solidity improved even more. The convertible, in particular, displayed far less flex and twist. A GTS model, priced $1200 less than the GT but equipped with the same V-8, was introduced for the model year.

Significant change came with the '96 models, when Mustang shelved its pushrod overhead-valve V-8s for two new overhead-cam V-8s. GT models got a single-cam 4.6-liter with two valves per cylinder and 215 horsepower in place of the 215-horse 5.0. Cobras got a double-overhead-cam V-8 of the same displacement but with four valves per cylinder and 305 horsepower; this engine replaced a 240-horse version of the 5.0-liter. Although the base 3.8-liter V-6 returned, its horsepower rating rose from 145 to 150. All engines had platinum-tipped spark plugs designed to last 100,000 miles. The GTS model was dropped.

Exterior changes for '96 included new vertical taillamps and a mesh insert behind the Mustang emblem in the grille. Standard with GT and Cobra models was a new anti-theft system.

That anti-theft feature became standard on the base Mustang for 1997. Other changes for the model year: a monotone color scheme (except on the dash); gray leather upholstery optional with the base convertible; and optional "diamond-cut" 17-inch alloy wheels for the GT.

By the time the 1998 model year rolled around, Mustang had been America's best-selling sporty car 12 years running, and was outselling Camaro and Firebird *combined*. The GT picked up 10 additional horsepower, to 225. The Cobra's version of the same 4.6-liter V-8 remained unchanged at 305 bhp. As with most other Fords for '98, Mustang's dual air bags were depowered to deploy with less force while still meeting federal requirements. Inside, all Mustangs came with two front cupholders instead of a single cupholder and an ashtray. Buyers were pleased, and by the end of the 1998 model year, Mustang sales had topped '97's figures by 30 percent.

Model-year 1999 marked the 35th Anniversary of Ford's ponycar and the event was celebrated with Mustang's first sheetmetal makeover since 1994. The new car offered a stronger "pyramid" form that was narrower at the greenhouse and wider toward the wheels, for a lower visual center of gravity. This was the most angular Mustang yet, a bold iteration of the "New Edge" design philosophy originally introduced by Ford's origami-like GT90 concept car. Key body lines were angular, body

creases sharp. And yet the design team managed by Ken Grant retained the familiar Mustang "look"; it was a car for the end of the century, yes, but clearly a ponycar, as well.

Slim, wraparound headlamps were new, as were pronounced, muscular wheel arches above flat spokes on new 15-, 16-, and 17-inch road wheels. A dramatic side scoop also was new, as were stepped tri-bar taillights. For the first time, Mustang's rear decklid was made of a weight-reducing, rust-resistant sheet molded compound.

The galloping chrome pony dramatically centered on the grille was again encircled by a chrome "corral" band, as it had been on the original Mustang. In addition, all '99 Mustangs carried on their front fenders a 35th-Anniversary version of the tri-color-bar emblem.

The powertrain engineering team, headed by Bill Koche, was busy also, fulfilling a self-imposed mandate to give Mustang engines more muscle. The split-port 3.8-liter V-6 gained 40 horsepower, to 190. The power boost was accomplished via a new intake manifold; improvements to cylinder-head flow; new aluminum main and thrust bearings; and new, high-tech piston coatings designed to reduce friction. A first-order balance shaft provided additional refinement.

The GT's 4.6-liter sohc V-8 power increased by 25, to 250. Intake airflow above 2000 rpm was boosted by bigger valves; new, higher-lift, longer-duration camshafts; improved aluminum upper main, upper thrust, and rod bearings; and revised intake manifold runners. The improved airflow, plus an improved combustion-chamber shape, ensured more thorough burning of the air/fuel mixture.

The GT's V-8 came with coil-on-plug ignition that provided increased

reliability, and higher-energy spark for more efficient combustion.

And for the limited-production '99 Cobra, Ford's Special Vehicles Team tweaked the 4.6-liter to 320 bhp, an increase of 15 over 1998. Standard transmission for base, GT, and Cobra models was again a 5-speed manual; a 4-speed automatic with overdrive remained optional on base and GT. Both had a performance-oriented 3.27:1 rear-axle ratio.

Janine Bay, chief Mustang program engineer, led a team that brought all-speed traction control to all models. The system used ABS sensors to detect excess drive-wheel spin. Wheel slippage was reduced by retarding ignition timing, controlling fuel flow reduction, and cylinder cutoff—all in conjunction with brake application. The driver could control the system with a console-mounted on/off switch.

Other improvements included reductions in noise and vibration, and a three-feet reduction in turning circles. Overall handling was improved by a 1.4-inch increase to rear track, and an additional 1.5 inches of rear jounce travel.

Convertible Mustangs gained under-body rail extenders designed to reduce mid-car shake.

Inside, the front-seat track was increased by one inch; and an available 6-way power seat replaced the previous 4-way unit. Heavier materials were added to seats and door-trim panels, and the front seats of all '99 Mustangs were adorned with a 35th Anniversary pony emblem embossed on the seatback.

New Mustang, New Edge, New Challenges—new challenges well met. The ponycar that defined youthful exuberance for a previous generation drives on, eager to meet the 21st century, still lively and unfettered, still treasured by the young and by the young at heart.

# 1994

- Israel and Jordan sign a historic peace accord

- Despite sharp price hikes industrywide, the Big Three post record net earnings as an economic recovery gathers momentum

---

- Mustang unveils a dramatic restyle reminiscent of the first-generation model; the intimate, redesigned cockpit evokes memories of classic Corvettes, with the added appeal of a standard passenger-side air bag

- Mustang's hatchback body style is dropped, leaving the two-door coupe and companion convertible in base and GT trim; the LX model is axed

- The top engine is a 5.0-liter V-8 producing 215 bhp, up from last year's 205; base engine is a 145-bhp 3.8-liter V-6

- Four-wheel disc brakes are now standard

- ABS is available on V-6 and V-8 models

- Other new standard features: tilt steering wheel and power driver's seat

- Z-rated 16-inch tires are standard on the GT

- A limited-edition Cobra is introduced; its sequentially fuel-injected 5.0-liter V-8 cranks out 240 bhp

- Model-year production totals 137,074 for 1994, signaling that the restyled Mustang is a hit

The conception of the fourth-generation Mustang was a long, involved process that boiled down to three different designs, seen here as sketches. Internal Ford designations were, from the top, Rambo, Arnold Schwarzenegger, and Bruce Jenner. Like the porridge sampled by Goldilocks, Rambo was too hot, Jenner was too cold, and Schwarzenegger was just right. Ford relied on consumer opinion from "Gallop Poll" market surveys to be sure the new shape would wow the Mustang cognoscenti. It did.

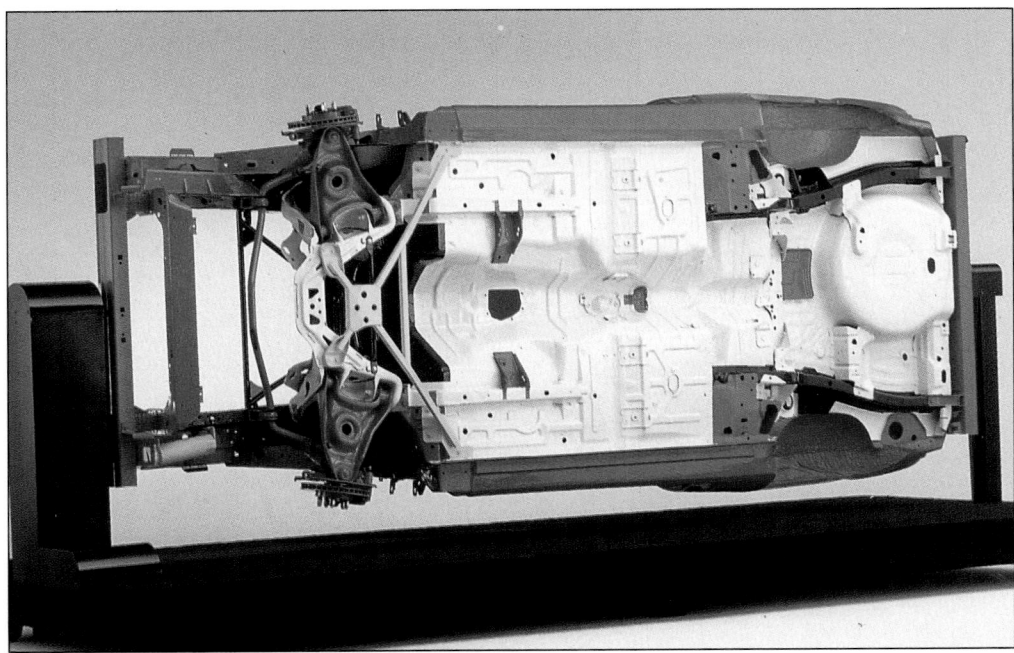

*Top row, from left:* In October 1990, at Ford's Design Center, fiberglass copies of the Jenner, Rambo, and Schwarzenegger Mustang concepts were presented to reps from Ford sales, marketing, product development, and upper management. Opinion was divided evenly between Rambo and Schwarzenegger. However, Schwarzenegger was the overwhelming choice at Ford Gallop Polls on the West Coast, and it was approved for production in November 1990. *Above left:* Although many components from 1979-93 Mustangs were carried over for '94, the chassis was almost entirely new. *Above:* A modified MacPherson strut continued to dominate the front-suspension layout for '94, but with a longer, lower control arm, increased caster, and stronger tubular anti-roll bars that allowed wider and taller tires. *Left:* Under-skin components were color coded: White indicated a carryover from 1993, yellow was convertible only, green was GT only, blue was modified from '93, and red was new and common to coupe and convertible, V-6 and V-8.

*Right:* Mustang's FOX-4 (for Fox-1994) platform was the strongest ever, allowing engineers to tune the suspension for optimum ride and handling and eliminate reliance on the chassis as the "fifth spring." *Below:* The '94 could have assumed the jelly-bean shape that typified auto styling of the time, but Team Mustang listened to enthusiasts and reinterpreted many styling cues that distinguished the original car. *Below right:* The new shape was at once modern and nostalgic—a perfect summation of the fun for which Mustang has been known. *Bottom left:* The two-door fastback came standard with the V-6; in GT trim the 302 HO was standard. *Bottom right:* The model year's other body style was a convertible, which offered the same engine choices as the coupe. The three-door hatchback was dropped because of the difficulty in building one with required levels of torsional stiffness. LX models were also eliminated.

*Top:* Ford's SVT (Special Vehicle Team) put together another limited-edition Cobra for 1994, set off by discreet Cobra fender badges, a Cobra-exclusive rear wing, and unique 17 × 8-inch wheels mounting P255/45ZR-17 Goodyear Eagle tires. *Above:* The Cobra 302 HO had GT-40 heads and produced 240 horsepower @ 4800 rpm; the less-potent GT version of the 302 was rated at 215 horses @ 4200 rpm. *Left:* Mustang dispensed with "fleet-style" models for '94, which meant no four-cylinder base models were offered. Every Mustang had to be zippy, which explains the base 3.8L (232-cubic-inch) V-6 with 145 horsepower @ 4000 rpm and 215 lbs/ft of torque @ 2500 rpm.

**227**

*Right:* The 1994 convertible was 65-percent more resistant to bending than the '93, resulting in a tight body with drastically reduced cowl shake. *Below:* The convertible top sank into a well that allowed it to sit evenly with the rear deck, even without the snap-on rear boot. *Below right:* The triangulated brace connecting the shock towers was stock on GTs and cut down body flex when the car was pushed progressively harder into a corner. The 302 HO's 215 horsepower (down from the previous year's 225) gave pleasing performance. *Bottom left:* The dual-cockpit instrument panel was a design theme of the original Mustang, engineered in contemporary trim for the '94. *Bottom right:* The convertible's rear seat did not fold down.

*Top row:* The new Mustang was the logical choice to pace the Indy 500 on May 29, 1994. *Left:* Race-car driver Parnelli Jones and a USAC representative paced the race in a 1994 Cobra convertible prepared by Jack Roush. A second Mustang pace car was built for A.J. Foyt and a third for Alex Trotman, Ford's CEO. *Middle right:* Ford supplied 108 "Festival" cars for Indy officials and VIPs. *Above:* Mustang paced the Indy 500 in 1964, 1979, and 1994.

*This page:* Team Mustang discovered that Mustang owners wanted galloping horses, so the running-horse logo (*top left*) returned to the grille. The '94 convertible was built on the assembly line alongside the rest of the Mustang line—the first time this had occurred since the '73 model. The structural rigidity of the convertible made it nearly as comfortable as the coupe, and occupants could carry on a conversation with the top down. As the '94 model year wound down, ragtops accounted for about one-third of total Mustang production. The 302 HO V-8 (*right*) was identical in coupe or convertible. Every '94 GT had the 302 HO, and every 302 HO Mustang was a GT.

# 1995

- Israeli prime minister Yitzhak Rabin is assassinated in Tel Aviv
- U.S. space shuttle *Atlantis* docks with Russian space station *Mir*
- More than 5500 people are killed by a 7.2-magnitude earthquake in Kobe, Japan
- Islamic extremists, upset with French stand on Algeria, initiate terror bombings throughout France
- The Chevy Camaro picks up optional traction control and a more muscular V-6
- Chrysler Corp.'s subcompact Neon bows at Dodge and Plymouth dealers
- FoMoCo raises the stakes in the compact class with its new Ford Contour and Mercury Mystique
- The compact Pontiac Sunfire is introduced as the replacement for the venerable Sunbird

- Mustang buyers who want the 240-bhp Cobra engine must purchase the full Cobra package, as the engine is not available with the GT
- A slightly softened suspension cushions occupants against road defects
- Mustang convertibles display considerably less body flex on rough pavement
- The previously standard power driver's seat is now optional

Few changes were needed after the successful 1994 redesign. With production of 185,986 in 1995, Mustang was the most popular sporty car in America. *Top:* The ragtop looked good in Dark Jewel Green. The convertible was available in base, GT, and Cobra models. Shown is the base version, which used a 145-horsepower 3.8-liter V-6. *Bottom:* The GT added a sport suspension and a 215-horsepower 5.0-liter V-8. This was the last year the 5.0 was offered in the Mustang; the trusty pushrod engine descended from the original Mustang V-8 of 1964.

*Top:* Ford's Special Vehicle Team (SVT) engineering group designed the Cobra R for road racing and just 250 were built in 1995—its only year of production. The $35,000 R was street-legal, but was sold only to sanctioned racers. *Above and right:* The R shared its instrument panel with the regular Cobra, but saved weight by eliminating the back seat, air conditioning, power windows, power door locks, radio, and sound insulation. The regular Cobra weighed 3400 pounds. The Cobra R, with a heavier engine and 20-gallon racing fuel cell, weighed 3326.

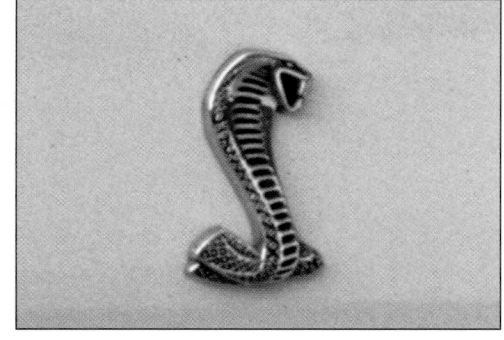

*Left:* The Cobra R used a special fiberglass hood bulged to clear its special engine. *Bottom left:* Exclusive to the R was a 5.8-liter (351 cid) V-8 packing 300 bhp at 4800 rpm and 375 lbs/ft of torque at 3750. It was developed from the Ford F-150 Lightning sport truck engine. The SVT crew added a brace between the strut towers to stiffen the front end and teamed the 5-speed manual with a 3.27:1 final-drive ratio instead of the regular Cobra's 3.08:1. *Car and Driver* ran a Cobra R against a '95 Camaro Z28. The Ford did 0-60 mph in 5.4 seconds, the quarter-mile in 13.8, and had a top speed of 151 mph. The 275-horsepower Z28 did 0-60 in 5.5 seconds, the quarter-mile in 14.1, and topped out at 156. *Above:* This Mustang deserved its Cobra badge. *Below:* The R's 17×9-inch alloy wheels were an inch wider than the standard Cobra's, and a stiffened suspension with Koni shock absorbers gave better handling. The only color offered was Crystal White.

*Top:* A stiffened body structure for 1995 made the drop-top more stable on bad roads. All Mustangs rode a little better with softer suspension. The standard Cobra had a 240-horsepower 5.0-liter V-8. Cobras were the only Mustangs with anti-lock brakes as standard equipment. The power driver's seat made optional on other 1995 Mustangs, was still standard on the Cobra. The suspension was firmer than the base or GT. At $25,605 the Cobra convertible was the most expensive Mustang after the Cobra R. *Right:* The price of the base coupe increased more than $1000 for '95, but at $14,530, it was the least-expensive Mustang. For that price you got 4-wheel disc brakes, dual air bags, tachometer and full instrumentation, tilt steering wheel, and other features. At $14,495, the V-6 Camaro coupe didn't have 4-wheel disc brakes, but it did have a cassette player, theft-deterrent system, anti-lock brakes—and 55 more horsepower.

# 1996

- Bill Clinton handily defeats GOP challenger Bob Dole to win a second term as U.S. President

- Researchers in Scotland clone a lamb they call "Dolly"

- Chrysler Corp.'s popular minivans are redesigned

- GM closes the book on its full-size, rear-drive trio: Chevy Impala/Caprice, Buick Roadmaster, and Cadillac Fleetwood

- Saturn's sedan and wagon get their first redesign since their 1990 debut

- Pontiac's Firebird gains two new performance packages and a more powerful V-8

- Mustang GTS is dropped, leaving a 2-door convertible and 2-door notchback in base, GT, and Cobra iterations

- Two new 4.6-liter V-8s debut: an overhead-cam, 215-horsepower mill for the GT and Cobra; and a double overhead-cam, 305-horse variant available with the Cobra only

- The base Mustang's 3.8-liter V-6 is now rated at 150 horsepower; 5 more than in '95

- All Mustang engines have new, platinum-tipped spark plugs designed to last 100,000 miles

- Taillamps switch from horizontal to vertical

- A passive anti-theft system is standard on GT and Cobra models

- Mustang grille emblem is now backed with a mesh insert

The big change for 1996 was introduction of the 4.6-liter overhead cam V-8. The old pushrod V-8 was tough and powerful, but Ford didn't think it could meet coming emission standards. The new engine had horsepower and torque similar to the old, but was more refined and didn't run out of power after 5000 rpm. The GT convertible *(top)* and the GT coupe *(bottom)* both used the the 215-horsepower single-overhead-cam 2-valve version of the engine. This V-8 (with up to 210 horsepower) was also used in full-sized Crown Victoria.

*Right:* Three-section vertical taillights added in 1996 were intended to recall the taillamps of the original Mustang. *Below left:* The interior design was unchanged for '96, but GT and Cobra models got a smoother shifting, stronger 5-speed manual transmission. *Below right:* Space taken up by the power-top hardware made the convertible's rear seat even more cramped than the coupe's. *Opposite page top:* An added benefit of the fresh engine was better handling. It required a redesigned front crossmember that helped stiffen the car's forward structure and allowed engineers to fit an improved front suspension. *Opposite page bottom left:* An iron block with aluminum heads and a single overhead camshaft per bank of cylinders were features of the GT's new 4.6. The ohc design, platinum tipped spark plugs, and the latest fuel injection and distributorless ignition systems reduced emissions and allowed 100,000 miles between tune-ups. The 4.6 was quieter than the old 5.0, but the dual exhaust retained the familiar V-8 rumble. Despite all these advances, the new GT was slightly slower 0-60 mph than the '95 model. The '96 did the sprint in 6.6 seconds compared to 6.1 for the '95. Quarter mile times were identical at 14.9 seconds according to *Car and Driver.*

*Above:* Only 2500 Cobra convertibles were built for North America in 1996. While the GT got a single overhead cam V-8 shared with the Crown Victoria, the Cobra got a dual overhead cam, 4-valve V-8 shared with the Lincoln Mark VIII. With 305 horsepower the standard Cobra had five more horsepower than the Cobra R of the previous year, but it had less torque. *Right:* Other Mustangs had gauges with black faces, but the Cobra's instruments had white faces. *Opposite page top:* Ford's estimated performance times for the Cobra were: 0-60 mph in 5.9 seconds and the quarter mile in 14.0 seconds at 101.6 mph. *Opposite page bottom left:* For 1996, the Cobra's hood bulge was slightly bigger to clear the new engine. *Opposite page bottom right:* Laser Red was one of four Cobra colors; the others were Crystal White, Black, and Mystic. Mystic was a special blue/purple/green paint that shifted color with light and angle.

*Opposite page top:* The Cobra 4.6-liter engine (center) is shown with two other hot Ford V-8s. To the left of the 4.6 is the Boss 429 of 1969-70 that used overhead valves, while the SOHC 427 of 1965 on the right was an earlier attempt by Ford at an overhead cam V-8. The SOHC had a successful drag racing career, but was never used in a production car. *Opposite page lower left:* This cutaway engine shows the chain used to turn the Cobra's dual overhead camshafts. While some makers use belts to drive overhead cams, Ford used the noisier, but more durable chain. *Opposite page lower right:* Even though the Cobra engine was similar to the Lincoln Mark VIII's it had 100 different parts and 25 more horses. Special attention was paid to engine's breathing. Four valves per cylinder and careful intake manifold design ensured power from idle to the 6000-rpm redline. *This page:* The engine was assembled at Ford's Windsor, Ontario plant, but the aluminum block was cast in Italy and the crankshaft was forged in Germany.

# 1997

- The United Kingdom's 99-year lease on Hong Kong expires, and the Asian financial center is handed over to Chinese control

- Humanitarian Mother Teresa dies at 87

- Diana, Princess of Wales, dies at 36 in a Paris automobile crash

- NASA's Pathfinder spacecraft lands on Mars

- Plymouth introduces the retro hot rod Prowler

- Pontiac's Grand Prix grows larger and sports aggressive new styling

- A redesigned, more powerful Ford Escort is introduced

- Chevy introduces the Malibu as a replacement for the Corsica

........................................

- Passive Mustang anti-theft system made standard in '96 GT and Cobra models is now standard on the base Mustang, as well

- Other Mustang changes are minor: monotone interior scheme; new "flecked" seat-fabric pattern on the GT; optional grey leather upholstery in the base ragtop; and optional "diamond-cut" 17-inch alloy wheels for the GT

After adding a new V-8 engine in '96, Ford made few changes for '97. *Top:* The Mustang convertible continued to be one of the most popular open cars in America. A GT convertible is shown. *Bottom:* This GT coupe has the optional diamond-cut alloy wheels that were new for '97. Also new for the GT was a flecked seat fabric pattern. The ride remained firm, but was considered more comfortable than the Camaro or Firebird competition. Gas mileage for the GT was around 15 mpg in urban driving. As expected of musclecar buyers, GT buyers tended to be males in their 30s and 40s.

*Top:* The base Mustang attracted younger (20s and 30s) buyers and more women than the GT. The base V-6 got a 5-bhp boost to 150 horsepower in '96. Gas mileage was about 19 mpg in urban driving. The Camaro's base 3.8-liter V-6 had 200 horsepower and similar fuel economy. Enthusiasts often overlooked the V-6 Mustang, but it sold well because it was cheaper to run and insure than the V-8 models. The theft-deterrent system that reduced thefts of the '96 GT and Cobra was made standard on the '97 base models. Those ordering automatic transmission got a new, thicker shift handle with an overdrive lock-out button on the handle instead of the console. The spoiler on this base convertible was optional. *Bottom:* Ford used this opening box to introduce the Cobra at auto shows. In spite of the elaborate introduction, little was new with the '97 Cobra after the introduction of its dual overhead cam engine in '96.

*Top:* Ford sold 10,049 Cobras in '97. *Bottom:* The low-volume Cobra V-8 was built by a two-person team that signed each engine. There were 12 teams. The signatures can be seen on the left cam cover. *Opposite page top:* Previous Mustangs had two-tone interiors, but for '97 the interior was one color—except for the dashboard. The 5-speed manual was the only transmission available on the Cobra. Camaro and Firebird V-8s offered 6-speeds beginning in 1993. *Opposite page bottom left:* One intake valve per cylinder was fed fuel below 3250 rpm, above both intake valves were given fuel. Ford said "This system gives the Cobra the best of all worlds: low speed torque and horsepower that grows as the tachometer needle swings higher." *Opposite page bottom right: Road & Track* said this about the Cobra's engine: "The V-8 is docile at idle and part throttle. Always lurking, though, is the soul of a high-performance machine."

*Top:* The round fog lights in the lower bumper and a different hood bulge with larger scoops distinguish a Cobra from the other Mustangs. The hood scoops are nonfunctional on all models. *Bottom:* The rear was identified by a "Cobra" bumper. The rear spoiler is subtler than that of some cars offering far less performance. *Opposite page: Road & Track* did a comparison test of a Cobra and a Camaro Z28. Both had 305 horsepower, but the Camaro's 5.7-liter ohv V-8 had more torque, 335 lbs/ft to the Cobra's 300. The Cobra did 0-60 in 5.7 seconds and the quarter mile in 14.2 at 99.5 mph. The Camaro was faster: 0-60 in 5.4 and the quarter mile in 13.9 seconds at 102.5, but *Road & Track* thought the Cobra was more fun to drive. "You sit higher and look out bigger windows. The shift action seems lighter. The Cobra maneuvers more nimbly, and takes a set more quickly when tossed into a corner. Trail-brake it too hard into a tight kink, stand on the throttle, and the Mustang will luridly swing its tail out into a crazy smoky drift."

# 1998

- The U.S. economy is at its most robust in 30 years, but financial crises cripple Japan, Indonesia, and other Asian nations

- Promising new developments in cancer treatment are announced

- Legendary singer/actor Frank Sinatra dies at age 82

- Chevy's Camaro picks up a detuned version of Corvette's aluminum V-8, rated at 305 horsepower, an increase of 20 over '97; an SS version cranks out 320 horses

- Daimler-Benz merges with Chrysler Corp.; the new entity is called DaimlerChrysler

- A hunky, all-new Chevy Corvette debuts

...............................................................

- Mustang's GT wrings 225 horsepower, ten more than last year, from its 282-cid ohc V-8; the Cobra's 282-cid dohc V-8 remains at 305 horsepower

- As per federal regulations, dual airbags, Mustang's included, are depowered

- Front cupholder and ashtray are replaced by dual front cupholders

*Opposite page top:* For 1998, the GT got 10 more horsepower for a total of 225. *Opposite page bottom:* The base and GT Mustangs gained standard air conditioning, cassette/CD player, power windows and door locks, remote keyless entry, and power decklid release. The GT also added a power driver's seat, fog lights, and leather-wrapped steering wheel. This GT has the optional leather upholstery. *Top:* The spoiler already standard on the GT convertible was made standard on the GT coupe in '98. *Bottom left and right:* Cobras got a new five-spoke alloy wheel.

*Top:* While slow sales had GM pondering the discontinuation of its Camaro and Firebird ponycars, Mustang sales for '98 were running 30 percent above '97 levels. More than 7 million Mustangs have been sold since its introduction. One hundred thousand Mustang owners are enthusiastic enough to join a Mustang club. There are 450 Mustang owners' clubs worldwide. *Bottom:* A high percentage of Mustangs have manual transmissions. Forty percent of Mustangs had manuals compared to 28 percent of Camaros. The Cobra interior was little changed except for the addition of a standard cassette/CD player.

# 1999

- Mercury Cougar returns as a compact coupe, with FoMoCo's New-Edge styling

- For its 35th Anniversary, Mustang boasts evolutionary new styling highlighted by knife creases characteristic of Ford's New-Edge design philosophy, aggressive fender flares, wraparound headlights, and a new vertical taillamp treatment

- Base 3.8-liter V-6 gets a boost of 40 horsepower, to 190; torque is increased by five foot-pounds, to 220

- Mustang GT's 4.6-liter sohc V-8 gains 25 horses, to 250, and torque increases by five foot-pounds, to 295

- All-speed traction control is available on all models

*Top right:* For Mustang's 35th anniversary in 1999 the body got its first restyling since the 1994 redesign. The car was narrower in the greenhouse and wider around the wheels. The pony on the new honeycomb grille was surrounded by a "corral" band as on the first Mustang. *Above:* The sharp edges on the hood and fenders were inspired by the "New Edge" style of the '96 GT90 concept car. *Bottom right:* The Ford blue oval badge was only on the base model. The rear track was 1.4-inches wider for better handling. Traction control was available for the first time on a Mustang.

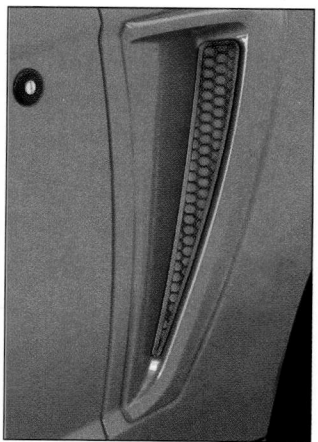

*Opposite page top:* A GT convertible is in the foreground and a base coupe is behind. The driving lights under the front bumper helped distinguish the GT from the base. The convertible body structure was again strengthened to reduce mid-car shake. All Mustangs were quieter with revised floorpan sealing and extra insulation in the rocker panels. *Opposite page bottom left:* The dual hood scoops of the previous generation were replaced by a single scoop in the center of the hood. *Opposite page bottom center:* The bigger side scoop got the same honeycomb as the grille. *Opposite page bottom right:* The taillights retained the three-segment look inspired by the original Mustang. *Top left:* A higher-lift cam, improved intake manifold, revised combustion chambers, and bigger valves added 25 horsepower to the GT's 4.6-liter ohc V-8 for a total of 250. *Bottom left:* With 190 bhp, the base V-6 had gained 40 horsepower from better-breathing heads, dual-runner intake manifolds, and high-tech piston coatings. The engine was smoother because of a stiffer block and a first-order balance shaft. *Top:* The new alloy wheels had flat spokes. Maneuverability was improved with a tighter turning circle. The base Mustang's turning circle was reduced 37 inches (from 40-feet 1-inch to 37-feet) while the GT's was reduced 33 inches (from 40-feet 8-inches to 37-feet 11-inches). The front disc brakes featured new 2-piston aluminum calipers.

*Top:* Convertibles traditionally accounted for 25 percent of Mustang sales and the GT convertible expected to help continue that tradition. *Left:* Headlights were slimmer for '99. *Bottom:* All Mustangs had a 1.5-inch increase in drive tunnel height at the back axle for more rear suspension travel. A decklid made of a light-weight sheet-molded compound replaced the steel decklid. While the base had a single exhaust outlet, the GT got dual 3-inch diameter exhaust outlets.

# CHAPTER 11

# Mustang at a Glance

*1965 Mustang hardtop*

## 1964½-66

### Model-Year Production

| No. | Model | 1964½-1965* | 1966 |
|---|---|---|---|
| 63A | Fastback, standard | 71,303 | 27,809 |
| 63B | Fastback, deluxe | 5776 | 7889 |
| 65A | Hardtop, standard | 464,828 | 422,416 |
| 65B | Hardtop, deluxe | 22,232 | 55,938 |
| 65C | Hardtop, bench seat | 14,905 | 21,397 |
| 76A | Convertible, standard | 94,496 | 56,409 |
| 76B | Convertible, deluxe | 5338 | 12,520 |
| 76C | Convertible, bench seat | 2111 | 3190 |
| — | Shelby Mustang GT-350 fastback | 562 | 2380 |
| — | Shelby Mustang GT-350 convertible | — | 18 |
| | TOTAL | 681,551 | 609,966 |

*\* 1965 = April 1964-August 1965*

### Prices

| No. | Model | 1965 | 1966 |
|---|---|---|---|
| 07 | Hardtop, I-6 | $2372 | $2416 |

| No. | Model | 1965 | 1966 |
|---|---|---|---|
| 07 | Hardtop, V-8 | 2480 | — |
| 08 | Convertible, I-6 | 2614 | 2653 |
| 08 | Convertible, V-8 | 2722 | — |
| 09 | Fastback, I-6 | 2589 | 2607 |
| 09 | Fastback, V-8 | 2697 | — |
| — | Shelby Mustang GT-350 fastback | 4547 | 4428 |

### General Specifications

| | 1964½-1965 | 1966 |
|---|---|---|
| Wheelbase (in.) | 108.0 | 108.0 |
| Overall length (in.) | 181.6 | 181.6 |
| Overall width (in.) | 68.2 | 68.2 |
| Curb weight (lbs.) | 2445-2904 | 2488-2650 |
| Standard trans. | 3-sp. man. | 3-sp. man. |
| Optional trans. | overdrive | overdrive |
| | 4-sp. man. | 4-sp. man. |
| | 3-sp. auto | 3-sp. auto |

### Engine Availability

| Type | cid | bhp | 1964½ | 1965 | 1966 |
|---|---|---|---|---|---|
| I-6 | 170 | 101 | Std. | — | — |
| I-6 | 200 | 120 | — | Std. | Std. |
| V-8 | 260 | 164 | Std. | — | — |
| V-8 | 289 | 200 | Opt. | Std. | Opt. |
| V-8 | 289 | 225 | Opt. | Opt. | Opt. |
| V-8 | 289 | 271 | Opt. | Opt. | Opt. |
| V-8 | 289 | 306 | — | Std. GT-350 | Std. GT-350 |

## 1967-68

### Model-Year Production

| No. | Model | 1967 | 1968 |
|---|---|---|---|
| 63A | Fastback, standard | 53,651 | 33,585 |
| 63B | Fastback, deluxe | 17,391 | 7661 |

*1968 Mustang fastback*

| No. | Model | 1967 | 1968 |
|-----|-------|------|------|
| 63C | Fastback, bench seat | — | 1079 |
| 63D | Fastback, del. bench seat | — | 256 |
| 65A | Hardtop, standard | 325,853 | 233,472 |
| 65B | Hardtop, deluxe | 22,228 | 9009 |
| 65C | Hardtop, bench seat | 8190 | 6113 |
| 65D | Hardtop, del. bench seat | — | 853 |
| 76A | Convertible, standard | 38,751 | 22,037 |
| 76B | Convertible, deluxe | 4848 | 3339 |
| 76C | Convertible, bench seat | 1209 | — |
| — | Shelby Mustang GT-350 fastback | 1175 | 1253 |
| — | Shelby Mustang GT-350 conv. | — | 404 |
| — | Shelby Mustang GT-500 fastback | 2050 | 2073 |
| — | Shelby Mustang GT-500 conv. | — | 720 |
| | TOTAL | 475,346 | 321,854 |

### Prices

| No. | Model | 1967 | 1968 |
|-----|-------|------|------|
| 01 | Hardtop, I-6 | $2461 | $2602 |
| 03 | Convertible, I-6 | 2698 | 2814 |
| 02 | Fastback, I-6 | 2592 | 2712 |
| — | Shelby Mustang GT-350 fastback | 3995 | 4117 |
| — | Shelby Mustang GT-350 conv. | — | 4238 |

### General Specifications

| | 1967 | 1968 |
|---|------|------|
| Wheelbase (in.) | 108.0 | 108.0 |
| Overall length (in.) | 183.6 | 183.6 |

| | 1967 | 1968 |
|---|------|------|
| Overall width (in.) | 70.9 | 70.9 |
| Curb weight (lbs.) | 2568-2738 | 2635-2745 |
| Standard trans. | 3-sp. man. | 3-sp. man. |
| Optional trans. | 4-sp. man. | 4-sp. man. |
| | 3-sp. auto | 3-sp. auto |

### Engine Availability

| Type | cid | bhp | 1967 | 1968 |
|------|-----|-----|------|------|
| I-6 | 200 | 120 | Std. | — |
| I-6 | 200 | 115 | — | Std. |
| V-8 | 289 | 195/200 | Opt. | Opt. |
| V-8 | 289 | 225 | Opt. | — |
| V-8 | 289 | 271 | Opt. | — |
| V-8 | 289 | 290 | Std. GT-350 | — |
| V-8 | 302 | 230 | — | Opt. |
| V-8 | 302 | 250 | — | Std. GT-350 |
| V-8 | 302 | 350 | — | Opt. GT-350 |
| V-8 | 390 | 320/325 | Opt. | Opt. |
| V-8 | 390 | 335 | — | Std. GT-350 |
| V-8 | 427 | 390 | — | Opt. |
| V-8 | 427 | 390 | Opt. GT-500 | — |
| V-8 | 428 | 360 | — | Opt. GT-500 |
| V-8 | 428 | 400 | Opt. GT-500 | Opt. GT-500 |

*1969 Mustang Boss 302*

## 1969-70

### Model-Year Production

| No. | Model | 1969 | 1970 |
|-----|-------|------|------|
| 63A | Fastback, standard | 56,022 | 39,470 |
| 63B | Fastback, deluxe | 5958 | 6464 |
| 63C | Fastback, Mach 1 | 72,455 | 40,970 |
| 65A | Hardtop, standard | 118,613 | 77,161 |
| 65B | Hardtop, deluxe | 5210 | 5408 |
| 65C | Hardtop, bench seat | 4131 | — |

| No. | Model | 1969 | 1970 |
|---|---|---|---|
| 65D | Hardtop, del. bench seat | 504 | — |
| 65E | Hardtop, Grandé | 22,182 | 13,581 |
| 76A | Convertible, standard | 11,307 | 6199 |
| 76B | Convertible, deluxe | 3439 | 1474 |
| — | Shelby Mustang GT-350 fastback | 1085 | 350 (all GT-350s) |
| — | Shelby Mustang GT-350 conv. | 194 | |
| — | Shelby Mustang GT-500 fastback | 1536 | 286 (all GT-500s) |
| — | Shelby Mustang GT-500 conv. | 335 | |
| | TOTAL | 302,971 | 191,363 |

## Prices

| No. | Model | 1969 | 1970 |
|---|---|---|---|
| 01 | Hardtop, I-6 | $2635 | $2721 |
| 02 | Fastback, I-6 | 2635 | 2771 |
| 03 | Convertible, I-6 | 2849 | 3025 |
| 04 | Grandé, I-6 | 2866 | 2926 |
| 01 | Hardtop, V-8 | 2740 | 2822 |
| 02 | Fastback, V-8 | 2740 | 2872 |
| 02 | Boss 302, V-8 | 3588 | 3720 |
| 03 | Convertible, V-8 | 2954 | 3126 |
| 04 | Grandé, V-8 | 2971 | 3028 |
| 05 | Mach 1 fastback, V-8 | 3139 | 3271 |
| — | Shelby Mustang GT-350 fastback | 4434 | 4500[1] |
| — | Shelby Mustang GT-350 conv. | 4753 | 4800[1] |
| — | Shelby Mustang GT-500 fastback | 4709 | 4800[1] |
| — | Shelby Mustang GT-500 conv. | 5027 | 5100[1] |

[1]Prices estimated

## General Specifications

| | 1969 | 1970 |
|---|---|---|
| Wheelbase (in.) | 108.0 | 108.0 |
| Overall length (in.) | 187.4 | 187.4 |
| Overall width (in.) | 71.3 | 71.7 |
| Curb weight (lbs.) | 2690-3210 | 2721-3240 |
| Standard trans. | 3-sp. man. | 3-sp. man. |
| Optional trans. | 4-sp. man. | 4-sp..man. |
| | 3-sp. auto | 3-sp. auto |

## Engine Availability

| Type | cid | bhp | 1969 | 1970 |
|---|---|---|---|---|
| I-6 | 200 | 115/120 | Std. | Std. |
| I-6 | 250 | 155 | Opt. | Opt. |
| V-8 | 302 | 220 | Std.[1] | Std.[1] |
| V-8 | 351 | 250 | Opt.[2] | Opt.[2] |
| V-8 | 351 | 290/300 | Opt. | Opt. |
| V-8 | 351 | 290 | Std. GT-350 | — |
| V-8 | 390 | 320 | Opt. | — |
| V-8 | 428 | 335 | Opt. | Opt. |
| V-8 | 428 | 335[3] | Opt. | Opt. |
| V-8 | 428 | 375 | Std. GT-500 | — |
| V-8 | 429 | 375[4] | Opt. | Opt. |

[1]290 bhp std. Boss 302
[2]std. Mach 1
[3]with Ram Air
[4]Boss 429 only

*1972 Mustang Sprint*

## 1971-73

### Model-Year Production

| No. | Model | 1971 | 1972 | 1973 |
|---|---|---|---|---|
| 63D | Fastback, standard | 23,956 | 15,622 | 10,820 |
| 63R | Fastback, Mach 1 | 36,499 | 27,675 | 35,440 |
| 65D | Hardtop, standard | 65,696 | 57,350 | 51,480 |
| 65F | Hardtop, Grandé | 17,406 | 18,045 | 25,674 |
| 76D | Convertible, standard | 6121 | 6401 | 11,853 |
| | TOTAL | 149,678 | 125,093 | 135,267 |

### Prices

| No. | Model | 1971 | 1972 | 1973 |
|---|---|---|---|---|
| 01 | Hardtop, I-6 | $2911 | $2729 | $2760 |
| 02 | Fastback, I-6 | 2973 | 2786 | 2820 |
| 03 | Convertible, I-6 | 3227 | 3015 | 3102 |
| 04 | Grandé, I-6 | 3117 | 2915 | 2946 |
| 01 | Hardtop, V-8 | 3006 | 2816 | 2897 |
| 02 | Fastback, V-8 | 3068 | 2873 | 2907 |

| No. | Model | 1971 | 1972 | 1973 |
|-----|-------|------|------|------|
| 02 | Boss 351, V-8 | 4124 | — | — |
| 03 | Convertible, V-8 | 3320 | 3101 | 3189 |
| 04 | Grandé, V-8 | 3212 | 3002 | 3088 |
| 05 | Mach 1 fastback, V-8 | 3268 | 3053 | 3088 |

### General Specifications

| | 1971 | 1972 | 1973 |
|--|------|------|------|
| Wheelbase (in.) | 109.0 | 109.0 | 109.0 |
| Overall length (in.) | 187.5 (6) 189.5 (8) | 190.0 | 194.0 |
| Overall width (in.) | 75.0 | 75.0 | 75.0 |
| Curb weight (lbs.) | 2907-3261 | 2908-3147 | 2995-3216 |
| Standard trans. | 3-sp. man. | 3-sp. man. | 3-sp. man. |
| Optional trans. | 4-sp. man. 3-sp. auto | 4-sp. man. 3-sp. auto | 4-sp. man. 3-sp. auto |

### Engine Availability

| Type | cid | bhp | 1971 | 1972 | 1973 |
|------|-----|-----|------|------|------|
| I-6 | 250 | 145 (gross)[1] | Std. | Std. | Std. |
| V-8 | 302 | 210 (gross)[2] | Std. | Std. | Std. |
| V-8 | 351 | 240 (gross) | Opt. | — | — |
| V-8 | 351 | 285 (gross) | Opt. | — | — |
| V-8 | 351 | 280 (gross) | Opt. | — | — |
| V-8 | 351 | 330 (gross) | Std.[3] | — | — |
| V-8 | 429 | 370 (gross) | Opt. | — | — |
| V-8 | 351 | 168 (net) | — | Opt. | Opt. |
| V-8 | 351 | 200 (net) | — | Opt. | Opt. |
| V-8 | 351 | 275 (net) | — | Opt. | Opt. |

[1] Rated 95 bhp (net) 1972-73
[2] Rated 136 bhp (net) 1972-73
[3] Std. Boss 351 only

## 1974-78

### Model-Year Production

| No. | Model | 1974 | 1975 | 1976 | 1977* | 1978 |
|-----|-------|------|------|------|-------|------|
| 60F | 2-door coupe, std. | 177,671 | 85,155 | 78,508 | 67,783 | 81,304 |
| 60H | 2-door coupe, Ghia | 89,477 | 52,320 | 37,515 | 29,510 | 34,730 |
| 69F | 3-door coupe, std. | 74,499 | 30,038 | 62,312 | 49,161 | 68,408 |
| 69R | 3-door coupe, Mach 1 | 44,046 | 21,062 | 9232 | 6719 | 7968 |
| | TOTAL | 385,693 | 188,575 | 187,567 | 153,173 | 192,410 |

* Includes vehicles produced as 1978 models but sold as 1977 models.

*1978 Mustang II King Cobra*

### Prices

| No. | Model | 1974 | 1975 | 1976 | 1977 | 1978 |
|-----|-------|------|------|------|------|------|
| 02 | 2-door, I-4 | $3134 | $3529 | $3525 | $3702 | $3731 |
| 03 | 3-door, I-4 | 3328 | 3818 | 3781 | 3901 | 3975 |
| 04 | Ghia 2-door, I-4 | 3480 | 3938 | 3859 | 4119 | 4149 |
| 02 | 2-door, V-8 | 3363 | 3801 | 3791 | 3984 | 3944 |
| 03 | 3-door, V-8 | 3557 | 4090 | 4047 | 4183 | 4188 |
| 04 | Ghia 2-door, V-6 | 3709 | 4210 | 4125 | 4401 | 4362 |
| 05 | Mach 1, V-6 | 3674 | 4188 | 4209 | 4332 | 4430 |

### General Specifications

| | 1974 | 1975 | 1976 | 1977 | 1978 |
|--|------|------|------|------|------|
| Wheelbase (in.) | 96.2 | 96.2 | 96.2 | 96.2 | 96.2 |
| Overall length (in.) | 175.0 | 175.0 | 175.0 | 175.0 | 175.0 |
| Overall width (in.) | 70.2 | 70.2 | 70.2 | 70.2 | 70.2 |
| Curb weight (lbs.) | 2620-2886 | 2660-2879 | 2678-2822 | 2627-2975 | 2646-2751 |
| Standard trans. | 4-sp. man. | 4-sp. man. | 4-sp. man. | 4-sp. man. | 4-sp. man. |
| Optional trans. | 3-sp. auto | 3-sp. auto | 3-sp. auto | 3-sp. auto | 3-sp. auto |

### Engine Availability

| Type | cid | bhp | 1974 | 1975 | 1976 | 1977 | 1978 |
|------|-----|-----|------|------|------|------|------|
| I-4 | 140 | a | Std. | Std. | Std. | Std. | Std. |
| V-6 | 171 | b | Opt.[d] | Opt. | Opt. | Opt. | Opt. |
| V-8 | 302 | c | — | Opt. | Opt. | Opt. | Opt. |

a: Rated 85 bhp 1974; 83 bhp 1975; 92 bhp 1976; 89 bhp 1977; 88 bhp 1978
b: Rated 105 bhp 1974; 97 bhp 1975; 103 bhp 1976; 93 bhp 1977; 90 bhp 1978
c: Rated 122 hp 1975; 139 bhp 1976-78
d: Standard Mach 1

*1980 Mustang 3-door*

## 1979-81

### Model-Year Production

| No. | Model | 1979 | 1980 | 1981 |
|-----|-------|------|------|------|
| 02 (66B) | 2-door coupe, base | 143,382 | 117,015 | 69,994* |
| 03 (61R) | 3-door coupe, base | 108,758 | 86,569 | 68,111 |
| 04 (66H) | 2-door coupe, Ghia | 48,788 | 20,288 | 11,991 |
| 05 (61H) | 3-door coupe, Ghia | 31,097 | 17,192 | 12,497 |
|  | TOTAL | 332,025 | 241,064 | 162,593 |

* Includes 4418 units with "S" (economy) option.

### Prices*

| No. | Model | 1979 | 1980 | 1981 |
|-----|-------|------|------|------|
| 02 (66B) | Base 2-door coupe | $4494 | $4884 | $5980 |
| 03 (61R) | Base 3-door coupe | 4828 | 5194 | 6216 |
| 04 (66H) | Ghia 2-door coupe | 5064 | 5369 | 6424 |
| 05 (61H) | Ghia 3-door coupe | 5216 | 5512 | 6538 |

* Initial model-year retail prices. All figures exclusive of options.

### General Specifications

|  | 1979 | 1980 | 1981 |
|--|------|------|------|
| Wheelbase (in.) | 100.4 | 100.4 | 100.4 |
| Overall length (in.) | 179.1 | 179.1 | 179.1 |
| Overall width (in.) | 69.1 | 69.1 | 69.1 |
| Curb weight (lbs.) | 2530-2672 | 2582-2614 | 2601-2692 |
| Standard trans. | 4-spd. man.[1] | 4-spd. man.[1] | 4-spd. man.[1] |
|  | 4-sp./OD man.[2] | 4-sp./OD man.[2] | 4-sp./OD man.[2] |
|  | 3-sp. auto[3] | 3-sp. auto[3] | 3-sp. auto[3] |
| Optional trans. | 3-sp. auto | 3-sp. auto | 3-sp. auto |
|  | 5-sp. man.[4] | 5-sp. man.[4] |  |

[1] Std. with 4-cyl.; [2] Std. with 6-cyl.; [3] Std. with V-8; [4] Optional 4-cyl. only

### Engine Availability

| Type | cid | bhp | 1979 | 1980 | 1981 |
|------|-----|-----|------|------|------|
| ohc I-4 | 140 | 88 | Std. | Std. | Std. |
| ohc I-4 Turbo | 140 | 131 | Opt. | Opt. | Opt |

| Type | cid | bhp | 1979 | 1980 | 1981 |
|------|-----|-----|------|------|------|
| ohv V-6 | 171 | 109 | Opt. | — | — |
| ohv I-6 | 200 | 85 | Opt.[1] | Opt. | Opt. |
| ohv V-8 | 255 | 117 | — | Opt. | Opt. |
| ohv V-8 | 302 | 140 | Opt. | — | — |

[1] Replaced V-6 option mid-model year.

*1985 Mustang SVO*

## 1982-86

### Model-Year Production

| Model | 1982 | 1983 | 1984 | 1985 | 1986 |
|-------|------|------|------|------|------|
| 2-door coupe, L/GL | 45,316 | — | — | — | — |
| 2-door coupe, GLX | 5828 | — | — | — | — |
| 3-door coupe, GL | 45,901 | — | — | — | — |
| 3-door coupe, GLX | 9926 | — | — | — | — |
| 3-door coupe, GT | 23,447 | — | — | — | — |
| 2-door coupe | — | 33,201 | 37,680 | 56,781 | 106,720[1] |
| 3-door coupe | — | 64,234 | 86,200[2] | 84,623[2] | 117,690[2] |
| Convertible | — | 23,438 | 17,600 | 15,110 | — |
| TOTAL | 130,418 | 120,873 | 141,480 | 156,514 | 224,410 |

[1] Includes convertibles.
[2] Includes SVO: 4508 (1984), 1954 (1985), 3382 (1986).

### Prices

| Model | 1982 | 1983 | 1984 | 1985 | 1986 |
|-------|------|------|------|------|------|
| 2-door coupe, L | $6345 | $6727 | $7088 | — | — |
| 2-door coupe, GL | 6844 | 7264 | — | — | — |
| 2-door coupe, LX | — | — | 7290 | $6885 | $7189 |
| 2-door coupe, GLX | 6980 | 7398 | — | — | — |

| Model | 1982 | 1983 | 1984 | 1985 | 1986 |
|---|---|---|---|---|---|
| 3-door coupe, L | — | — | 7269 | — | — |
| 3-door coupe, GL | 6979 | 7439 | — | — | — |
| 3-door coupe, LX | — | — | 7496 | 7345 | 7744 |
| 3-door coupe, GLX | 7101 | 7557 | — | — | — |
| 3-door coupe, GT | 8308 | 9328 | 9578 | 9885 | 10,691 |
| Turbo 3-door coupe, GT | — | 9714 | 9762 | — | — |
| Convertible, LX | — | — | 11,849 | 11,985 | 12,821 |
| Convertible. GLX | — | 12,467 | — | — | — |
| Convertible, GT | — | 13,479 | 13,051 | 13,585 | 14,523 |
| Turbo cvt., GT | — | — | 13,245 | — | — |
| 3-door coupe, SVO | — | — | 15,596 | 14,521 | 15,272 |

### General Specifications

| | 1982 | 1983 | 1984 | 1985 | 1986 |
|---|---|---|---|---|---|
| Wheelbase (in.) | 100.4 | 100.4 | 100.4 | 100.4 | 100.4 |
| Overall length (in.) | 179.1 | 179.1 | 179.1 | 179.3[1] | 179.3[1] |
| Overall width (in.) | 67.4 | 69.1 | 69.1 | 69.1 | 69.1 |
| Curb weight (lbs.) | 2568-2636 | 2684-2975 | 2736-3124 | 2657-3165 | 2795-2853 |
| Standard trans. | 4OD man. | 4OD man. | 4OD man. | 4OD man. | 4OD man. |
| Optional trans. | 5OD man. | 5OD man. | 5OD man. | 5OD man. | 5OD man. |
| | 3-sp. auto | 3-sp. auto | 3-sp. auto | 3-sp. auto | 3-sp. auto |
| | — | — | 4OD auto | 4OD auto | 4OD auto |

*SVO: 180.8 in.*

### Engine Availability

| Type | cid | bhp | 1982 | 1983 | 1984 | 1985 | 1986 |
|---|---|---|---|---|---|---|---|
| ohc I-4 | 140 | 88 | Std. | Std. | Std. | — | — |
| ohc I-4 Turbo | 140 | 145[1] | — | Opt. | Opt.[2] | Opt.[2] | — |
| ohc I-4 Turbo | 140 | 205 | — | — | — | — | [2] |
| ohv I-6/1 bbl | 200 | 88 | Opt. | — | — | — | — |
| ohv V-6/2 bbl | 232 | 105 | — | Opt. | — | — | — |
| ohv V-6 TBI | 232 | 120 | — | — | Opt. | Opt. | Opt. |
| ohv V-8/2 bbl | 255 | 111 | Opt. | — | — | — | — |
| ohv V-8/2 bbl | 302 | 157 | [3] | — | — | — | — |
| ohv V-8/4 bbl | 302 | 175 | — | [3] | [3] | — | — |
| ohv V-8 TBI | 302 | 165 | — | — | Opt. | — | — |
| ohv V-8/4 bbl | 302 | 210 | — | — | — | [3] | — |
| ohv V-8 TBI | 302 | 180 | — | — | — | Opt. | — |
| ohv V-8 PFI | 302 | 200 | — | — | — | — | Opt.[3] |

[1] *Rated 155 bhp 1985*
[2] *Standard Turbo GT 1984-85, SVO 1986*
[3] *Standard GT*
*Note: **TBI** = throttle-body fuel injection; **PFI** = port ("multi-point") fuel injection; **bbl** = barrel(s) (carbureted engines)*

*1989 Mustang GT*

## 1987-93

### Model-Year Production

| 1987 | 1988 | 1989 | 1990 | 1991 | 1992 | 1993 |
|---|---|---|---|---|---|---|
| 159,145 | 211,225 | 209,769 | 128,189 | 98,737 | 79,280 | 114,228 |

### Prices

| Model | 1987 | 1988 | 1989 | 1990 | 1991 | 1992 | 1993 |
|---|---|---|---|---|---|---|---|
| 2-door coupe, LX | $8043 | $8726 | $9050 | $9456 | $10,157 | $10,215 | $10,719 |
| 3-door coupe, LX | 8474 | 9221 | 9556 | 9962 | 10,663 | 10,721 | 11,224 |
| Cvt., LX | 12,840 | 13,702 | 14,140 | 15,141 | 16,222 | 16,899 | 17,548 |
| 2-door, LX 5.0 Sport | — | — | 11,410 | 12,164 | 13,270 | 13,422 | 13,296 |
| 3-door, LX 5.0 Sport | — | — | 12,265 | 13,007 | 14,055 | 14,207 | 14,710 |
| Cvt., LX 5.0 Sport | — | — | 17,001 | 16,183 | 19,242 | 19,644 | 20,293 |
| 3-door coupe, GT | 11,835 | 12,745 | 13,272 | 13,986 | 15,034 | 15,243 | 15,747 |
| Cvt., GT | 15,724 | 16,610 | 17,512 | 18,805 | 19,864 | 20,199 | 20,848 |
| 3-door coupe, Cobra | — | — | — | — | — | — | 20,000 |

| Model | 1987 | 1988 | 1989 | 1990 | 1991 | 1992 | 1993 |
|-------|------|------|------|------|------|------|------|
| 3-door coupe, Cobra-R | — | — | — | — | — | — | 25,692 |

## General Specifications

| | 1987-93 |
|---|---|
| Wheelbase (in.) | 100.5 |
| Overall length (in.) | 179.6 |
| Overall width (in.) | 68.3 |
| Curb weight (lbs.) | 2754-3350 |
| Standard trans. | 5OD manual |
| Optional trans. | 4OD automatic |

## Engine Availability

| Type | cid | bhp | 1987 | 1988 | 1989 | 1990 | 1991 | 1992 | 1993 |
|------|-----|-----|------|------|------|------|------|------|------|
| ohc I-4 | 140 | 90/105[1] | Std. | Std. | Std. | Std. | Std. | Std. | Std. |
| ohv V-8 | 302 | 225[2] | Std. | Std. | Std. | Std. | Std. | Std. | Std. |
| ohv V-8 | 302 | 245[3] | — | — | — | — | — | — | Std. |

[1] 4-cyl. LX models only; 90 bhp 1987-90, 105 bhp 1991-93
[2] Optional 1987-88 LX models, std. 1989-93 LX "5.0L" models; rerated for 1993 models to 205 bhp.
[3] 1993 Cobra models only

# 1994-99

## Model-Year Production

| 1994 | 1995 | 1996 | 1997 | 1998 | 1999 |
|------|------|------|------|------|------|
| 137,074 | 185,986 | 135,620 | NA | NA | NA |

## Prices

| Model | 1994 | 1995 | 1996 | 1997 | 1998 | 1999 |
|-------|------|------|------|------|------|------|
| 2-door notch. | $13,365 | $14,330 | $15,180 | $15,355 | $16,070 | NA |
| 2-door notch., GT | 17,280 | 17,905 | 17,610 | 18,000 | 20,070 | NA |
| 2-door conv. | 20,160 | 20,795 | 21,060 | 20,755 | 20,570 | NA |
| 2-door conv., GT | 21,970 | 22,595 | 23,495 | 23,985 | 24,070 | NA |
| 2-door notchback, Cobra | 22,425 | 21,300 | 24,810 | 25,335 | 25,630 | NA |
| 2-door convertible, Cobra | 23,535 | 25,605 | 27,580 | 28,135 | 28,430 | NA |

## General Specifications

| | 1994-1998 | 1999 |
|---|---|---|
| Wheelbase (in.) | 101.3 | 101.3 |
| Overall length (in.) | 181.5 | 183.2 |
| Overall width (in.) | 71.8 | 73.1 |
| Curb weight (lbs.) | 3055-3565 | 3069-3429 |
| Standard trans. | 5-sp. man. | 5-sp. manual |
| Optional trans. | 4-sp. auto | 4-sp. auto |

## Engine Availability

| Type | cid | bhp | 1994 | 1995 | 1996 | 1997 |
|------|-----|-----|------|------|------|------|
| ohv V-6 | 232 | 150 | Std. | Std. | Std. | Std. |
| ohc V-8 | 281-302 | 205-215 | Std. | Std. (GT only) | Std. (GT only) | Std. |
| dohc V-8 | 281-302 | 305 | Std. (Cobra | Std. (Cobra | Std. (Cobra) | Std. |

| Type | cid | bhp | 1998 |
|------|-----|-----|------|
| ohv V-6 | 232 | 150 | Std. |
| ohc V-8 | 282 | 225 | (GT) Std. |
| dohc V-8 | 282 | 305 | (Cobra) Std. |

| Type | cid | bhp | 1999 |
|------|-----|-----|------|
| ohv V-6 | 232 | 190 | Std. |
| sohc V-8 | 280 | 250 | (GT) Std. |
| dohc V-8 | 281 | 320 | (Cobra) Std. |

*1999 Mustang GT*

# INDEX